THE CATLOPAEDIA

A complete guide to cat care

J.M. Evans and Kay White

HENSTON

First published, 1988

ISBN 1-85054 113 2

Cover photograph by Marc Henrie

Henston Ltd., Friary Court, 13–21 High Street, Guildford, Surrey, England

Typeset by M.C. Typeset Ltd., Gillingham, Kent, England
Printed and bound by Cradley Print PLC, Cradley Heath, Warley, West Midlands, England

CONTENTS

INTRODUCTION

Cats are in the ascendancy again. All the indications are that by the time we enter the 21st century cats will be the most popular, and indeed the most suitable household pet, in many countries in the world. After a long history of semi-neglect in many aspects of their lives, the tide has turned on the availability of information about cat care. Feline medicine and surgery has made tremendous strides in recent years, and illness and injuries are understood and cured as never before. Commercially produced cat foods are widely available in the most tempting number of varieties which also provide excellent balanced nutrition. As well as being popular, cats are going to be better cared for and better appreciated, and we hope that our book will go a long way to make information about cats more readily available and more easily understood.

We show you how your cat is built and how its body systems work. We try to indicate, as far as possible, how the cat thinks and how it behaves, and make suggestions to enable owners to bring natural cat-behaviour into line with what is acceptable within the home. And we reveal just a little magic to help bring that errant cat into line. We describe the illnesses which affect cats, and the signs cats show which will indicate that the owner should consult the vet, and we include a section on 'What did the veterinary surgeon mean?' to help you amplify what was said at the consultation. There is also a section on nursing the sick cat, to save the owner anxiety and to promote quick recovery.

Also included are many paragraphs which answer the question 'What if . . .?' on all kinds of topics, from cats which refuse to use a litter tray to cats which pretend they are stuck up a tree. Because we believe that you and your cat-owning friends will want to consult *The Catlopaedia* often, and in a hurry, you will find that all the topics are cross-indexed for quick and easy retrieval.

Our intention is that *The Catlopaedia* shall fill the role of a very knowledgeable cat-owning friend, forever at your elbow to answer the questions which do not get answered elsewhere, and most importantly, to help you, your family and your cat to enjoy a happy, lifelong relationship.

J.M. Evans

Kay White

ACKNOWLEDGEMENTS

Encyclopaedias traditionally carry a wide range of information of an educational nature. This, the Cat Encyclopaedia or Catlopaedia for short, represents a concerted input of knowledge from a number of acknowledged experts on various aspects of the feline world.

We, the nominal authors of the book, know that we have been fortunate to be able to draw upon the experience and resources of writers of the calibre of Andrew Edney BA, BVetMed, MRCVS; Barry Kirk, Editor of the *Feline Advisory Bureau Bulletin* and regular contributor to the weekly magazine, *Cats*; David Sutton, BVetMed, MRCVS; Geoff Skerritt, BVSc, FRCVS; The Waltham Centre for Pet Nutrition, particularly I.H. Burger and G.G. Loveridge; and Jo Wills, BVetMed, MRCVS and ex-FAB scholar. We should also like to thank the artists who provided such clear and informative diagrams for the anatomical section, and also livened up the text with other illustrations. Without the gentle prodding and sometimes more frantic urging of the production team at Update-Siebert Publications, the book might not be with you today. We are grateful to Sara Green and Sally Wells for their sympathetic support when the going got hard.

Most of all we want to acknowledge with especial thanks, the support we have received from Pedigree Petfoods, the makers of the cat's all-time favourite food, Whiskas. The company's sponsorship of this book, as a companion volume to *The Doglopaedia*, is an act of generosity to all present and prospective cat owners.

CHAPTER 1
BREEDS

Introduction

Despite their use to man, the cat has not evolved in the same way as the dog, which has developed physically in different ways in order to fulfil the many tasks set by its master. The cat has just two main roles as servant to the human race – as vermin exterminator and as companion. The attributes required for these functions are acute senses, speed, agility, and intelligent forbearance.

The cat has fulfilled these roles since the beginning of time, so there has been little need to change its appearance or physiology. The cats of today are easily recognizable and comparable to those of the ancient Egyptians. The only major changes have been at the hands of man.

In fairness to most of the world's Cat Fancies, they have not allowed the extremes of cosmetic breeding seen in the dog world, where man's apparent eye for beauty can, and has, determined the shape of a breed, often to the detriment of its natural physiology. The multi-coloured cats in feral colonies seen throughout the world are a good example of natural selection, where only the fittest kittens survive. To some extent this also applies to the domesticated cat, but foraging and hunting for food is of less importance here. The greatest changes in the cat can be seen in the pedigree world, where new breeds are appearing from cross-matings with existing breeds.

This has led to the establishment of pedigrees for the different varieties and the setting up of organizations world-wide catering for their care and administration.

In Britain at the turn of the century there were a number of clubs which each registered cats' names and pedigrees for their own members. Such a confused situation could not long persist, and they therefore combined to form one organization, the Governing Council of the Cat Fancy (GCCF) which today is still the major registration and legislative body.

There are currently over six million cats in the United Kingdom, of which the largest percentage, approximately 90 per cent, are non-pedigree. However, although pedigree cats are fewer in number, they occupy the largest amount of time and activity in an ever-growing Fancy. There are seven main categories of pedigree cats and these are described below.

Longhaired cats (Persian)

Major characteristics:

- Placid
- Quiet voice
- Affectionate disposition
- Adapt well to closed environment
- The most popular show cat in USA and UK
- Small litters
- Spectacular looking
- Constant grooming
- Moult and lose fur

Fig. 1.1

Longhaired cats (non-Persian)

Major characteristics:
- Lively and inquisitive
- Less grooming than Persian types
- Adapt to new environment
- Affectionate

Fig. 1.2

Shorthaired cats (British)

Major characteristics:
- Affectionate nature
- Very robust and hardy
- Easy grooming
- Adaptable to home environment

Fig. 1.3

Shorthaired cats (Foreign)

Major characteristics:

- Very affectionate
- Easy grooming
- Can be quite vocal
- Very active and inquisitive
- Large litters
- Time-consuming
- Need warmth

Fig. 1.4

Foreign and oriental shorthaired cats (Siamese type)

Major characteristics:

- Very graceful
- Low grooming requirement
- Very vocal
- Very affectionate
- Demanding in time and toleration
- Inquisitive and lively
- Do everything at top speed

Fig. 1.5

Burmese

Major characteristics:

- Striking, muscular cat
- Very affectionate
- Adaptable to home environment
- Fun-loving and inquisitive
- Large litters
- Low grooming requirement
- Longevity

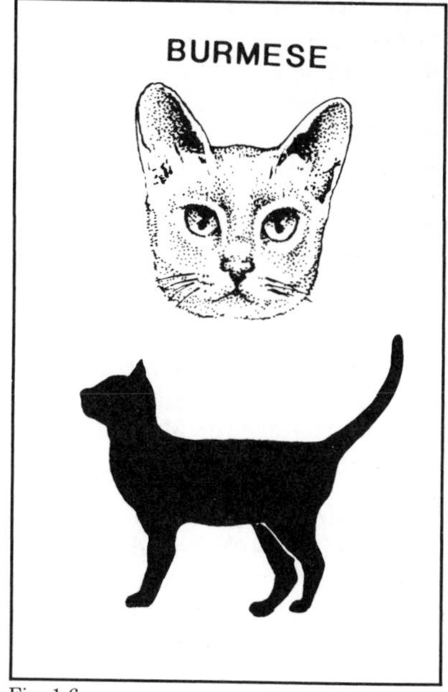

Fig. 1.6

Siamese cats

Major characteristics:

- Striking appearance
- Extremely affectionate
- Very vocal and demonstrative
- Active and inquisitive
- Can be destructive
- Low grooming requirement
- Short show career for some colours

Fig. 1.7

Other varieties

Of the varieties and breeds already mentioned, all have been recognized or are in the process of being accepted by the GCCF. This means that the cats and their parents and progeny are registered and are allowed to compete at cat shows held throughout Britain. There are a number of breeds that have not reached this status, either by lack of numbers or because the breeding programme is in its early stages. However, some breeds have been refused recognition because of a deformity or some other reason which would be to the detriment of the cats concerned. An example is the Scottish Fold, which appeared as a mutation in the 1960s. The folded, bent foward, dog-like ears characteristic of these are in fact a deformity, and it is not considered correct to breed from them.

Breeds from other countries are making appearances in Britain, but are very highly priced because they are in short supply. Two varieties increasing in popularity are the Maine Coon from North America and the Norwegian Forest Cat.

Maine coon

A very old and established native of North America. The cats are extremely hardy. They are slow to mature, taking four years to reach full size. With no restrictions on the coat colours, they come in a full blaze of spots, patches, stars and stripes. The coat is longer than that of a shorthaired cat's and they were given their name because of their resemblance to the Racoon.

Norwegian Forest Cat

Very similar to the Maine Coon in looks and temperament. The large coat is ideal for the extremes of climate found in its native country, with the outer fur being resistant to snow and rain. The coat is very easy to groom and maintain. All colours are permitted.

To the casual observer and single cat owner, the range and variety of the breeds may seem confusing. Describing in detail each colour and variety of the feline race is a mammoth undertaking, particularly as new colours of cat are constantly being introduced making it difficult to keep an up-to-date list.

Furthermore, identifying breeds of cat is not easy and indeed to the untrained eye many of the breeds look alike. Table 1.1 should help the novice to identify the more obvious types of cat.

Each breed has its own characteristics and to appreciate the beauty and grace of cats, a visit to an all-breed cat show is recommended to those who wish to further their knowledge of cats or just to enjoy a day out. There are several shows being held in the UK virtually every weekend at different locations around the country. The procedure of a typical cat show is described in Chapter 11. The GCCF issue lists of shows and venues on request and details of how to apply can be found in Chapter 11.

Table 1.1. Breed identification

Characteristic	Longhairs		Shorthairs				
	Persian	Non-Persian	British	Foreign	Burmese	Other foreign	Siamese
Head shape							
Round	●	○	●	–	–	–	–
Wedge	–	○	–	●	●	●	●
Nose							
Short	●	○	–	–	–	–	–
Long	–	○	●	●	●	●	●
Ears							
Short	●	●	○	–	–	–	–
Tall	–	–	○	●	●	●	●
Eyes							
Round	●	●	●	○	○	–	–
Oval	–	–	–	○	○	●	●
Body shape							
Short	●	○	○	○	–	–	–
Long	–	○	○	○	●	●	●
Legs							
Short	●	○	●	●	–	–	–
Long	–	○	–	–	●	●	●
Tail							
Short	●	○	–	–	–	–	–
Long	–	○	●	–	–	–	–
Tapering	–	○	–	●	●	●	●

Key: ●, characteristic present;
○, characteristic present but not marked;
–, characteristic absent

CHAPTER 2
CAT MANAGEMENT

Choosing the right kitten

The first decision you must make is what type of kitten: pedigree or non-pedigree; if pedigree what breed; male or female; and precisely what the kitten is for – do you want it simply as a pet, or do you intend to go in for showing or breeding? One fundamental point however must be borne in mind: a cat is for life and not to be discarded if your mood changes.

Pedigree cats

A large percentage of the people who want a pedigree cat are intent on entering the breeding and showing world, although a substantial number of pedigree kittens do not meet the required standards for the show world and are sold as pets. Choosing the type of cat that will suit is difficult, but reference to Chapter 1, a visit to an all-breed cat show and talking to breeders should make the decision easier. It is not advisable to buy a pedigree kitten from a pet shop. Apart from the questions of choice and price, the new owner would not be able to see the parents or kittens from the same litter, or be in a position to judge the nature or temperament of an animal in a strange and potentially stressful environment. Another factor is the advice and help the new owner often needs in the early days will not be available, such assistance a breeder will happily and freely give. There are plenty of breeders and clubs more than willing to help and a list of specific breed clubs, plus show list, can be obtained from the governing bodies mentioned in Chapter 11.

Longhaired pedigree cats

The problems of maintenance are obvious with careful grooming of the cat taking as much as an hour a day. During the warm weather, or all the year round in warm homes, the cat sheds hair profusely. Inevitably the hair attaches itself to home furnishings and clothes, but the quiet and adaptable personality of the breed make them ideal house cats. The breeding season means kittens are usually available from late spring onwards.

Shorthaired pedigree cats

These cats need less grooming, but variation across the varieties is very great. Temperament is probably the largest single variant and this may range from quiet to extremely boisterous. The virtually constant breeding season means kittens are available all year round.

Non-pedigree

Recognized to be generally hardier than their pedigree cousins, the non-pedigree cat comes in a myriad of colours and coat patterns, and usually has a benign attitude and temperament provided the kittens have been handled frequently during the socialization period. Newspaper advertisements, rescue organizations and charities are the most obvious places to look for kittens and there is usually no limit on availability, although there is an abrupt increase during the summer months. Included in this explosion in the feline population are numbers of adult cats who, for one reason or another, are unwanted. Unless there is some peculiarity in their nature, the older cat should be regarded just as favourably as a kitten when seeking a new pet, but with the added bonus of being already trained. Avoid feral cats or kittens. They are the semi-wild strays that have not been domesticated. Often originating from colonies living around industrial and hospital buildings, these kittens and cats rarely make good house pets, retaining most of their wild characteristics and being aggressive, fearful, destructive and showing little affection.

Male kittens

Males usually grow larger than the females and in some breeds the male kitten can become sexually aware at six months and will start pungent marking of his territory soon after. Cat urine has a very strong smell and is corrosive, so unless it is the intention to keep the cat as a stud, castration is the only answer if you want to keep a male as a pet. Your vet will advise on the timing of what is quite a minor operation if done early, usually at about six months. It is advisable to make an appointment with the vet some time before. Although neutered males can grow to huge proportions, they are very clean and home loving. The alternative is a cat who wanders in search of females and fights for territorial mastery, often returning from forays dirty and battle scarred, and very often requiring veterinary attention for abscesses and other ailments.

Female kittens

Once again, unless the intention is to keep the kitten for breeding, to have a female spayed is the kindest and most sensible procedure. It is a mistaken belief that a female cat should have one litter before spaying. Every year thousands of unwanted kittens are destroyed. Having a litter does nothing for the cat, and precious little for the offspring. Siamese and some foreign breeds come into oestrus at a very young age and can reproduce before they are really adult, so a guideline would be to book the kitten in to be spayed at about four to five months of age.

Suitability

The home environment plays an important part in determining the type of cat to be introduced. Longhaired cats are very adaptable and are well suited to an enclosed home and adapt as well to a flat as to large open spaces. Some shorthaired varieties have similar natures, the British for instance, but in general the foreign and Siamese prefer space, as do the non-pedigree. Another point to bear in mind is the nature of the home. Cats are very clean but do not necessarily respect property. Longhaired cats leave their fur on the furniture, driving the houseproud to despair. Shorthaired cats also moult, and are also known to be somewhat destructive in their natures.

Cats are particularly vulnerable to being injured on roads. Injuries sustained are often fatal or at least require prolonged veterinary attention. There is little by way of training that can be done to give cats road sense. If you live close to a busy main road, you may have to think twice before having a cat at all, or you may decide to make arrangements to keep your cat totally indoors.

Choosing a cat

Having decided on the type of kitten you require, the next step is to ensure it is a healthy one. Most breeders welcome visits by prospective owners. This gives the buyers an idea of the conditions the kitten has been reared in, and the breeders can assess the suitability of the purchasers. One or both of the kitten's parents can usually be seen as well as the remaining kittens in the litter. Points to note are listed below and you should select a kitten that fulfils all or most of these criteria. A good choice will:

Appear alert – a lively kitten is interested in its surroundings and notices every movement.

Be healthy looking – the coat should be shiny or glossy and clean.

Show playfulness and curiosity – a healthy kitten should be active, playing and stalking its littermates, although don't be worried if the kitten is a little wary of strangers.

Kittens possessing these qualities are well worth considering, but care should be taken before choosing a kitten which shows any of the following traits and characteristics:

Lack of activity – though not necessarily a sign of illness, the quiet kitten in a lively litter is unusual and best avoided as there may be some underlying nervous problem.

Watery eyes and sneezing – either of these conditions can require veterinary treatment and could be the precursor to major problems and high treatment costs. If you already own another cat or cats you would be wise not to take any kitten from this breeder at this time as infectious conditions quickly spread throughout a cattery or a house and to your cats too.

Poor coat – the coats of unhealthy kittens can be described as 'staring', the hair appearing dull and standing away from the body.

Undersized or pot-bellied – to choose a small kitten is not necessarily bad, but remember that failure to grow properly may be associated with illness. Small kittens with pot-bellies can be harbouring worms or some other malady and are best avoided.

Never pick a kitten because you feel sorry for it, for without doubt problems will appear later which can be very distressing and expensive to cure. Responsible pedigree breeders will not sell a kitten unless it is in peak condition, and will not usually object if the buyer asks for a veterinary inspection or report. If there is any doubt about the fitness of a kitten, resolve the problem before making an agreement to buy. Never take a sickly kitten as a gift, it could cost you a great deal of money and heartbreak.

Age

Pedigree kittens are usually weaned by the time they are three months old, and the ruling bodies of the Cat Fancy recommend that kittens do not leave home before that time. However, some breeds mature faster than others and may be available considerably earlier. Non-pedigree kittens are, more often than not, taken into a new home far too young and are often still learning to eat solid food, although they do learn very quickly. Care should be taken with these kittens and it is recommended that veterinary advice is sought. It is essential that both pedigree and non-pedigree kittens are fully vaccinated against infectious diseases. Pedigree kittens are usually vaccinated before purchase at about 12 weeks. Non-pedigrees are rarely vaccinated before sale, so the new owner must have the kitten protected as close to 12 weeks as possible, and certainly before neutering or spaying.

Price

People are usually only too glad to find a home for a non-pedigree kitten and make no charge but some may ask for a contribution to a charity. Animal care organizations may make a small charge for help with their running costs.

The pricing structure for pedigree kittens is, however, quite different. Breeding pedigree cats is an expensive hobby and the price asked for kittens probably does not even reflect a fraction of the costs actually borne by the breeder.

The price varies with the standard of kitten required. Pedigree kittens which do not match up to the standard of breed points are often sold at very reasonable cost, longhaired breeds are always the most expensive. As a rule of thumb, it can be said that a pedigree kitten suitable for breeding from costs twice as much as a pet quality pedigree kitten, and a show kitten will cost almost three times as much as a pet.

Pedigree kittens are usually registered by the breeder when a few weeks old. They will normally bear the breeder's own prefix plus an individual name. When purchasing a kitten, a duly signed and completed pedigree, a transfer certificate to register the kitten in the new owner's name, and a certificate of vaccination against feline enteritis must accompany the kitten. If you are in doubt about the health of the kitten, seek veterinary advice at once. Do not leave it several days to see if it improves. Breeders are often the best people to go to for advice in respect of general after care as they can speak with the knowledge of the breed as well as familiarity with the kitten you have purchased.

Wise breeders sell their kittens with a short term insurance cover, so that if the kitten falls ill or is injured during the first few weeks in the new home, veterinary fees are covered. If the kitten should die, the insurance policy will refund the purchase price. It is wise for the new owner to extend this insurance to an annual policy so that provision is made for any emergency illness or accident which may befall the cat.

The first few days

Settling into a new home is probably the most traumatic time for a young kitten, having been separated from its mother and littermates and brought into an unfamiliar environment where there are often other animals. Great care must be exercised in introducing the newcomer to its new home, giving the kitten lots of comfort and reassurance. Keep the windows and doors closed to prevent escape, as the strange surroundings can quickly disorientate the kitten and if it gets away the chances of it finding its new home again are slim.

Show the kitten the preparations you have made to welcome it, starting with the prepared litter tray, followed by the feeding area where some food is already set out. It is important not to change the locations of the litter tray and feeding place as this will confuse the kitten. Then introduce the kitten to any other animals in the house. Elder cats in particular can be jealous of any newcomer and they will need reassuring that their place in the hierarchy is not usurped. Feeding the elders before, and some distance away from, the newcomer over a period of time usually works and, although it may not be completely accepted, the kitten will generally be tolerated. Provide the kitten with an escape route or bolt-hole, a cardboard carton will do, so that it can escape from the well-meant investigations of dogs and other cats.

Bring your kitten into the home at a time when you and other members of the family are going to be at home for a few days. Collect your kitten early in the day so it has some time to get acclimatized to your home before bedtime. Doubtless the little cat will have become tired during play and exploration and will have spent some time already in the bed you have prepared for it, so that it will not mind so much when you leave it for the night. Make the kitten comfortable with a well-wrapped hot-water bottle in its box. Turning a cardboard box on its side so that it has a roof may make the kitten feel more secure.

Above all, patience is required in these formative days. The kitten will soon accept its new home and quickly become a part of the family, though it must be treated with kindness during this period.

Equipment

The cat's basic requirements are very simple – a cat carrier, a feeding bowl, water bowl, litter tray and a bed. The latter is not absolutely necessary as the newcomer usually finds its own most comfortable spot, but in the early days the kitten needs a secure den before it has had the opportunity to choose its own. After the initial first days, other items of equipment will be required such as grooming implements. Ask the breeder to show you the grooming technique and what combs and brushes should be used.

Toys and a scratching post are best introduced early on as the kitten, once it has grown in confidence, will start to look around for items with which to play and exercise its claws. A carrying basket or fold-up cardboard box, available from veterinary surgeons or pet shops, will be required for trips to the vet or boarding cattery. It is never a good idea to carry the cat in your arms or on your lap in the vet's waiting room, on a bus or in the car. Accustoming the kitten to travel in a carrier will pay dividends later on.

The first steps into the great outdoors are the next adventure the kitten will face. For an initial period, it is a good idea to buy the kitten a light collar with a name and address tag. Though the initial outings may be in the owner's sight, there will be the first solo trip and the collar may prove invaluable. There are various types of collar available, most of which are perfectly safe, though care should be taken that it fits correctly and is not too loose. A badly fitting collar can trap the cat as it squeezes through tight gaps. The addition of a bell to the collar may have a significant effect on the survival rate of the surrounding wildlife.

The final piece of equipment to be acquired is a cat flap. This simple device saves the tiresome opening of doors and windows on demand, and also obviates the security risk of leaving windows open, so it quickly repays the outlay. Security is an important aspect of cat flaps, so it is a good idea to place the flap well away from the door handles and bolts.

Check list for cat flaps

1. Make sure that the flap allows for rapid entry if the cat is escaping from an enemy.
2. The flap should be constructed from lightweight materials to avoid bruising the cat's head and body.
3. A perspex door is ideal so that the cat can see that no enemies are waiting on the other side.
4. Hinges and fastenings should be of stainless steel or brass – any other material will corrode when sprayed with tom-cat urine.
5. An average sized cat-flap is 7½ × 9½ inches, but a cat which weighs over 18 lb may need a larger entrance.
6. In order to prevent other cats getting in, or prey being brought into the house by your own cat, consider having two cat flaps, one leading into a garage, utility room or conservatory and a second one leading into the rest of the house.

Care and maintenance

Once the cat has settled into your home, it will want to play and explore. This is the most time-consuming period for kitten and owner. During this time the kitten is rarely still, chasing anything that moves including the owner and family, and as these days are shortlived it is a time to be enjoyed by both parties. The owner's responsibilities grow with the kitten, and more time and effort must be spent on maintenance.

Grooming

Start a grooming routine early. All cats need grooming so the sooner the kitten becomes used to it the better, and most cats will find it pleasurable. Longhaired cats obviously need the most care and daily grooming with a long tooth comb, with wide spaces between the teeth, is recommended. The teeth of the comb go deep into the coat, taking out any dead hair but also keeping the coat loose. Comb away from the head, i.e. with the natural lie of the fur, but afterwards use a stiff bristle brush and sweep up the coat in the direction of the head. Some longhaired cats have very fine hair and may be helped by the occasional weekly application of baby powder. Obviously this depends on the colour of the coat, but it does help in preventing knots and tangles, particularly in damp weather or when the cat is moulting. Never use force on a knot or tangle. Any form of tangle should be teased apart gently from the root up. The very last resort is to cut the matt through the middle and attempt to prise it apart, but be very careful. If you are in the least unsure, consult your vet or possibly a breeder. A badly neglected longhaired cat may have to have all its fur clipped down to the skin while under a general anaesthetic at the veterinary surgery.

Shorthaired cats need less grooming than their longhaired counterparts but they benefit from a weekly comb through with a short tooth comb and a brush with a stiff bristle brush or rubber brush to remove dead hair. Some breeds, like the Rex, require a soft brush as their coat is very delicate. The breeder should advise on this.

Bathing

Not all cats need a bath, although most longhaired show cats get one a few weeks before a show. Unless they like water, it can be a difficult few hours for both cat and owner. Experienced breeders use a shower and let the cat stand with its paws on the edge of the bath to give it some stability. Most cats usually tolerate this and save all their energy for protesting during the drying process which is carried out with a hair dryer, comb, powder and lots of patience.

Vaccination

The most important thing to remember is the need for primary and annual booster vaccinations, particularly for cat 'flu and enteritis, see Chapter 9. Pedigree kittens are usually innoculated before they leave the breeder, but non-pedigree kittens are generally not vaccinated and they must be given this protection as soon as your veterinary surgeon advises it. It is most distressing watching an animal fight these dreadful diseases which can often be fatal.

The vet is a skilled professional and is always ready to give advice and help. Always consult the vet if in the slightest doubt, for it could save your cat's life.

General health care

Most cats do not need any regular attention apart from the occasional wipe of the ears. Longhaired cats can, however, have some problems with weepy eyes which need attention on a regular basis – a wipe with a pad of moist cotton wool is generally all that is required. The same applies to the nose, although any persistent problems should be seen by the vet. Cats' ears are very delicate and any problem associated with cleaning should be tackled very carefully. Unless you are experienced, it is not a good idea to use any instrument in the ear other than a soft pad of cotton wool. Irreparable damage can only be easily be caused with something like a cotton bud. The most frequent invaders of cats' ears are minute mites. Their presence is indicated by large amounts of wax (see Chapter 9, Ectoparasites).

A good scratching post is much appreciated but claws may get very sharp and need trimming from time to time. If you are unsure in any way, ask the vet to clip them for you, as the claw has a good blood supply and bleeds profusely if cut too far back. Declawing, i.e. surgical removal of the claws to prevent the cat spoiling furnishings, is banned by the British governing body.

Boarding

Rescue organizations dread holiday periods as the number of stray cats increases enormously. Some people seem to think that the cat will be able to fend for itself while they are away, and wonder why it is not there to greet them on their return. Unless the cat can be left with a very responsible and watchful neighbour or a cat sitter, the only alternative is to entrust it to a boarding cattery to be looked after.

All such institutions should be licensed by the local authority and regularly checked for the standard of accommodation. A list of the local establishments can be obtained from the authority, local press or yellow pages, but it is advisable to obtain more personal recommendations from either the vet or another cat owner.

Make an appointment to visit the cattery. The proprietors are usually more than happy to allow prospective customers to see their premises, and refusals should be viewed with caution.

Make arrangements very early, as the most popular catteries are usually fully booked early in the year. The cattery will have its own rules, but in general all cats must be vaccinated against enteritis (FIE) and male cats must be neutered. It helps to prepare a diet sheet of the cat's likes and dislikes beforehand, as well as a note of any tendencies that would help in the care of the cat. Some cats prefer something like their own bedding to remind them of home. Cat boarding is a business enterprise, which, if properly done, involves a lot of care and expertise, so boarding your cat is bound to cost a great deal more than just the cost of its food.

Check list when choosing a boarding cattery

1. Is the cattery officially licensed? The licence should be prominently displayed in the reception area. If you use an unlicensed cattery you have no means of complaint should anything go wrong.
2. Are dogs boarded as well? If so, the accommodation for each species should be well-separated, as most cats are nervous of unfamiliar dogs, and dogs are noisier in a boarding situation.
3. The cat accommodation should not smell, neither of cats nor of disinfectant.
4. Are the empty cat pens clean and dry?
5. Does the cattery insist on seeing up-to-date vaccination certificates? Any other regime puts *your* cat at risk.
6. Is the cattery insured with a reliable company which covers the cost of any veterinary attention the boarders may need? Or will you have to pay

separately on your return if the vet was called to your cat while you were away?

7. The cat's accommodation should have outdoor runs, of smooth concrete, not grass which is impossible to disinfect.
8. Avoid places where the cats are accommodated in stacked cages within sheds, with many cats sharing the same airspace.
9. If the cats have individual houses, check that their neighbours are not within sneezing or spitting distance, as this is the way infection is passed on.
10. Look at escape opportunities. Is there a safety passage between the cages, and are there double entrance doors?
11. Is there good ventilation but non-opening windows?
12. Check that wiring and runs are secure, not rusted or sagging.
13. Are individual diets catered for?
14. Ideally, the same people should see the cats several times a day, so that they get a continuity of observation and care.

Quarantine catteries

Importing an animal into the UK is costly but the law requires that all animals coming from overseas, except for the Channel Islands, the Isle of Man and Ireland, are quarantined for six months. Specialist quarantine catteries are abundant and lists and specific regulations are obtainable from the Ministry of Agriculture Fisheries and Foods (MAFF), Hook Rise South, Kingston by Pass, Surbiton, Surrey KT6 7NF. Your veterinary surgeon should be able to give you advice in respect of quarantine catteries in the area.

Flat cats

It may seem to be against the nature of a cat to be confined permanently indoors. Some owners, however, feel happier if their cats are protected from the many hazards which cats can encounter outdoors, especially in urban situations.

It is quite possible for cats to live in an airy, sunny flat all their lives without going outdoors if the needs of the cat are always given consideration. It would obviously be better to have two cats in such a situation so that there is some feline company and interplay, and the owners must also expect to spend some time every day playing with the cat. It may in fact be risky to allow a cat which lives indoors nearly all the time to have occasional outings 'as a treat'. Such a cat will have no ranking among local felines and may panic if attacked.

For cats kept indoors most or all the time, hygiene is an essential and it is important to pay attention to the choice and siting of the litter tray or box. By their very nature, faeces and urine are smelly and unpleasant, so the location of the tray or box requires careful thought.

There are a considerable number of designs of litter tray on the market. Some are just open plastic trays, others have tops that can be lifted off, and the most sophisticated are totally enclosed with a cat flap entrance. The costs vary from under a pound for the simplest tray to considerable sums for the deluxe varieties. Generally the covered-in types are good value and provide some degree of privacy for the cat and containment of unpleasant odours.

The size of the tray is an important consideration. There is a lot of common sense in supplying a large receptacle, though it is worth considering a smaller size tray if the cat refuses to use the original one – sometimes the sheer size frightens them.

The most common reason for cats refusing to use a litter tray is the state of the contents. Being very fastidious, cats will reject a dirty tray and use your carpet instead. Trays should be cleaned and washed on a regular basis in dilute disinfectant that does not contain phenol, a particularly toxic substance to cats. The frequency depends on the use, and a good guideline for a single cat is at least once a day though no amount of cleanliness is ever wasted.

Types of cat litter

- Garden earth
- Peat
- Sawdust or wood shavings
- Shredded newspaper
- Commercially prepared cat litter frequently based on fuller's earth

The many types of commercially prepared cat litter have a lot of advantages over the other materials that are sometimes used. This type of litter is handy to carry, convenient to use and being very absorbent, masks most of the unpleasant smells. Cleaning the trays is further helped by the litter forming clumps, when wetted by urine and faeces, which are easy to remove with a scoop.

Even if your cat has constant access to the outside, through a catflap it may still be necessary to provide a litter tray in case the cat is not inclined to use the garden when the ground is very wet, or when it is frozen.

If a clean tray is provided most cats will use that and not your carpet, unless there is some psychological reason for aberrant behaviour (see Chapter 4).

Elderly cats

The average lifespan of a cat is 14 years, although many live longer, with 21-year-olds being not unusual. Of all animals, the cat tends to grow old most gracefully. The movements get a little slower, the old cat feels the cold more through slowing of the metabolic rate, more time is spent sleeping and the muzzle tends towards a distinguished greying. Hearing and sight degenerate as in most animals, but the one problem cats seem to suffer from most is kidney failure. The first signs are not easily noticed but as the failure gets more pronounced, excessive drinking can be noticed. Constipation is a common difficulty associated with old cats, and veterinary advice should be sought in respect of treatment and prevention of the problem.

Probably the most difficult decision owners have to make is whether the time has come for their ageing cat to be painlessly put to sleep by the veterinary surgeon (euthanasia). The quality of life for the cat may be such that it can be selfish and cruel to allow it to continue to suffer. There is no comfort in grief, only the knowledge that after a lifetime of care, the owners have carried out their final duty to their pet by making its closing days as painless and comfortable as possible.

Although it is not easy to do, a wise owner will discuss in advance with the veterinary surgeon the question of body disposal. The veterinary surgeon will be able to describe the alternative methods of disposal in the locality, together with the approximate cost.

CHAPTER 3
MOTIVATION AND INTELLIGENCE

The senses

Cats have the well-developed senses of a successful hunter – sight, smell, touch, taste and hearing – which they use to the full.

Sight

Cats have a reputation for being able to see in the dark. Although this is an exaggeration, as no animal or human can see without the presence of light rays, it is true that cats can see very much better in dim light than humans. This is due to the setting and construction of the eyes.

Sitting well forward on the head, the eyes give a wide angle of vision with a three-dimensional field of view. This is caused by the curvature of the large lens and cornea with the lens set well back, thus allowing the maximum amount of light through: up to five times more than in humans.

Vision in low light is further aided by a mirror-like structure covering the back of the retina called the tapetum lucidum, which gives the familiar glow of a nocturnal animal's eye when caught in a beam of light in the dark. Unabsorbed light within the eye is reflected by this structure onto the rods and increases the intensity of light falling onto the light sensitive cells.

In proportion to their body size, cats have very large eyes, nearly two-thirds the size of human eyes. Cats can also see gradation of colour, although they have only a few colour sensitive cone cells in comparison with man.

Kittens are born with their eyes closed, the eyelids generally open about five to 10 days later. However, it is not until three months later that their vision develops fully. Cats are able to change their range of vision much more quickly than man, but are unable to see an object at short range except when it moves.

Smell and taste

These senses are very highly developed in cats, and this attribute is the basis of the cat's reputation as a fastidious eater, even though cats can and will eat and drink things which are harmful or even poisonous to them. Cats are attracted to the aroma given off by a substance, and it is noticeable that cats suffering from some kind of nasal congestion, perhaps during cat 'flu or a similar illness, stop eating altogether unless tempted by strong smelling food. Cats are not carrion eaters, and they will not eat putrid meat. They also dislike the smell of a stale litter tray.

The cat's tongue is long, muscular and rough. It is covered in minute rasps called papillae, which enable the cat to effectively clean a bone, a plate or its own coat. The tongue can also be curled in from the sides to form a spoon-like shape to lap up liquids.

There are taste buds all over the tongue, with particular concentration at the tip and at the back of the throat. A variety of tastes please cats, meat and fish are the favourites, but chocolate, fruit and olives are sometimes liked although sweet tastes generally do not appeal.

The experience of taste gives rise to one of the few feline facial expressions which can be identified, this is the flehmen reaction, seen in other animals, notably horses, as well. The top lip is drawn up in a slightly sneering expression, caused by the cat trapping airborne molecules on the taste buds of the tongue and flicking the tongue back on to a sac in the roof of the mouth which transmits chemical information to the brain. Flehmen is seen most frequently in toms which are sampling the pheromones of passing females in oestrus, but it is also seen in cats which are intoxicated by cat nip.

The sense of smell and taste are also vital for territory marking. Cats, especially males, indicate their territorial boundaries by a series of marker points on which the cat sprays urine, or makes visible signs from scratches. The chemical content of the urine used for territory marking is said to vary according to the intention of the spraying action. The urine sprayed before a fight is different in chemical composition and is much more pungent than that passed in the normal way as body waste. The urine sprayed indicates to passing cats, and probably also to dogs, the territorial limits of the resident cat.

Touch

The nose pads and paws are very sensitive areas of touch in cats. Receptors in the tip of the nose can determine the difference between warmth and cold. The whiskers of the cat growing stiffly out of the muzzle, the vibrissae, are also important sensory organs. They can be fanned out in front or straight to the side to define objects close by.

The vibrissae are extremely delicate and should never be touched or pulled; indeed cats are touch sensitive all over their bodies. Guard hairs on the coat also contain touch receptors which are powerful enough to determine the proximity of objects which the cat cannot see.

Hearing

The cat's hearing is extremely acute. It is able to pick up even the most minute sound, with the highest pitch being in the region of 65 kHz, even higher than the range of a prick-eared dog. Both dogs and cats can hear a range of sound completely beyond human ability. At the base of the ear flap the cat has a number of muscles which allow the ear to be moved through 180 degrees and become 'pricked' towards the location of the sound.

The balancing mechanism in the inner ear must have some unique property in the cat, as they rarely suffer from motion sickness while travelling. While they may not enjoy the experience, they do not vomit, as many dogs do.

Some cats are genetically deaf, others may become deaf by some accident or old age. In most cases this does not seem to bother them, although care should be taken when approaching a sleeping deaf cat.

Movement and agility

Cats have 230 bones in their skeletons, 25 more than in man. The extra vertebrae which the cat has at the top of the spinal column contribute to the flexibility of the body, as does the open construction of the shoulder joint which permits the forelegs to be turned in a wide arc. The clavicle, the collar bone, which limits man's ability to turn the head, is very small in the cat. Cats can therefore turn their heads at right angles to their backs, twist their bodies into any curve, and raise their forelegs freely. Except for the Manx breed, all cats have between 18 to 23 bones in the tail, again allowing for great range of movement and the ability to use the tail as a steering and balancing mechanism when needed.

Cats can retract their claws while walking, and they only use them unsheathed if on a very slippery surface. Retracting the claws keeps them sharp for killing prey.

It is extremely rare to see a cat, with the possible exception of the Manx, which does not have a free and unconsciously graceful style of movement which is pleasing to the eye. Cats are by nature sprint animals. They are built for pursuit and for evading predators, so they can swiftly summon enormous bursts of energy for short periods. The rest of the time they are content to lead a very relaxed life, spending at least two-thirds of their time sleeping.

Hunting

The natural predatory instincts of cats are never far below the surface, and cats will hunt and kill whether they are well-fed or not, although this behaviour sometimes shocks owners who have regard for all wildlife. Kittens are taught to hunt by their mothers quite early in life, and they soon learn to co-ordinate their body movements so that their hunting is successful. The cat kept totally indoors will still hunt, even if the quarry is confined to moths and beetles.

Even more disturbing to many owners is the cat's apparent pleasure in torturing its prey by catching and letting it go, only to pounce once more just as the small rodent is getting away. The cat is, however, almost certainly fulfilling its need to practise the 'catch and kill' technique. Cats are constantly sharpening up their reflexes so that they keep in top hunting form. This is not delinquent behaviour, as cats have no sense of right and wrong, and they do not seem to feel guilt at their owners' displeasure.

Although they are solitary hunters, cats like to share their kill with their human family. Cat psychologists say that owners must avoid recoiling in horror at a multilated rodent or bird which has been brought into the house, but should rather praise the hunter with a stroke or a few kind words. The number of trophies brought in may even increase if the cat feels it needs to prove its worth or that it is not getting sufficient attention.

Body language

Aggression

The cat's coat is supplied with erector muscle which will cause the hair to stand on end and the tail to bush out, making the cat look twice the size, in order to terrify an enemy.

The ears and eyes are used as battle flags as the cat advances on its opponent. A fearful cat is very precise in its movements, keeping its body close to the ground, with ears and whiskers flattened and eyes large and round. Anger inspires an opposing range of movement, the gait is more rigid, the ears erect but held back on the head, the eyes reduced to slits and the whiskers projected forward. In both fear and anger, there will be a lot of growling, and also high pitched hissing and yowling. Spitting is a sign both of anger and defensive behaviour. It is usually accompanied by an arched back and raised fur. See Figure 3.1 for visual emotions.

Lashing the tail from side to side is another indication of anger, but when the tail is held stiffly extended behind it is a sign that the cat is about to attack.

Pleasure and invitation to play

A gentle waving tail means the cat is quietly pleased, but a tail moved gently from side to side while the cat is sitting is an invitation to another cat or kitten to play.

Kneading

Cats will stand on their owner's lap or on a soft surface and gently knead with their front paws, sometimes with claws extended. This is said to be a sign of contentment and affection, a memory action from earliest kittenhood when it kneaded at its mother's mammary glands. However, this lap kneading is often performed on complete strangers, and very often they turn out to be people who are not very cat orientated. No-one knows why cats sometimes delight in showing overt affection to people who are not cat-minded.

Vocalization

Cats can convey a whole range of emotions through body language and by their voices. Kittens can purr from one week old. Purring is a sign of pleasure, used when comfortable and being petted, but a louder and deeper purr can also be a sign of pain. Queens ofter purr deeply in the first stage of labour when some pain or discomfort is being felt, and it has been noticed

Normal expression

Pleasure and contentment
- half closed eyes.

Play or hunting - eyes wide open
and ears pricked and alert.

Fright or fear - eyes wide open
but ears and whiskers flat

Anger - ears erect but turned back.
eyes - pupils constrict and whiskers
bristle forwards.

Fig. 3.1 **The visual emotions**

that cats which are incubating feline influenza will often purr deeply for hours at a time. Mewing varies in tone and pitch. Different breeds vary very much in vocal tone, some of the longhaired cats making an almost inaudible mew, while the Siamese has the biggest tonal range, with about 40 different calls having been identified.

Screeching and howling in sexual combat can be a loud, penetrating and almost frightening scream. Cats tend to be vocal when in pain, and many will moan frequently especially when injured.

Grooming

The fastidious nature of the cat means it spends a lot of time grooming itself, though not all the actions of this type are performed for fur cleaning. Licking performs four different functions:

1. It is a way of smoothing down the fur so that it acts as a body insulator.

2. In warm weather licking spreads saliva which cools the cat as it evaporates. This compensates for lack of sweat glands in the skin.
3. Sebum, an oily secretion from the sebaceous glands, is spread over the fur and the action of the sun on this secretion produces vitamin D, an essential dietary requirement.
4. Licking also stimulates glands at the base of the hairs which waterproof the coat.

Boredom

This behaviour is most frequently seen in cats which are confined to a small area. They pace up and down along the same path for hours on end, head down, and body swaying from side to side.

Burying faeces

This is an instinctive behaviour in cats which kittens learn from their mothers. A kitten which has left home too early may need some tuition by the new owner but the idea is readily accepted by all cats except ferals. There are several suggestions as to why the cat is so discreet with its faeces: one is that it is a manifestation of the extreme cleanliness of the cat. Another is the need for small animals to hide their presence from predators.

The odour of their own faeces triggers a cat to perform the scratching-burying action, even if there is no loose material to cover the faeces with. Having praised the cat for its neat ways, it must be said that the cat is an opportunist animal and will seek out some friable earth or sand to use if there is any available. For this reason, children's sand-pits and heaps of potting soil should be covered, or they will become polluted, and seed-beds in the garden should be protected with netting or wire directly they are planted. Advise your neighbours to do likewise or you may fall out over the cat's natural behaviour.

Greeting and contentment

In greeting, the cat arches its back and head, and the tail is usually erect. Rubbing movements are more than affection – the cat is depositing its scent from glands at the base of the ear and tail.

The ultimate symbol of contentment is a cat curled up on the mat by a glowing log fire or basking in the sun, usually asleep or with half closed eyes. This is often accompanied by a gentle purring.

Curiosity

The old saying is right – curiosity does kill cats. But cats are very curious indeed, downright inquisitive in fact. They have a compulsion to explore any new place or object brought into the home and curiosity can lead to a cat being shut into cupboards, being nailed up under floor boards, or carried off in vans and cars. When you own a cat you must be constantly vigilant about where it is, and before disposing of any carton, you must be sure there is not a cat inside.

Cats are extremely fond of sitting in boxes, bowls and containers, and at cat shows you will see many glorious champions fast asleep in their litter trays, because this is the only container allowed in their cage until judging is over.

Cat mint

An owner may be mystified by the sight of a cat rolling about in an almost demented way on or near the blue herbaceous plant *Nepeta cataria* (cat mint or catnip). This commonly grown plant exudes the chemical nepetalactone, a very effective insect repellent but one which induces almost compulsive addictive behaviour in some adult cats, although kittens seem almost unmoved by it. Rolling in nepeta is usually harmless but if the cat persistently 'goes on a trip' under its influence, the area may have to be wired off while the plant is in flower or, in extreme cases, it may be necessary to forgo growing this particular plant. Warn neighbours too if your cat is an addict, so that they can protect their flower beds. Cat toys containing small amount of catnip do not induce such extravagant behaviour, and they are especially enjoyed by many cats during the winter, particularly those which live in the house.

Sexual activity

Reproductive function is described elsewhere in this book but some aspects of sexual activity need to be mentioned here as, to new owners, the behaviour of the queen at this time may seem to be so bizarre as to indicate pain and illness what in fact they are normal behaviour patterns.

Queens in oestrus, familiarly known as 'calling', display uniquely overt sexual invitations which may cause alarm in those who have not owned a queen before.

'Calling' is literally interpreted with the queen uttering loud and long cries, especially noticeable in the Siamese and other Oriental breeds. The queen will be excessively affectionate to her owners and yet will take every opportunity to escape to seek a feline mate. She will roll and writhe on the floor, in yoga-like contortions, and may fling herself about violently, as if taking revenge on her own body because she cannot get her freedom. It is understandable that novice owners may interpret these antics as an expression of intense pain and in a way it is, because the female cat has such an intense compulsion to be mated. However, it is no kindness at all to satisfy her desire, as if she is let out, it is likely she will be away for several days, and will return, if she returns at all, battered, bitten and also pregnant.

Inevitably some queens will not return at all, as mating calls frequently lead to both males and females being killed on the roads. If her owners are not merciful enough to have her spayed, the queen will repeat this mating behaviour probably every few weeks until the end of her life, and if she is allowed her freedom, she will undoubtedly be mated and produce kittens at every opportunity.

Feral cats

As one of the last animals to be domesticated, the cat finds it easy to revert to a free-living state, but it is only in the last 50 years or so that many countries in the Western world have found they have a problem group of animals in the feral cats. Ferals are not wild cats. They are domestic pets which have either been turned out of their homes or have chosen to take up a semi-wild existence, and are now living and breeding in colonies of up to 50 cats where several generations will manage to live together in relative harmony.

Feral colonies are almost always established close to where man will provide some food or shelter, even if involuntarily, and it is estimated that up to two million cats live in derelict buildings around the grounds of hospitals, churches, dockyards, factories and railway stations, and even in the heart of major cities.

Feral cats become increasingly less tame, and it is almost impossible to handle them, although they will congregate for feeding, especially when the food arrives regularly at one place. Many people get pleasure from providing food for these cats and for some, feeding the cats becomes an obligation which they impose upon themselves often to the detriment of their own health and well-being. Urban ferals thrive on the contents of the plastic rubbish sacks put outside restaurants and shops, and it is said that this method of rubbish disposal has done much to help the feral to survive.

Feral cats can be a nuisance. They spray urine liberally to mark their territory, they yowl and fight, they proliferate fleas which can migrate on to humans, they get trapped in ventilation ducts and under building works. When the food supply is plentiful, ferals breed in prolific fashion, but if they fall ill they are unlikely to get any veterinary attention as even a sick feral is difficult to catch. The life expectancy of ferals is poor, because of disease, malnutrition, cold and traffic risk. Feral kittens will never make good pets even if taken into the home, they will always be almost impossible to tame and they may always be unhealthy.

Local authorities are often asked to eliminate colonies of feral cats which have become a nuisance, but total elimination seems not to be a good proposition, as if the site is a good one the from cats' viewpoint it soon fills up with a new colony of cats.

Several charities now spend a lot of time and energy in raising funds to control colonies by trapping the cats, taking them to a veterinary surgeon to be spayed or castrated, deloused and wormed, and vaccinated against cat 'flu. The cats which have been treated have a nick taken out of the tip of one ear, so that they will be recognized and not be trapped again. Trapping is cold, unpleasant work, and unfortunately it does not always have the intended effect as haphazard trapping means that only the most tame cats in the colony will be caught. When treated and fully recovered, cats which are healthy are put back into the colony, but it is doubtful if this is a completely successful solution to the problem as a neutered male, for instance, cannot resume his previous place in the hierarchy. Some workers would rather the treated cats were sent to sanctuaries, but this is a doubtful kindness to cats which are impossible to handle and which have enjoyed a free-living, if precarious, existence.

CHAPTER 4

TRAINING AND THE CORRECTION OF BEHAVIOUR PROBLEMS

Ability to learn

A cat, unlike a dog, really cannot be trained to obey. Behaviour patterns which are unacceptable to the owner often arise because the cat is displeased by some event, individual or new element in the household. Inappropriate elimination behaviour often seems to be used as a 'weapon' when the cat is displeased in some way, but it may be equally used if the cat feels threatened by some event or new arrival. The owner must look at each behaviour problem as it arises, trying to see the situation from the cat's point of view, and seeking to alter, as far as possible, the situation which appears to give rise to this behaviour.

Your veterinary surgeon can often give advice, and no behaviour which worries you should be considered too trivial or commonplace to be discussed, because much cat behaviour can be modified.

Cat Discouragement Plan

If the behaviour pattern defies analysis and seems to indicate wilful naughtiness then the 'Cat Discouragement Plan' is worth a try at least. Chastising the cat is never any use, since the cat will only bear a grudge against the person delivering the punishment. The Cat Discouragement

Plan has the advantage of keeping the owner remote from the cat and the scene of the crime. Quite simply, it involves squirting a jet of water at the cat with such force as to surprise and disconcert it, just at the time it is about to, or is actually, performing the behaviour pattern the owner wants to curb. The cat dislikes this treatment intensely, but only its feelings are hurt and no physical damage is done. Additionally, the owner is not obviously involved with the incident.

Water holders should be kept filled and ready for instant use. Indoors a water pistol or spray used for misting houseplants may be used. If the problem to be cured is an outdoor one have the garden hose ready connected for instant use, or keep a knapsack sprayer loaded for this purpose only, but beware of confusion with one used for insecticides – such containers must be clearly labelled.

The answers to the following frequently asked questions may help to solve some problems of unacceptable behaviour in cats.

Behavioural 'what ifs'

What if my cat stops eating?

Changes in the cat's routine can easily upset their attitude to food. They are very sensitive to the environment in which they are fed, particularly the location, noise level and the food container. When the appetite is poor these factors should be looked at and if necessary corrected.

Sometimes 'hiding' food near the usual eating place will stimulate the cat's natural instinct to steal food.

Try warming the food to 38°C; this not only releases pleasant odours, but provides the cat with food which is as warm as that of freshly killed prey. The temperature level is quite critical, for if it is above 40°C cats begin to lose interest in the food.

Make sure that your cat is not getting fed elsewhere. Some cats have a regular route of points of call at which sympathetic people feed them – your cat may be having lunch out every day!

What if my cat is spraying or urinating in the house?

This is a behaviour pattern often adopted by entire males and sometimes by queens, so neutering is usually the answer to curbing fouling of this kind. Even if neutering is carried out when the cat is mature, it can be just as effective in reducing hormone-related spraying. Hormone medication with tablets or by injection may be used by veterinary surgeons to aid the diagnosis of the cause and to treat certain cases. The few males, and some females, which do not respond fully to neutering may need medical treatment as well. Some spraying may be associated with stress in multi-cat households. Provide a safe refuge within the house for each cat, and consider sending one cat to board at a cattery to see if the problem eases.

Spray the polluted area with a deodorant suitable for use around cats, and try spreading the area usually soiled with sheets of aluminium foil, as cats will not walk on this surface. If only one area is used for spraying, the situation may be eased by putting the cat's feeding dish or even its bed in this place, as cats will seldom soil their own area in this way.

It may be that the cat is expressing its resentment against the arrival of a human or animal addition to the household, or some other change in its preferred environment. If you think that this is the case it may pay to consider whether it is possible to return to the original situation or at least minimize the change.

If all else fails, try the Cat Discouragement Plan, if necessary by setting up the situation and lying in wait for the cat to come by with the intention of spraying – you may only have to do it once if you time it absolutely correctly.

What if my cat runs up the curtains and pulls the whole lot down?

Cats are tempted to do this, especially if the curtain is blowing in the breeze. If you are forewarned that this act will take place, be prepared with the Cat Discouragement Plan. In future choose curtain material which is unsuitable for climbing, something in which their claws cannot get a grip. A bad experience, such as the curtains and supports falling down around them, deters most cats from repetition. Maybe you could set up such a booby trap!

What if my cat chews the house plants?

Many house plants are poisonous (see Chapter 10) but cats usually only ingest tiny amounts, so actual poisoning from the source is rare. You can discourage your cat from eating plants in the following ways:

1. Put the plants in areas which do not invite the attention of cats, preferably do not put them on a windowsill or in the direct path of the cat's usual patrol route.
2. Put the plants in hanging baskets suspended from shelves or the ceiling.
3. Cover the plants should you have to leave the cat in the room with them – or simply remove the plants!
4. Try the Cat Discouragement Plan.
5. Try growing some grass in a seed tray especially for the cat.

Fig. 4.1 **What if my cat chews the house plants?**

What if my cat is depositing all its urine and faeces in the house?

First check with the veterinary surgeon to make sure there is no physical reason for this behaviour. This is particularly important if the consistency of the faeces is in any way abnormal. Consider the possibility that something or someone has frightened the cat when it was outside.

There may be some reason why the cat is disinclined to use its litter tray.

- Is the tray located too close to the cat's sleeping and eating area?
- Has the cat too little privacy? Try covering the tray with a hood, a large cardboard carton is ideal.
- Is the litter tray large enough? Longhaired cats seem to require a larger tray.
- Have you changed the type of litter being used, or has the formula of the brand you always choose changed? Deodorants may discourage the cat from using the tray, as it may not recognize its own scent.
- Has the cat become allergic to the litter being used? Some contain dust particles which can irritate the nose and throat.
- Is the tray cleaned out often enough? The litter tray should be emptied, washed inside and out and refilled at least once a day.

It may be that the tray is quite satisfactory but that the cat has found a particular surface which it prefers. The answer must be to exclude the cat from the parts of the house which it is inclined to soil, or cover these areas with plastic while encouraging the cat to go elsewhere. It may even be necessary to indulge the cat by providing the cat with a small piece of the favoured carpet alongside its litter tray.

Finally, it is possible that this behaviour is the result of the arrival of a new animal or baby. In such cases, you must be patient as the behaviour may only be temporary. If you think the introduction of a new animal is to blame then it may help to feed the new arrival last, but in view of the resident animal and before it has finished its food.

What if my cat persists in stalking birds?

This is a natural behaviour pattern which offends many owners, but an attempt to stop the cat doing it may result in frustrations which may be expressed in other ways, for instance by spraying in or around the house. Wearing a collar with a bell on it does not handicap the hunting cat very much, but if you decide to use one, make sure that the collar has an elastic link to prevent accidents.

Fig. 4.2 **What if my cat persists in stalking birds?**

What if my cat persists on jumping on the worktop and cooker?

This is behaviour which is both annoying and unhygienic, as well as potentially dangerous to the cat. Try the Cat Discouragement Plan, and also in this instance as the cat jumps on to the forbidden surface, try shouting 'No!' loudly. When you are out of the kitchen, cover the worktops and cooker with aluminium foil, as the cat will not walk over this material.

What if my cat goes outside, but comes back in to relieve itself indoors?

Try putting the litter tray near the door, or even outside.

What if my cat does damage by digging the garden?

The Cat Discouragement Plan can be effective for this problem. When you realize the cat is digging in a particular spot, set your hose up ready. Deliver the water jet accurately but from as far away as possible so that the cat does not associate you with the wetting, it is important that the cat is caught in the act.

If the cat digs in the neighbour's garden some action must be taken. It is unnecessary to fall out and to pursue a long-running vendetta over an animal's behaviour when it can easily be stopped. Give your neighbour permission to apply the Cat Discouragement Plan perhaps even more vigorously than you do at home.

Cat repellents should also be used, if the neighbour does not want your cat in his garden at all. Tabasco, pepper, mustard or proprietory repellents may be used on the seed or flower beds and, as a last resort, fine plastic netting may be used on seed beds. However, your neighbour should be warned not to be friendly to the cat in any way, and not to feed it while you are trying to discourage it from entering his property.

Fig. 4.3 **What if my cat does damage by digging the garden?**

What if my cat eats large holes in woollen clothing?

This behaviour is generally associated with Oriental cats or crosses with those breeds. Unfortunately the chewing habit is often not confined just to wool; cats may make holes in almost any fabric and, to their own danger, will swallow strands of fabric which may obstruct the intestine and need surgical removal. There is no real remedy for this behaviour as it usually takes place when the owner is not present, but as the behaviour pattern is said to be strongest in some lines of Siamese, serious consideration should be given to discontinuing those lines.

Boredom can play a considerable part in inducing wool sucking and other kinds of aberrant behaviour. If this is the cause, much can be done to enrich the cat's life. Providing a companion cat is most effective, but conflict may arise when unneutered males are kept together. Patience and tact are needed when introducing a kitten to an adult cat, and owners should be prepared for some sulking behaviour, and perhaps inappetence for a few days.

Catnip-filled toys and table tennis balls keep even quite elderly cats amused, so will one of the commercially made cat posts which have a spring loaded fixture to the ceiling, and include several platforms and houses with many exits and entrances to fill the need the outdoor cat fulfils by tree climbing.

What if my cat scratches the furniture?

Scratching is a normal behaviour which does not offend until it is done in an inappropriate place. Save your furniture by creating a scratching post from a fairly substantial piece of grainy wood about 36 inches high fixed in a vertical position. Site the post near the door or cat flap so the cat can limber up before going outside. Alternatively the scratching post can be situated near the cat's bed so that it can stretch and claw immediately on waking up.

Liberal applications of perfumed wax polish will often prevent cats scratching polished wood.

Damage to soft furnishings can be prevented by choosing fabrics with a horizontal weave, or by installing vinyl covered furniture. Try pinning portions of fresh orange peel on fabrics which your cat stratches, for cats hate the smell and the zest. After a while the cat will be completely turned off from attacking that piece of furniture, and you need no longer renew the orange peel.

Finally you may have to resort to using the Cat Discouragement Plan.

What if my cat chews its own fur and sometimes breaks the skin?

The well-entrenched habit of self-grooming seen in all the cat family can be taken too far, and grooming can become continuous and obsessional. Tail chasing and biting can also be a normal reflex taken to an extreme state. Both conditions can be attention-gaining strategies, especially in Siamese. If a kitten starts this behaviour, the simple act of the owner walking out of the room may reduce the purpose of the behaviour. Taking notice of the kitten at this time may only reinforce the behaviour pattern. Great care is needed if any deterrent substance is put on the skin, but as most cats dislike the juice of fresh oranges, the application of this fluid to the bitten part can be safe and effective. The determined tail-or-hindquarter-biter may be frustrated by a plastic or cardboard Elizabethan collar, but ask your veterinary surgeon's advice first. Very severe cases will almost certainly require professional attention and medication. Tranquillizers and anti-convulsants have been used successfully but may be needed for several weeks.

What if we move house, will my cat stray?

A cat needs about a week of careful restriction to establish the location of its new home and the food supplies and comforts it is used to finding there. If you are moving to a house which is not yet in good order, it may be preferable to board your cat until you can offer the standard of living it has been used to. Once the cat has moved in, it will require a further week to discover the amenities of the locality and how to fit in with the feline society in the vicinity. The first unsupervised trips outside should be organized to be near feeding time, so that the cat is motivated to come back quickly. Cats are usually very conscious of the benefits their human family can offer and they soon readjust, provided there is nothing in the new location to offend them. If they are not carefully integrated into their new society they may well make extraordinary efforts to return to their original home. Buttering the paws does nothing to make the cat settle down – cats dislike anything sticky on their feet – however neutering does tend to reduce the extent of wandering.

What if my cat refuses to use the bed I bought for it?

In general cats do not feel secure at floor level and they often prefer to be high up, so put a cushion on top of a high cupboard, preferably under an electric light fitting, so you can leave a 60 watt bulb burning as warmth for the cat when you do not feel justified in having room heating on.

Fig. 4.4 **What if my cat refuses to use the bed I bought for it?**

What if my cat is at risk from being run over?

All cats which are allowed outside are at risk, unless they live in a very remote area. Many owners believe that their cat never strays outside their own garden, but when the cat is a victim of a road accident they have to believe that the cat does regard the opposite side of the road as part of its territory. A luminous collar with elastic insert may show motorists that the cat is there at night, but the only sure protection is to keep the cat indoors.

What if my cat gets into fights?

Aggression may be directed to other animals in the house, those outside which stray onto the cat's territory, or to the owner.

Unneutered cats, especially males, may defend their territory very vigorously indeed and suffer painful wounds in the process. If a male or female cat is not intended for pedigree breeding, it will lead a much happier life if it is neutered. Discuss the procedure with your local veterinary practice. Entire tom cats invariably have torn ears and abscesses as a result of their attempts to dominate the locality. Castration, even at a mature age, makes for a much more socially acceptable cat.

If fighting occurs within the household it may be necessary to make sure that the subordinate cat always has the opportunity to retreat into a safe place. Some females hold long standing grudges against each other which can never be resolved. The only remedy is to find a new home for one, or to separate them behind closed doors in different parts of the house.

A cat which has not been properly socialized with people or with other cats will not know how to fit into the society of either. Many cats which live on farms, or around hospitals or factories, have always fended for themselves and they can be very difficult, probably impossible, to catch and handle even when they obviously need help. It may take many months for such a cat to adjust to human households, if it ever does, and it is often best to release such a cat into the environment from which it came, after neutering, worming and attention to any other physical disabilities.

What if my cat attacks me?

Cats react instinctively to what they recognize as danger, real or imagined. Domestication is only a gloss on the surface and if your cat is frightened it will bite and scratch the nearest person or animal. Cats do not seem to have the same inhibitions which many dogs have about not biting their owner. Despite that, kittens should be trained from an early age not to be aggressive to humans. Allowing them to play rough games with biting and scratching an opponent is asking for problems later in life.

Never try to pick up a cat which is frightened or angry. Use an ordinary sweeping broom to move one cat away to break up a fight, likewise move with a broom a cat which is threatening or actually attacking its owners. Cat scratches can often become inflamed and cause a problem to humans. It is wise to have any extensive scratches or bites, especially if inflicted by an unfamiliar cat, attended to at a hospital casualty department. Cat bites can only too readily become infected, very inflamed or may even form an abscess.

Finally, it is quite useless to punish cats for not being what we want them to be. Any physical chastisement is likely to make matters worse, especially where the cat has aggressive tendencies.

What if my cat will not use its cat-flap?

Check to see that the cat door is in the most convenient position for the cat. The bottom of the door should be not more than six inches above ground level, so that the cat can walk through rather than have to jump. Educate your cat to use the door, by beginning with the door propped open, and offering a favourite food just inside or just outside, according to the action you want to teach.

When the door has been accepted, the next stage is to close the flap, but to show the cat how to push it open to receive its reward. The final stage in education is to put the cat out, and then to quickly call it back again perhaps showing it the food reward through the partly open flap.

There are very few cats which cannot learn how to use a cat door, provided it is well-designed and sited so that the cat's head or tail does not get trapped, and that it does not make a crashing noise as the cat goes through. Give your cat a big welcome when it comes in through the flap for the first few weeks and it will soon become the preferred mode of entry to your home.

What if other cats come in through the cat flap?

This can be a great nuisance but it is less likely to occur if your own cat is neutered and is therefore of little attraction to other cats. One way to ensure that intruders never come in is to buy an electronically controlled model to which the key is worn on a collar around your cat's neck. The door will only open when your cat comes close enough to operate the mechanism.

It is wise to have some kind of lock or fixing on your cat door so that you can restrict your cat's freedom when you need to.

What if my doormat is fouled by other cats?

This fouling is likely to be done by unneutered males and may well occur if you have an in-season queen in the house. Some people advise sprinkling crushed moth-balls around the doorway but these are actually poisonous to cats and should not be used. One of the best deterrents in this situation is neat tomato juice poured on to the area where spray has been deposited.

What if I see that my cat, or another, is stuck up a tree?

This is actually very often a non-event. If everyone leaves the site you may well find the cat gets down on its own, but it is understandably disinclined to do so when a crowd of people gather below calling it and trying to entice it.

An unfamiliar person climbing the tree and trying to grab the cat may well make it retreat higher into the branches so that it really cannot get down. Leave some very attractive food, for example a few sardines, in a saucer on the ground as an attraction for the cat to descend.

If the cat is still in the tree 24 hours later, then the time has come to call the fire brigade for their help. They are very experienced with heights and ladders and it is much better to ask expert help if it is needed, rather than allowing other people to risk being badly scratched and bitten by an angry and frightened cat.

Have a secure cat carrier ready to pop the cat into when it is brought down as it is likely to be very frightened and not at all grateful to its rescuers.

If the fire brigade have helped, a donation to their funds would no doubt be very welcome.

CHAPTER 5

DOS AND DON'TS

Introduction

Size, natural curiosity, and play are the three characteristics of the cat which seem to lead the animal into trouble, sometimes with severe or even fatal consequences.

Cats will investigate new places, large and small, with the ever present risk of getting locked in or trapped. Any comfortable warm place can be appropriated as a feline bed, and a curled up cat can easily be missed.

Great care should be taken, particularly with kittens, as they are especially accident prone. By paying attention to the following dos and don'ts a lot of potential problems can be avoided.

Indoors

Do:

Washing machines

Do check the washing machine before and after loading the washing. Not only are cats and kittens attracted to the open door of the machine, but they can find a cosy bed in the linen basket and may be scooped up with the washing to be put into the machine. Particular care should be taken if

Fig. 5.1 **Do check the washing machine.**

washing is left in the machine some time before the wash. If you see your cat in the machine, once it has started to wash, the first priority is to get the door open; a problem with many modern machines is that they have time delay locks on the doors. Unless discovered quickly, this form of accident is often unfortunately fatal.

Other domestic appliances

Do check ovens, fridges and freezers before closing the doors. Though not as much of a problem as washing machines, some kittens have been known to get trapped in a refrigerator or deep freeze. Special care must be taken on premises where there are walk-in cold rooms. Emergency treatment should be to warm the cat but not too quickly, and then consult your vet without delay. Do not feed the cat while it is chilled and do not be tempted to give brandy, etc.

Cupboards

Do check cupboards, as they are another favourite hiding place, although in general they do not present much of a problem. However, a cat or kitten waking up in a dark place can do quite a lot of damage to itself and to the contents if the cupboard contains glass and crockery.

Kitchen cupboards containing toxic cleaning materials are an obvious danger, particularly if the tops to the bottles are loose. In all cases veterinary help is urgently required. Wash off the toxic substances in running water while at the same time preventing the animal from licking itself. Take note of the substance's name or, better still, take the bottle with you to your veterinary surgeon; this will save vital time and enable him to give the most appropriate treatment.

Toilets

Do ensure that toilets with a lid are kept closed when not in use. Small kittens have been known to jump onto the top and fall in, their small size preventing easy escape. There have been some instances of kittens being drowned after trying ineffectively to get out, but it is usually their pride that is hurt most.

House repairs

Do check carefully before replacing floorboards that may have been lifted and panelling which may have been removed during house repairs. If your cat does become trapped in this way, it is a good idea to walk heavily or tap the floor. This will usually move any animal towards a small aperture where you hope it will come out; a light or some form of illumination will help, particularly if the cat is lost in the labyrinth of rafters and beams.

Don't:

Doors

Don't slam doors without looking behind you. Many cats naturally follow their owner and have been subjected to serious injury by a door closing on them. The most common accident in this respect is for the tail to be caught. The resulting damage can mean amputation. In all cases where a door has been slammed on a cat it is best to seek veterinary help as there may be some internal damage.

Food

Don't leave unattended food on the kitchen tops. It acts like a magnet to cats and kittens who will leap into the unknown for the promise of food. The most obvious hazard is the cooker top or split level hob still hot from cooking. Cats' paws are very sensitive but their bodies do not carry many sense receptors and they can get badly burnt before they realize anything is wrong. Hot cooking oil is an attraction and cats tend to sample the liquid first, often burning their tongues.

Don't leave half open tins of food within easy access. This overwhelming temptation can lead to bad cuts from the lid. In the case of large tins, cats may push their heads into the tin to get at the contents and have trouble withdrawing. The same applies to plastic bags where a tempting morsal of food is just out of reach. Cats will push their heads into the bag or container, running the risk of getting stuck, with suffocation being the obvious danger.

Baths

Don't leave the bathroom door open when running a bath. The slippery surface of the bath top can make the cat lose its footing and fall into the water. As most people run the hot water first, the dangers of the cat being scalded as well as drowned are very high. The cat will be in pain and possibly shocked and will try desperately to escape. Veterinary help is urgently needed.

Hot liquids

Don't carry boiling or hot liquids with a cat underfoot. The cat can become entangled with your feet, causing you to spill the liquid over yourself and the cat. Make sure that way is clear before transferring any hot substances.

Skylights

Don't be tempted to leave skylight windows open for the cat, even though you may think that the natural climbing ability of the cat makes this method of entrance an easy way to save constantly opening doors. During cold weather when surfaces are slippery, it can be very dangerous crossing roofs or climbing onto small ledges. Another hazard is keeping a cat in a high rise flat. The small balcony rails which normally make very good tightropes become very slippery during cold weather. In both these situations the animal could lose its footing and plunge to the ground. Although the cat is renowned for its ability to land upright, it can nevertheless do serious damage to itself when falling from such a height. Any cat which has suffered such an accident should be taken to a vet for a thorough check-up, possibly involving the taking of X-ray pictures to look for possible internal injuries.

Electrical appliances

Don't keep electrical appliances at floor level. It is not unknown for cats to spray onto electrical and mechanical devices and over a period of time this can result in the machine grinding to a halt or even exploding through extreme corrosion.

To the determined animal, nowhere is totally safe, but generally some degree of safety can be achieved by removing the article from floor level. Favourite appliances to spray on seem to be video recorders and televisions. Both are often situated close to ground level, but are also extremely dangerous as they are high voltage appliances. It is not always obvious that the cat has been spraying on an electrical appliance but some, e.g. an electric toaster, do give off the most pungent smell of burnt urine.

Chewing electric cables is a favourite pastime of kittens and this leads to many electrocutions. It is advisable to hide or secure all such cables out of the kitten's reach by tying them behind the appliance or hiding them under the carpet.

In all cases of electrocution, veterinary help is urgently required with immediate first aid as described in Chapter 10.

Ornaments

Don't leave your precious ornaments in precarious places. Valuable ornaments are the most notorious casualties of feline climbing expeditions. To cats there are few inaccessible places in a home, although the breeds do vary in their skills. Cats frequently find a sleeping place in the tightest corner, often on high surface with crockery and glass seemingly occupying all the space. Once settled and curled up the animal will then send everything flying as it stretches in its sleep, or when it is disturbed by humans.

Outdoors

Do:

Water containers

Do cover up any form of water container. The majority of cats are not very good at swimming and any form of water should be viewed as a hazard. Fish ponds are a fascination and feline caution is often thrown to the wind in an attempt to secure a snack. Ponds and swimming pools with straight sides present the greatest risk as the cat will have difficulty in getting out, although a net or cover over the entire pool is usually enough to deter them.

Water butts need to be securely covered as a cat landing on a poorly fitting top can fall in with little chance of escape.

Cars

Do always check under your car before starting up. Cats often use a car to hide under or as shelter from the weather, sometimes preferring to sit close to the tyres. Not all cats have perfect hearing and may not be quick enough to move out of the way before the car moves off.

Another favourite place is a warm engine compartment from which there is little room to escape when the car is started. This risk can be avoided by blocking up any gaps between the outside and the compartment.

Fig. 5.2 **Do check the car.**

Sheds and garages

Do check garden sheds before closing them up for the day. There are many toxic hazards in these places, although the most obvious danger is if the shed is to be left closed for a long period of time. Garages and any other form of outbuilding are also hazardous in this way. If the family pet is missing, these places should be the first to be investigated.

Don't:

Nylon netting

Don't ever use nylon netting with holes bigger than an inch in diameter to protect trees or prevent your cat from using a gap in the fence. A cat will be able to get its head through the gap in the netting but not its body. It will struggle to release itself but this only results in the animal getting more tangled in the mesh and in serious danger of strangling itself. Small mesh size, under half-an-inch, is safer, but do bear in mind that this material stretches under pressure.

Weed killers

Don't let your cat have access to areas that have been sprayed or painted with any form of weed killer or wood preservative. Fence the area off or cover it up. Although it is unlikely that the cat will lick such substances on purpose, it will clean any foreign material from its paws and coat and thus ingest the toxic substance. Some forms of wood preservative are not toxic to cats, but it is safer to assume that all materials used for such purposes are hazardous and best avoided. As with all forms of poisoning, veterinary assistance is urgently required and you should be able to let the vet know the name of the product and its contents so that he can give the most effective treatment promptly.

Turning cats out at night

Don't put the cat out at night. Being creatures of comfort, cats prefer the warmth indoors to prowling around in the dark looking for shelter. Some cats like to go out hunting at night but they often tire of the chase and return in the early hours of the morning expecting someone to let them in. Although cats generally are very good at looking after themselves, severe weather can take its toll. Predators, particularly in urban areas are not much of a problem. Foxes have been known to give cats a wide berth, although weak elderly cats or small kittens may become victims to a hungry vixen searching for food.

Fig. 5.3 **Don't turn cats out at night.**

CHAPTER 6
FEEDING

Nutrient requirements

Cats are grouped zoologically in the order Carnivora and this classification seems to be particularly relevant to their nutritional requirements, since a large number of studies, mainly conducted over the last 10 to 15 years, have shown that the cat has many nutritional characteristics of a true carnivore. Cats require about 40 essential nutrients which they must obtain from their food.

Food supplies proteins, fats, carbohydrates, minerals, vitamins and water. With the exception of carbohydrate, all of these are essential components of the cat's diet. However, the key to proper feeding is balancing the various elements of the diet so that a given quantity of food contains adequate amounts of *each* nutrient. The quantity of nutrients required by the cat goes from protein → fat → minerals → vitamins in decreasing order of magnitude (Table 6.1), but for a diet to be balanced all of these nutrients must be present at the correct concentration. This raises the question of how much food is required each day by the cat and this is, in turn, determined by the energy content of the diet.

Energy

Energy itself is not a nutrient in that it is derived from protein, fat and carbohydrate in the diet. Energy is measured in kilocalories (kcal) and each

Table 6.1. Recommended minimum nutrient levels in cat foods

Nutrient	Units	Amount	Notes
Protein	g	28	a
Fat	g	9	b
Linoleic and arachidonic acids	g	1.0	b
Arachidonic acid	g	0.02	b
Calcium	g	1.0	
Phosphorus	g	0.8	b
Calcium to phosphorus ratio		0.8	
Sodium	g	0.2	
Potassium	g	0.4	
Magnesium	g	0.05	
Iron	mg	10	c
Copper	mg	0.5	c
Manganese	mg	1.0	c
Zinc	mg	4.0	c
Iodine	mg	0.1	
Selenium	ug	10	
Vitamin A	IU	550	
Vitamin D	IU	100	
Vitamin E	mg	8.0	b
Vitamin K	ug	8.0	d
Thiamin	mg	0.5	
Riboflavin	mg	0.5	
Pantothenic acid	mg	1.0	
Niacin	mg	4.5	
Pyridoxine	mg	0.4	
Folic Acid	ug	100	d
Vitamin B12	ug	2.0	
Choline	mg	200	
Biotin	mg	–	d
Taurine	mg	100	c

All values are expressed per 400 kcal metaboilizable energy which approximates to 100 g of dry matter (i.e. with all moisture removed) in commercial cat foods.

g = grammes, mg = milligrammes, ug = microgrammes, IU = International units.

Levels are those used by the Waltham Centre for Pet Nutrition – based on National Research Council (1986) Nutrient Requirements of Cats – to allow for all stages of the life cycle. The National Research Council is part of the National Academy of Sciences of the USA and publishes books on the nutritional requirements of many different animals including the cat.

(a) Protein levels assume a balanced amino acid content and satisfactory digestibility. (b) Fat content stated only as a guide. Key nutrients are the EFA linoleic and arachidonic acids. With high levels of EFA, vitamin E will need to be increased. (c) Figures assume high availability. It is particularly important to ensure that this is the case with these nutrients. (d) Cats do not usually require these nutrients in their diet. This is because bacterial normally present in the intestines of healthy cats can make enough of these nutrients to meet the needs of the animal. Nevertheless, supplementation may be necessary if antibacterial or antivitamin compounds are being given or are present in the diet.

gramme of protein and carbohydrate contributes about 3.5 kcal of energy while fat contributes just over double this. The cat obtains energy by oxidizing ('burning') food in a series of complex chemical reactions.

Energy is needed for muscular work such as exercise, maintenance of body temperature, breathing, heart function and other processes necessary for life. Thus even a sleeping cat is using energy. The normal active adult cat requires about 80 kcal of energy per kilogramme (kg) of bodyweight per day. Various factors affect this requirement: kitten growth, pregnancy and lactation all increase the amount of energy required by approximately two, one and a half, and three to four times respectively.

If a cat takes in too much energy, i.e. eats too much, this leads to accumulation of body fat, the principal component by which the body stores energy. However cats in general seem to regulate their food intake fairly well. Consequently obesity in cats is not particularly common, and is far less common than in dogs.

Protein

Proteins are large complex compounds which, like many other biological materials, consist of chains of smaller and simpler units. In proteins these units are the amino acids. There are only about 20 different amino acids which are found in proteins but, as the combinations in which they can be arranged is almost infinite, there is a very large variety of proteins all with different characteristics.

Cats need protein in their diet to provide amino acids which are reformed into new proteins to form essential parts of the body's structure and function. Proteins are required for tissue growth and repair, in the regulation of metabolism and in the body's defence mechanisms against disease. As might be expected, the protein requirements for growing kittens or queens during lactation are higher than those of normal adult cats because of the formation of new tissue and production of milk.

Owing to differences in their amino acid composition, proteins vary widely in their quality. Protein quality is a reflection of the extent to which a particular protein can be used by the animal consuming it and depends on the types of amino acids present. Most animals are unable to make 10 of the amino acids in sufficient amounts and these key nutrients must therefore be provided by the proteins in the diet. It follows that a diet completely lacking just one of these 'essential' or 'indispensable' amino acids is totally inadequate for the animal. In contrast, a diet with an amino acid content close to the requirement of the cat has a high nutritional value. Animal proteins generally have a more balanced amino acid profile than plant proteins. In practice, of course, proteins from various raw materials are mixed to provide an amino acid profile that is satisfactory for the particular animal.

The cat has a higher protein requirement than the dog both as a kitten and as an adult. This appears to be due to a high rate of protein breakdown which the cat cannot 'adapt' if fed a low protein diet.

Fat

Fat performs several functions in the diet of the cat. It is the most concentrated energy source (see above) and lends palatability and an acceptable texture to cat foods. It also acts as a carrier of the fat soluble vitamins (A, D, E and K, which are discussed later), and contains the essential fatty acids (EFAs). These are required for healthy skin, kidney function and reproduction. In many mammals the key EFA is linoleic acid. This compound can be converted into the other EFAs required by the animal – known as the 'derived EFAs' – by the normal process of metabolism. The cat has only a limited capacity to do this and therefore must have small quantities of the derived EFA supplied in its diet. Linoleic acid is found in large amounts in vegetable oil (for example corn oil contains 50 to 60 per cent linoleic acid) but the derived EFAs (such as arachidonic acid) are found almost exclusively in animal tissues. So this rather unusual metabolism of the cat means that any cat food designed as complete and balanced for all stages of the life cycle must contain some ingredients derived from animal sources.

Carbohydrate

There are three major types of carbohydrate in foods. There are simple sugars such as glucose (a single unit or monosaccharide) and sucrose (a disaccharide – two units); starches (polysaccharides) are long chains of the simple sugar units. Finally there are the indigestible polysaccharides like cellulose.

Carbohydrate is a useful, usually economical, source of energy in the diet. It is not essential as such because the key nutrient it provides, glucose, can be made by the cat from protein, assuming its concentration in the diet is adequate. Cats usually find the single unit sugars and *cooked* starch very digestible. Some disaccharides, notably lactose (milk sugar) can be digested only to a certain extent so if milk is given to cats the amount should be limited (see section on practical feeding). The indigestible polysaccharides are collectively grouped as roughage, bulk or, more accurately, dietary fibre. Many benefits are claimed for dietary fibre in man but it is unlikely that these also apply to the cat because of differences in the digestive systems. Nevertheless there may be some application for a limited amount of dietary fibre in the management of diarrhoea and possibly diabetes in cats. A word of caution is necessary as *too much* fibre in the cat's diet may result in increased faecal bulk, even diarrhoea, and may reduce the absorption of minerals.

Taurine

No discussion of the nutrient requirements of cats would be complete without at least a brief description of the importance of taurine. This substance is similar to, but not precisely the same as, the amino acids found in proteins. Unlike most other mammals, the cat cannot make sufficient taurine for its requirements and must therefore have taurine supplied directly in its diet. Taurine is a key nutrient. Its importance was first linked to the function and structure of the light-sensitive area of the eye (retina) but more recent studies have shown it is required for reproduction, growth and development, and possibly for healthy heart muscle as well.

Taurine is found almost entirely in animal-based raw materials – fish is probably the best source. Virtually none is found in plants, cereals or associated products. This is yet another illustration of the cat's dependence on a supply of animal tissue in its diet (see section on fat) and indicates the truly carnivorous nature of this animal's nutritional requirements.

Vitamins and minerals

Vitamins and minerals (especially the former) are required in smaller amounts than the other nutrients (protein and fat) but are all essential for normal health.

Vitamins

The vitamins are usually divided into two broad categories: fat-soluble and water-soluble. The fat-soluble vitamins A, D, E and K are retained in the body. This means that a daily intake of these vitamins is not essential as long as the overall intake over, say, several days to a week is satisfactory. However, retention of excessive quantities of the fat-soluble vitamins can have serious effects on a cat's health. For example, over-feeding of vitamins

Table 6.2. Vitamins

Vitamin	Dietary source	Main functions	Results of deficiency	Results of excess
Fat Soluble				
Vitamin A	Fish oils, liver, vegetables	Vision in poor light, maintenance of skin	Night blindness, skin lesions	Anorexia, pain in bones (malformation)
Vitamin D	Cod-liver oil, eggs, animal products	Calcium balance, bone growth	Rickets, osteomalacia	Anorexia, calcification of soft tissues
Vitamin E	Green vegetables, vegetable oils, dairy products	Reproduction	Infertility, anaemia, muscle weakness	*
Vitamin K	Spinach, green vegetables, liver, *in vivo* synthesis	Blood clotting	Haemorrhage	*
Water Soluble (B group)				
Thiamin (B_1)	Dairy products, cereals, organ meat	Release of energy from carbohydrate	Anorexia, vomiting, paralysis	*
Riboflavin (B_2)	Milk, animal tissues	Utilization of energy	Weight loss, weakness collapse, coma	n/k
Niacin	Cereals, liver, meat, legumes	Utilization of energy	Anorexia, ulceration of mouth (black tongue)	*
Pyridoxine (B_6)	Meat, fish, eggs, cereals	Metabolism of amino acids	Anorexia, anaemia, weight loss, convulsions	*
Vitamin (B_{12})	Liver, meat, dairy products	Division of cells in bone marrow	Anaemia	n/k
Folic acid	Offals, leafy vegetables	As B_{12}	Anaemia, poor growth	n/k
Pantothenic acid	Animal products, cereals, legumes	Release of energy from fat/carbohydrate	Slow growth, hair loss, convulsions, coma	n/k
Biotin	Offal, egg yolk, legumes	Metabolism of fat and amino acids	Loss of coat condition (scaly skin, scurf)	n/k
Choline	Plant and animal material	Nerve function	Fatty infiltration of liver, poor blood clotting	n/k

* Effects of excess have been reported in other animals under special circumstances but unlikely under normal conditions; n/k = not known.

A or D can result in malformation of the skeleton with painful joints (vitamin A) and calcification of the soft tissues, such as the kidneys (vitamin D). Vitamins E and K are much less toxic but the key point is that oversupplementation of an already adequate diet can actually be dangerous and must therefore be avoided.

The metabolism of vitamin A in the cat shows an unusual characteristic which once again demonstrates the cat's need for a carnivorous diet. In nature vitamin A is found, to a large extent, in the form of substances which can be converted into the active vitamin. These compounds are the carotenoids which occur as the yellow, orange and other coloured pigments in fruits and dark green vegetables. Most mammals can convert carotenoids to vitamin A and can satisfy a certain part of their requirement in this way. The cat cannot carry out this reaction and therefore requires a source of preformed vitamin A in the diet. Preformed vitamin A is not found in plants, only in animal materials, the best source being liver. In fact, liver contains such a high concentration of this vitamin that its inclusion in a balanced diet must be carefully controlled to avoid vitamin A overdosage.

The water-soluble vitamins are not retained in the body, so a regular frequent intake is necessary for the cat. The water-soluble group consists of the B complex. Unlike man, cats do not need vitamin C in the diet, as they can make it from other food components.

The characteristics of all the vitamins are summarized in Table 6.2.

Minerals

Minerals are usually subdivided into two groups: major minerals and micro-minerals on the basis of the amounts required in the diet. The minerals in the latter group are usually referred to as trace elements. The functions and other details of the minerals are listed in Table 6.3 but their role can be summarized under three main headings:

(a) As structural components of the skeleton and teeth, for example calcium and phosphorus.
(b) In the control of the body fluids and to ensure proper functioning of nerve impulses and muscle contractions, for example sodium and potassium.
(c) As components of various enzymes and proteins, the best example being iron in the haemoglobin of red blood cells.

Like the fat-soluble vitamins, many minerals are toxic if fed in excess.

Water

Although water is not always regarded as a nutrient it is essential to life. It can be argued that its provision is more crucial than a supply of food; a cat can survive much longer without food than it could without water. Water has many roles in the body:

- it transports nutrients and metabolites (in the blood);
- it is a vital part of the temperature regulation system;
- it is essential for the digestion and metabolism of food;
- it is the principal route of elimination of waste materials via the urine.

As with any nutrient, cats must balance their supply and demand for water. Output is via faeces (usually the smallest amount), urine (usually the largest proportion) and evaporation. Lactation is also a route of water loss and, in abnormal circumstances, vomiting and diarrhoea can increase the losses from the intestinal tract. Water is obtained by three routes: water

Table 6.3. Minerals

Mineral	Dietary source	Main functions	Results of deficiency	Results of excess
Calcium	Bones, milk, cheese, white bread	Bone formation, nerve and muscle formation	Poor growth, rickets, convulsions	Very high levels – bone deformities
Phosphorus	Bones, milk, meat	Bone formation, energy utilization	Rickets (rare)	Symptoms of calcium deficiency
Potassium	Meat, milk	Water balance, nerve function	Poor growth, paralysis, kidney and heart lesions	n/k
Sodium/chlorine	Salts, cereals	Water balance, muscle and nerve activity	Poor growth, exhaustion	Thirst
Magnesium	Cereal, bones, green vegetables	Bone formation, protein synthesis	Anorexia, vomiting, muscular weakness	Diarrhoea
Iron	Eggs, meat (liver), green vegetables	Part of haemoglobin (oxygen transport)	Anaemia	Weight loss, anorexia
Copper	Meat, bones	Part of haemoglobin	Anaemia	Anaemia – interferes with iron absorption
Zinc	Meat, cereals	In digestion, tissue maintenance	Hair loss, skin thickening, poor growth	Diarrhoea
Manganese	Tea, nuts, cereals	Fat metabolism, many enzyme functions	Reproductive failure, poor growth	Poor fertility, albinism anaemia
Iodine	Fish, dairy produce	Part of thyroid hormone	Hair loss, apathy, drowsiness	In other animals, symptoms similar to deficiency
Selenium	Cereals, fish meals	Associated with vitamin E function	Muscle damage	Toxic but cats may be more tolerant than other animals

Cats may also require molybdenum, fluorine, silicon, nickel, vanadium and chromium in very small amounts;
n/k = not known.

drunk, water taken in as part of the food, and metabolic water. The latter is produced by breakdown of protein, fat and carbohydrate and for typical cat diets under normal conditions, contributes about 10 per cent of the total water intake. Clearly, the daily requirement for water can depend on many factors and it is important that cats always have a plentiful supply of fresh, clean drinking water.

Choice of foods

There are two main feeding methods available to the cat owner, prepared pet foods and homemade diets.

Prepared pet foods

There are basically three types of prepared food available and they are categorized on the basis of their water content: wet, semi-moist and dry. The most familiar of the wet variety (and indeed of all the groups) are the canned foods, such as Whiskas. Table 6.4 summarizes the main types of prepared cat foods.

Prepared pet foods offer several advantages: convenience, palatability, safety, a specified nutritional role and, above all, the testing and expertise that is an integral part of any reputable manufacturer's development and preparation of their products. In addition the label will usually contain details of what type of nutritional role the product fulfils (for example adult maintenance or kitten growth), and guidelines on the amounts which should be offered.

Fresh foods

It is possible for the enthusiastic cat owner to prepare a homemade diet but achieving the correct nutrient balance needs skill and nutritional knowledge. Each raw material used must be assessed as to its contribution to and deficiencies in the overall diet. For example muscle meat is an excellent source of good quality protein and many B-group vitamins, but it is very low in calcium and phosphorus (especially the former) and the fat-soluble vitamins. A meat-based diet must therefore be balanced with, for example, bone meal to provide the correct quantity of minerals. This and other examples are summarized in Table 6.5. How can this problem with meat be reconciled with the fact that the cat is a true carnivore? In the wild, cats will not eat simply the muscle of their prey but the whole body including bones, brains, gut contents and skin. These other tissues will provide the nutrients missing from a purely muscle meat diet.

Some household scraps are highly palatable to cats. The most commonly fed items in this category are fish and chicken skins, cooked fat or meat (usually from the joint) and fried bacon. Care should be taken to make sure that sharp bones are either removed or thoroughly softened by cooking before such items are fed to cats. As a general rule, scraps are best fed at least lightly cooked as this will lessen any health risks from food spoilage organisms. One final point is that too many scraps fed in addition to the normal diet may lead to excessive energy intake. The emphasis should therefore be on giving just small quantities as and when they are available, particularly as today's wide range of prepared cat foods will satisfy all of the cat's nutritional requirements, and supply a balanced and enjoyable diet.

Table 6.4. Prepared cat foods

Type of food	Feeding	Major ingredients	Comments
Dry complete foods	May be fed alone, only water required	Cereals, animal and vegetable protein concentrates, fats, vitamins and minerals	Cheaper feeding regime, but may be problems with palatability and acceptance
Semi-moist foods	May be fed alone, only water required	Some cereals, protein concentrates, fats, vitamins and minerals	Higher water content leads to softer food which is more palatable
Wet foods	Complete, balanced diet	Mainly meat, poultry, fish, minerals, vitamins. Some vegetable protein or cereals	Soft moist texture, very high palatability

Table 6.5. Fresh foods

Food	Source of	Seriously deficient in	Comments
Meat (lean beef, mince, chicken)	Protein, fat, some B vitamins, some minerals	Calcium, phosphorus, iodine, copper, fat soluble vitamins, biotin	
Fish (fillets)	Protein, essential fatty acids some minerals, most vitamins	Calcium (if bones not cooked), iron, vitamin A	Some raw fish may contain anti-thiamin factor
Liver	Protein, fat, fat soluble vitamins, B vitamins	Calcium, phosphorus, other minerals	Excessive amounts of liver may lead to vitamin A toxicity
Milk	Most nutrients	Iron	Amount should be limited owing to lactose (see text)
Eggs	Most nutrients		High intake of raw egg white may lead to biotin deficiency
Bread/cereals	Carbohydrate (energy), some protein, some minerals and vitamins	Fat, essential fatty acids, fat soluble vitamins	High levels of phytate found in cereals may restrict absorption of minerals

Supplements

A balanced diet, by definition, does not need supplementation. Homemade diets will require a certain amount of supplementation, as discussed above, but it must always be remembered that enough is enough. Excessive supplementation can be dangerous as has already been discussed.

Practical feeding

Adult cats

Normal healthy non-breeding adults cats have the least demanding nutrient requirements and in general their problem is fussiness (or, rarely, overeating) rather than nutrient deficiency.

Cats prefer to eat small meals so they should be fed at least twice a day. As they seldom overeat they can have as much as they can eat at each meal.

Overeating

Cats that show a tendency to overeat should have a reduced amount of food offered at any one mealtime. In addition any titbits from the table should be stopped and between-meal treats reduced. It may also be useful to find out if the cat is getting food from a neighbour. Neutered cats, in particular, may have a tendency to take less exercise which can lead to a gain in weight.

Full grown cats may be fed entirely on canned cat food, such as Whiskas, Kitekat or Katkins. A complete, balanced and interesting diet can be provided from the wide range of varieties available. Dry cat food, such as Brekkies, is a useful way of providing a change of taste and texture and can be fed as a meal or a few at a time as a treat. As mentioned earlier, fresh drinking water should always be available to all cats whatever their diet.

Fussy cats

Cats are sometimes fastidious and can develop the habit of being over-fussy about their food, even to the point of almost starving themselves if they do not get the food they want. Obviously, this should be discouraged as it can be harmful to the cat's health. The range of varieties offered by proprietary ranges of cat food helps owners to overcome this problem. It is advantageous to get cats used to variety feeding so there will be no problems with them obstinately refusing any changes.

Cats prefer to eat their food at room temperature and food served straight from the refrigerator may not be acceptable to some cats. If food is kept in this way it should stand for a while to reach room temperature as that is how cats like it best.

Milk

Some cats enjoy drinking milk every day but there are a few individuals that react adversely to it; they can have trouble digesting it and may develop diarrhoea. If this is the case the cat should be restricted to water only. For all cats the amount of milk provided should be limited (see section on carbohydrates).

Pregnancy and lactation

From the start of pregnancy the queen will eat increasing amounts of food and, unless she is overweight, should be allowed as much as she can eat at each meal.

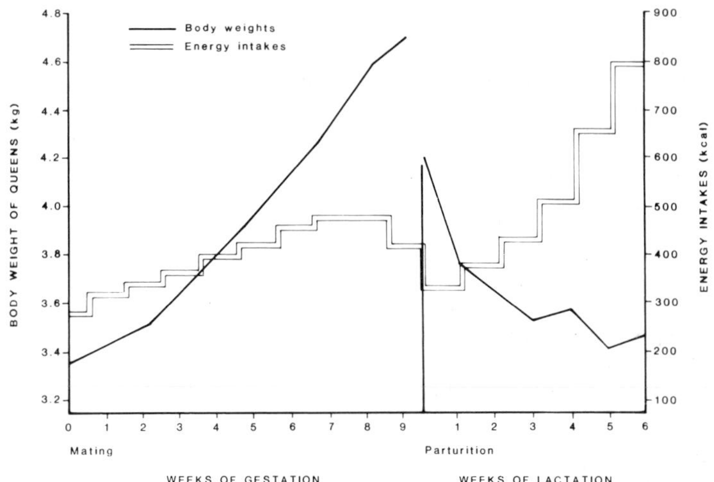

Fig. 6.1 **Weekly body weights and mean metabolizable energy intakes of queens during gestation and lactation. (Source: G. Loveridge (1986), The Waltham Centre for Pet Nutrition.)**

Figure 6.1 is taken from the National Research Council's Nutrient Requirements of the Cat (1986) and illustrates the pattern of body weight changes and energy intake during pregnancy and lactation.

It can be seen that these cats, which were fed commercially available canned food, steadily increased their energy intake starting at the beginning of pregnancy and reaching a peak in weeks six and seven.

As with many other animals consumption dropped immediately before birth (parturition). It appears that, for satisfactory reproduction, the queen lays down tissue in pregnancy over and above that needed for the foetal and placental tissue and uses this during lactation.

Food intake immediately after birth can be low due to the queen eating the placentas and associated fluids, but if low intake persists veterinary attention should be sought as prolonged food deprivation will limit milk production. In healthy cats, food intake should increase rapidly, with queens with larger litters eating substantially more.

As lactation is arguably the most nutritionally demanding time in a queen's life, it is not surprising that, as can be seen in Figure 6.1, the queen's body weight will decline despite increasing food consumption.

Kittens which are adequately fed by their mother are likely to be warm and quiet, whereas those receiving insufficient milk may be noisy and cold with individuals isolated from the rest of the litter.

At three to four weeks of age, kittens should be starting to show an interest in soft and palatable solid food and weaning will begin. A well-tried method of encouraging kittens to try solid food is to provide it at low level in shallow dishes. Gradually the kittens will take more food and demand less of the queen. This will allow her to decrease milk production and start to regain the bodyweight she will undoubtedly have lost in early lactation. Weaning should be completed by eight weeks.

Kittens

Food which is suitable for kittens must meet a number of demanding criteria. It must be palatable to ensure that it is eaten, balanced to provide the right mix of nutrients, and concentrated so that it can be eaten in the quantities which a kitten can manage. One specialist food available, Whiskas Kitten Food, has a recipe specially designed to fulfil these needs and take the worry out of feeding young kittens.

Like most young animals, kittens have relatively small stomachs and so it is essential to feed small meals at frequent intervals, four to five meals at eight weeks, decreasing to two meals at six months of age. Figure 6.2 shows the typical growth rate of kittens reared on commercially available canned cat food at the Waltham Centre for Pet Nutrition.

With all cats, but particularly kittens, any changes to the diet should be made gradually so that digestive upsets are avoided.

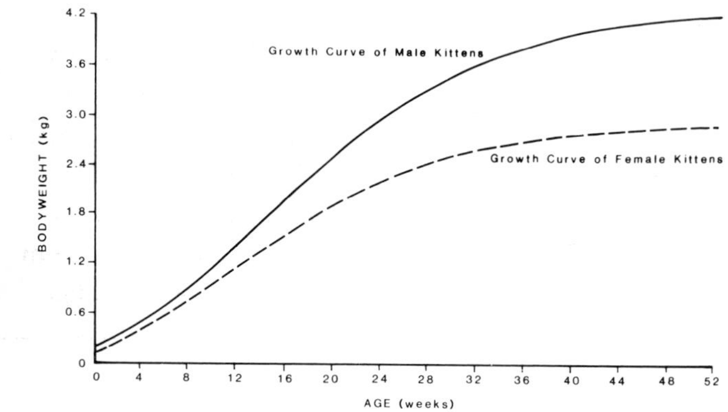

Fig. 6.2 **Growth curves of male and female kittens. (Source: G. Loveridge (1986), The Waltham Centre for Pet Nutrition.)**

Old and sick cats

Although correct feeding is an important part of the overall treatment for old or sick cats, each individual case is different, and care is necessary in offering any guidelines on this subject.

A few generalizations can be made. Old cats will usually become less active and will need less energy, and therefore less food. However they may also become more fussy. For older cats a highly palatable, easily digested food such as Whiskas should be given in controlled amounts, to prevent the cat becoming overweight. Careful supplementation under veterinary guidance may be necessary if the appetite is very poor.

For sick cats, professional guidance is clearly essential and your veterinary surgeon will be able to advise on any modifications to the diet that may be required.

CHAPTER 7
ANATOMY AND PHYSIOLOGY

Introduction

In order that owners can properly look after their pets and get the most out of them, it is important to have at least a fundamental understanding of how cats are 'made' and how they 'work'. Furthermore, owners who know the names of the various parts and organs, and their functions can more easily describe any signs and symptoms shown by their cats to a veterinary surgeon or breeder when seeking advice and can better understand why a specific treatment or course of action has been advised. The information given in this chapter is intended to provide this necessary information in an easily understandable and interesting way. It makes sense for all owners, and especially new ones, to read this chapter in its entirety as one would do with a manual for a new car. Thereafter, it should be necessary only to 'brush-up' on specific points. The information has been provided in such a way that details can be quickly retrieved when required.

The points of the cat

Note
- The flank refers to the side of the cat including the chest and the abdomen.

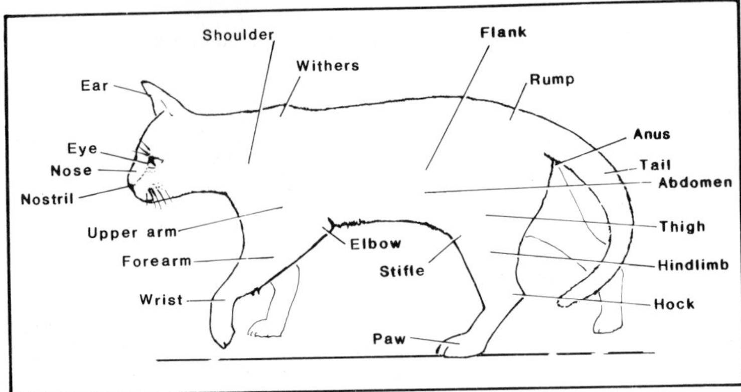

Fig. 7.1 **The points of the cat.**

- The paw is from the carpal joint to the ground in the foreleg and from the hock to the ground in the hindleg. See Figure 7.2.
- The ventral surface is the underneath side of any part of the cat.
- The dorsal surface is the upper side of any part of the cat.
- Recumbency is the term used to describe a cat that is lying down: dorsal recumbency, lying on its back; sternal recumbency, lying on its chest; lateral recumbency, lying on its side.

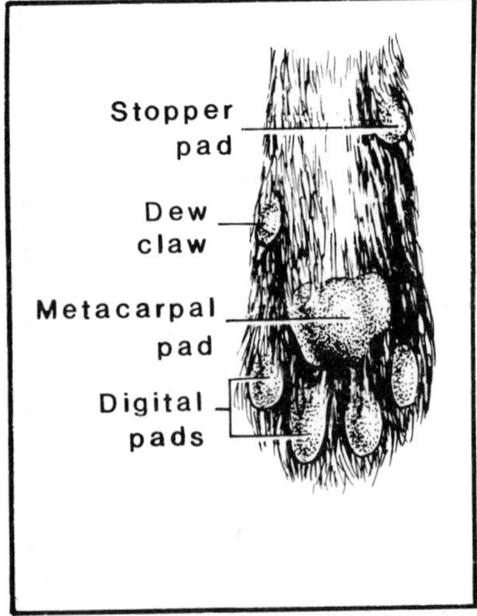

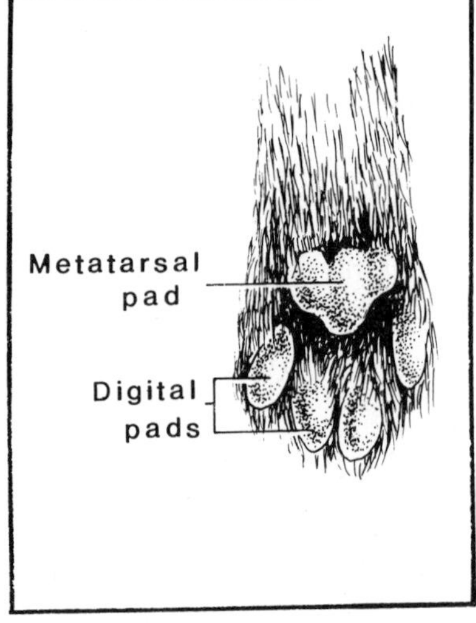

Fig. 7.2 **The paw.**

The paw

Lameness is frequently caused by problems in the paw, e.g.
- thorns in the pad;
- torn claws;
- cut pads.

In cases of lameness it always makes sense to examine the paw of the affected leg first, especially if the leg is being carried.

The skeletal system

Essentially the skeletal system is made up of bones joined by ligaments, muscles and tendons. The function of the skeleton is to support and protect the body organs and, through the muscles which are connected to the bones by tendons, to make locomotion possible.

The major bones in the skeleton

Note
- The long bones, e.g. the humerus, radius and ulna, the femur and the tibia, are most prone to fracture, particularly in road traffic accidents.
- In adult animals the bones usually break into two or more separate parts. In young animals the bone may bend and split, causing the so-called 'green-stick' fracture.
- The forelimb is not joined to the remainder of the skeleton, it is held in place simply by muscles. Unlike the dog, there is a collar bone (or clavicle) in the cat.

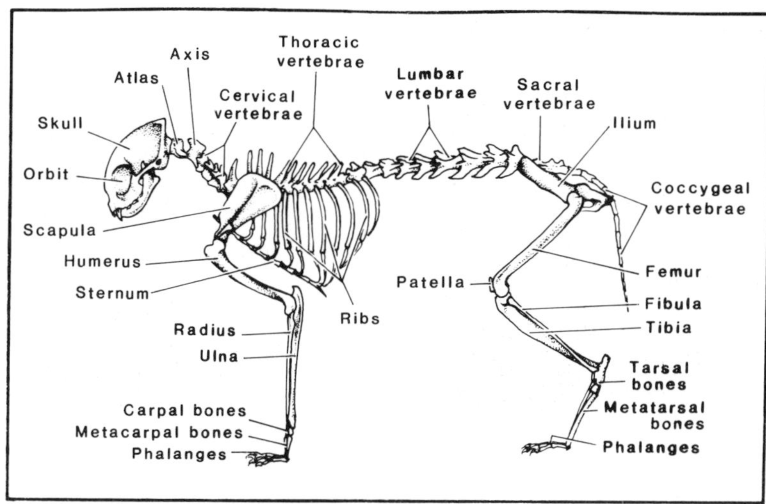

Fig. 7.3 **The skeleton of the cat.**

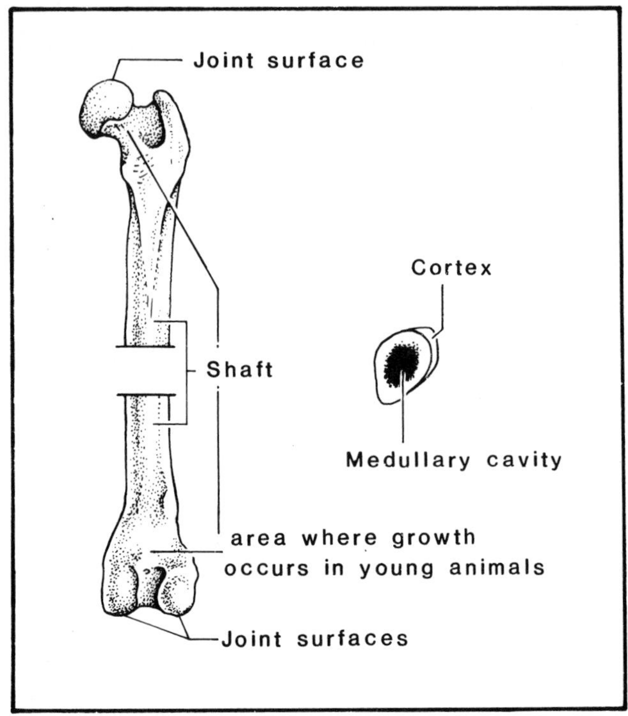

Fig. 7.4 **The structure of a long bone.**

The structure of long bones

Note

- Fractured bones can be repaired by placing a pin in the medullary cavity or by screwing a metal plate to the cortex where appropriate.

The structure of the vertebrae

There are a total of 30 neck and trunk vertebrae plus 21–24 in the tail. Seven cervical vertebrae make up the neck. Thirteen thoracic vertebrae make up the spine over the chest and articulate with the ribs. Seven lumbar vertebrae and three sacral vertebrae form the lower back. The number of coccygeal vertebrae depends on the length of the tail.

Note

- The spinal cord lies within the vertebral canal and is thus protected by bone.
- The vertebrae are separated by discs of cartilage which give protection against trauma and allow the spine to be more flexible. The centre of the disc may slip out of place and press on the spinal cord causing pain and paralysis.
- The vertebrae are joined together by ligaments and muscles which are anchored to the vertebral processes. Contraction of the muscles makes the spine bend vertically and from side to side.

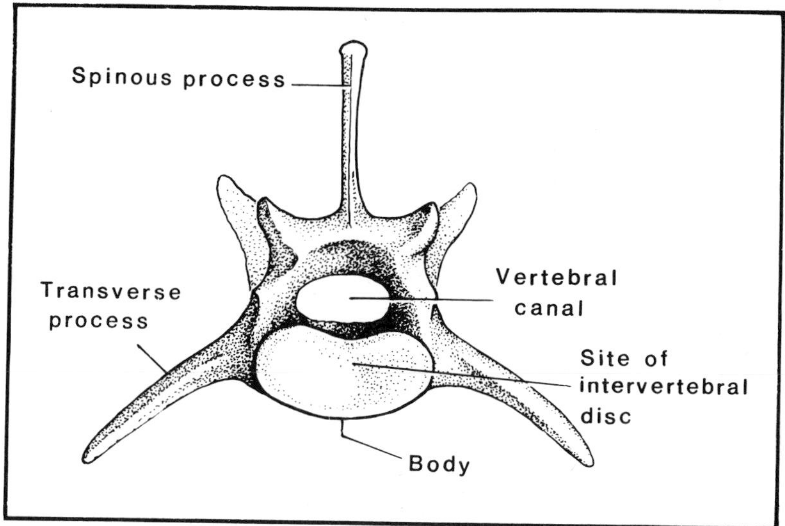

Fig. 7.5 **The structure of a vertebra.**

The structure of the skull

The upper jaw consists of the maxilla bone. The lower jaw is hinged to the skull and consists of the mandible which has both horizontal and vertical parts. These can quite easily become fractured in road traffic accidents. The

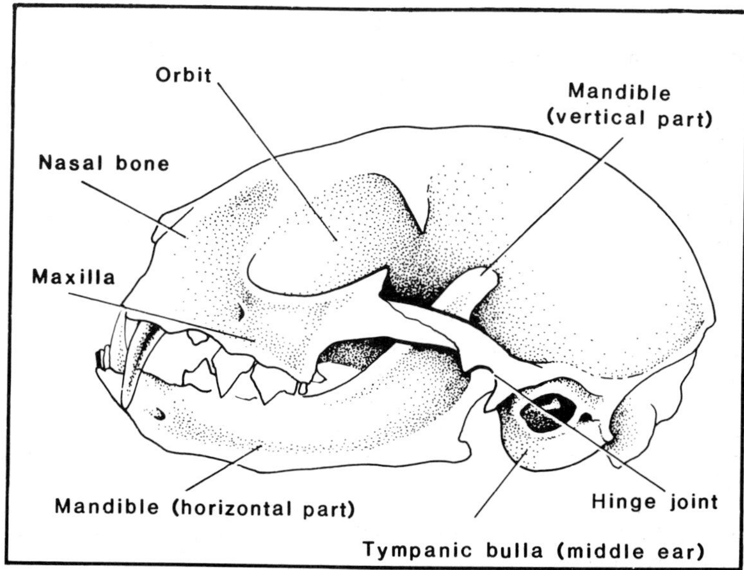

Fig. 7.6 **The structure of the skull.**

jaw may become dislocated by trauma but that is comparatively rare. It is quite common however for the left and right horizontal parts of the mandible, where they are joined in the front of the mouth, to become separated in traumatic accidents. Sometimes the bones that make up the roof of the mouth do not fuse properly giving rise to a cleft palate. Kittens with severe cleft palates cannot suck because they cannot form a vacuum in the mouth and so often die. It is sensible to check all kittens as they are born for this congenital abnormality.

The bony plates that make up the top of the skull are fused together in the middle of the forehead. In kittens born with the abnormality hydrocephalus, the skull bones do not fuse properly and a gap, or fontanelle, persists.

The teeth

Adult cats have a total of 30 teeth. These are made up as shown in Table 7.1.

Kittens begin to cut their milk teeth at about 14 days after birth. There are no molars in this set.

Milk teeth are shed and replaced by adult teeth at four to six months old. If any milk teeth persist which threaten to obstruct the correct growth of the permanent teeth, they can easily be removed by a veterinary surgeon.

Cats' teeth are shaped for tearing and cutting rather than grinding, thus particles of food do not tend to become lodged in the teeth and dental decay is therefore relatively rare.

Cats' teeth frequently accumulate 'tartar', a hard deposit, on their surfaces particularly if they only have access to soft food. This scale can be

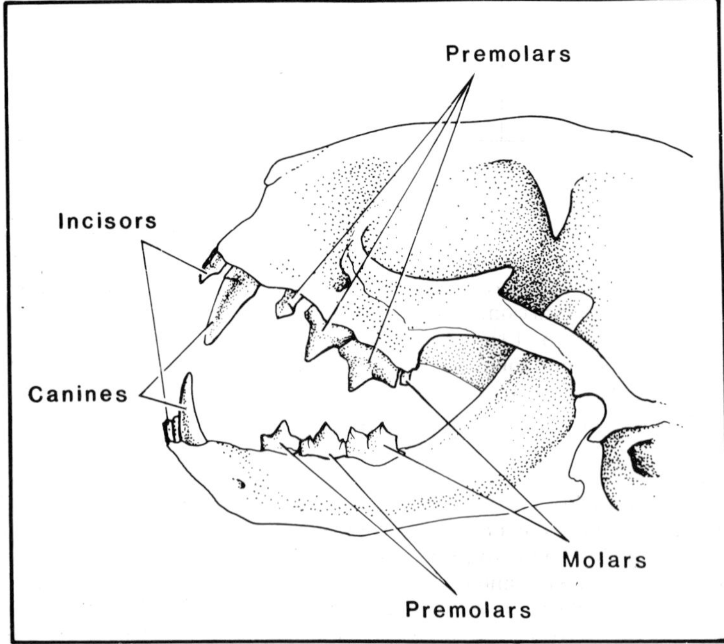

Fig. 7.7 The teeth.

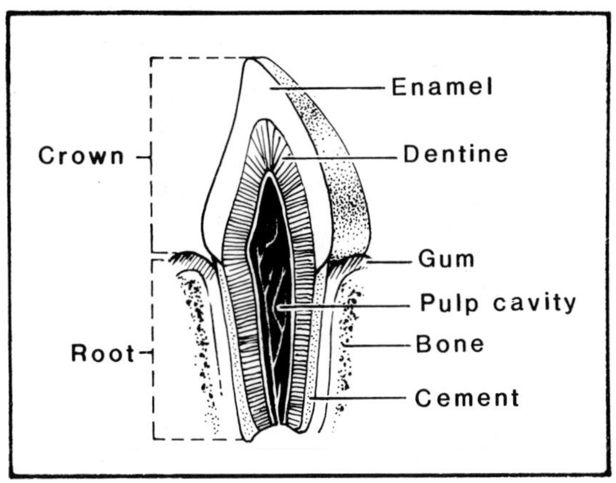

Fig. 7.8 **The structure of a tooth.**

Table 7.1. Teeth

Tooth type	Upper jaw	Lower jaw
Incisors	6	6
Canine	2	2
Premolars	6	4
Molars	2	2

fairly easily removed by veterinary surgeons and should not be allowed to accumulate as it can lead to gingivitis, inflammation of the gums, associated with smelly breath and premature loss of teeth. Tartar starts to accumulate at the tooth/gum junction. Infection can also enter at this level. Both can lead to inflammation of the gum.

The last upper premolar and the lower molar are much larger than the rest of the teeth. They are called the carnassial teeth. They have more than one root which can make them difficult to extract.

The joints

A joint is the region where two or more bones articulate with one another. Simple joints allow movement in one plane only, whereas ball and socket joints, e.g. the hip, allow rotation to occur. The ends of the bones which form joints are covered with smooth cartilage to facilitate movement and the joint itself is lubricated with a viscous liquid called synovial fluid. The bones are joined together with ligaments which may become damaged if the joint is 'sprained' by being bent or straightened beyond its normal limits. If the

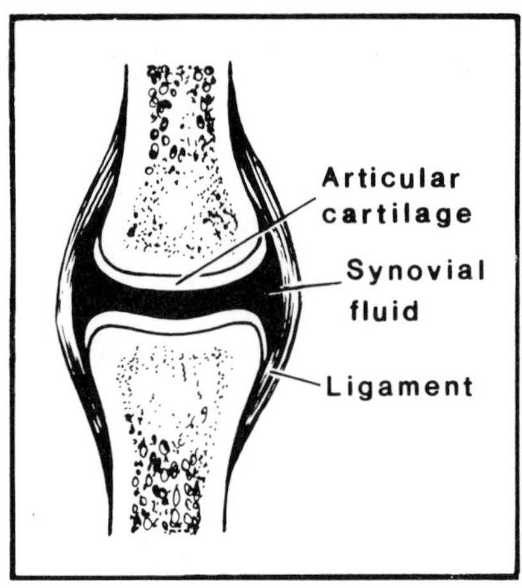

Fig. 7.9 **The structure of a simple joint.**

ligaments break, or are so stretched that the bones become separated, a 'dislocation' occurs. The stifle and hip joints are particularly prone to problems in cats. Their structure is shown in Figures 7.9, 7.10 and 7.11.

- In arthritis the articular cartilage becomes inflamed and makes movement painful.
- The upper part of the patella is joined by a tendon to the muscles which straighten the stifle.
- The lower part of the patella is joined by a ligament to the tibia.
- The patella fits in a groove in the femur and moves up and down as the leg is straightened and bent.

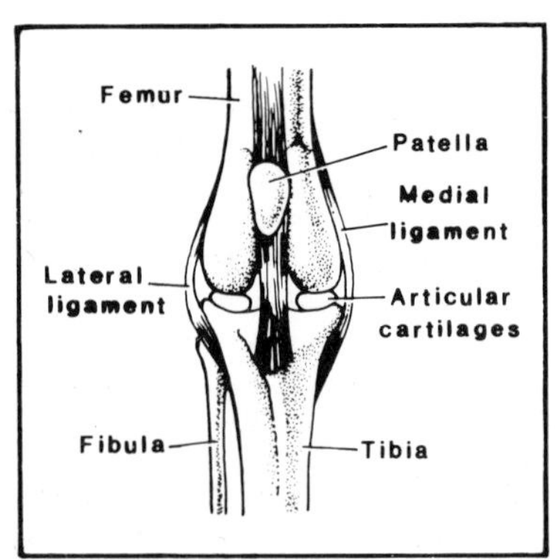

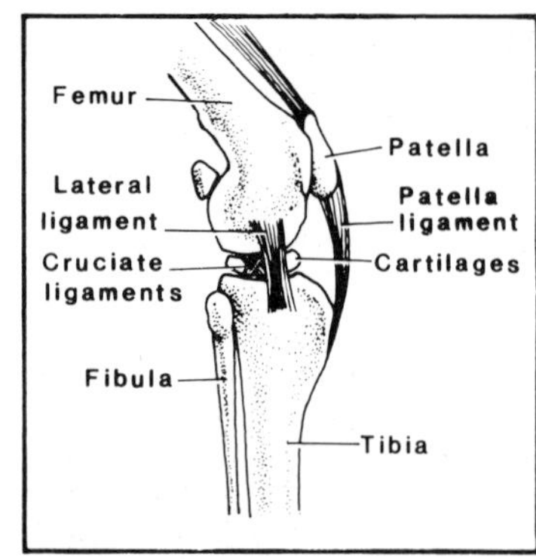

Fig. 7.10 **The structure of the stifle joint.**

(a) Front view. **(b) Side view.**

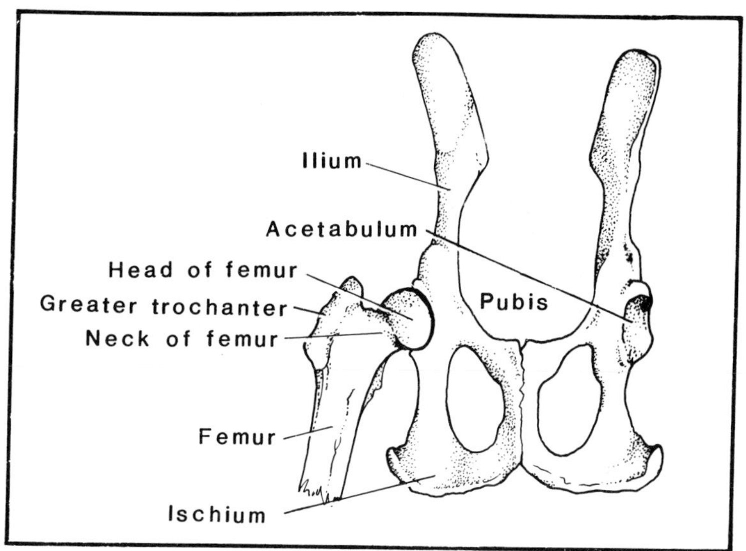

Fig. 7.11 **The hip joint.**

- The patella may be dislocated to either side if the joint is subjected to trauma. This can occur quite easily if the animal is born with a groove which is abnormally shallow.
- Within the joint lie two cartilages which cushion the joint against trauma, and promote the smooth movement of the joint. There are also two cruciate ligaments within the stifle joint. These structures may become ruptured so allowing excessive, sometimes painful, movement of the joint.
- The hip joint is a typical ball and socket joint.
- In spite of a ligament between the head of the femur and the acetabulum dislocation of the hip joint is quite common as a result of accidents.

The skeletal muscles

Muscles are made up of fibres which contract when stimulated by a nerve impulse. Some muscles, for example those making up the stomach wall, are flat and relatively thin, others are cylindrical and when contracted are quite fat (e.g. the biceps muscle which flexes the elbow and the quadriceps muscle which lies in front of the femur and straightens the hind leg). Since the ends of the muscles are attached to bone by tendons, contraction and relaxation causes movement in the joints, making them bend (flex), extend, move inwards (adduction), move outwards (abduction) or rotate. In principle each muscle is opposed by another which exerts the opposite effect, thus the animal can adjust the position of any joint very precisely.

Apart from their obvious actions in causing locomotion, the muscles also serve to generate body heat by shivering. The muscles over the chest contract and relax to bring about respiratory movements. The abdominal muscles come into play when a cat passes motions or gives birth, as well as helping to flex the spine when the cat is galloping. The shoulder muscles hold the fore leg to the cat's trunk.

Over-extension of muscles can cause damage and this is called a muscle strain. Myositis is the word used to describe inflammation of muscles, and is often accompanied by acute pain.

The skin

The overall purpose of the skin is to cover the body and protect the underlying tissues and organs, but it is also responsible for carrying information about objects that come in contact with the animal, and the environmental temperature. The skin is also, of course, sensitive to pain and will warn the animal of danger from sharp objects etc. The skin consists of two main layers – the epidermis and dermis.

The epidermis

This layer is made up of hardened plate-like cells which are formed continuously from the bottom layer and are shed or worn away from the top. The layer contains no blood vessels.

In places, the epidermis extends down into the underlying layer to form a hair follicle which produces a single hair by growth from the bottom. When this growth stops that hair is shed and usually another begins to grow in its place. In cats a number of hairs group together to emerge through a common opening. One hair in such a group is often thicker and longer than the others and is called a 'guard hair'. The rest of the coat is formed by the smaller,

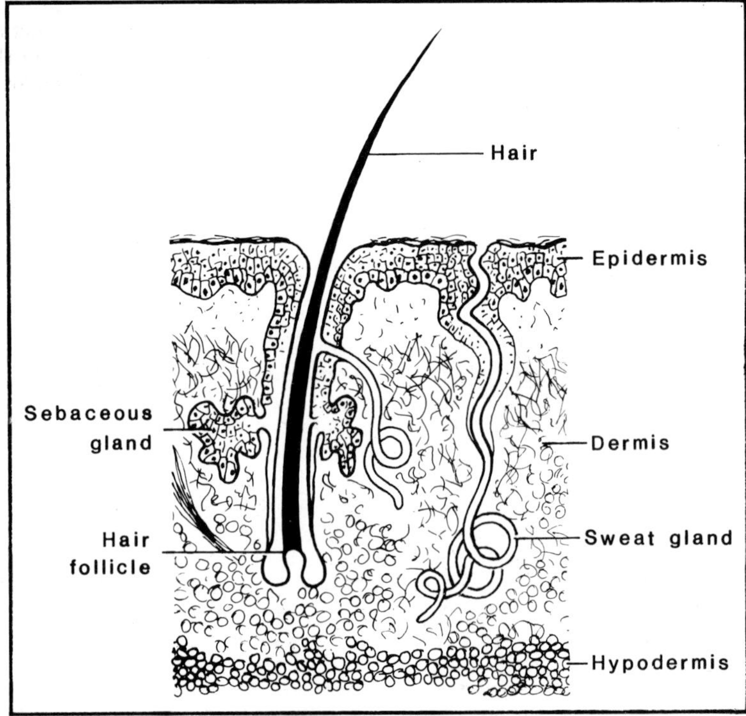

Fig. 7.12 **The structure of the skin.**

softer hairs in the bunch. The size of these hair bunches will vary according to the coat type. Sebaceous glands feed into the hair follicle producing a thick fluid that lubricates the skin and keeps it pliable.

Sweat glands also open up to the surface through the epidermis. In man, the evaporation of fluid produced by these glands is a major cooling mechanism. However, cats lose heat principally by panting over their tongues.

The dermis

This layer contains blood vessels, that nourish the lower layer of the epidermis, and connective tissue, which supports the hair follicles and sweat glands. It also contains nerve ends which are sensitive to pain and touch. Small muscle fibres in the dermis, which can lengthen and contract, alter the shape of the skin and erect or lower the hairs. This effect is particularly noticeable in the centre back area and tail when the cat is mentally aroused, aggressive or fearful.

Modified skin structures

- The mammary glands are skin glands that have become specially modified to produce milk.
- The anal sacs (or so-called scent glands) are inversions of the skin where it joins the end of the digestive tract. There are two sacs which lie on either side of the anus, producing a dryish secretion of varying consistency. Occasionally the opening of these cavities become blocked and, unless expressed, the sacs may become impacted and painful.
- The claws originate from the coronary border, the circular junction between the base of the claw and the skin. The claw grows down over the dermis that lies over the underlying phalanx. The dermis contains a lot of blood vessels and will bleed profusely if cut.

Note

In subcutaneous injections the needle passes though the epidermis and dermis and medicament is deposited in the hypodermis. Intramuscular

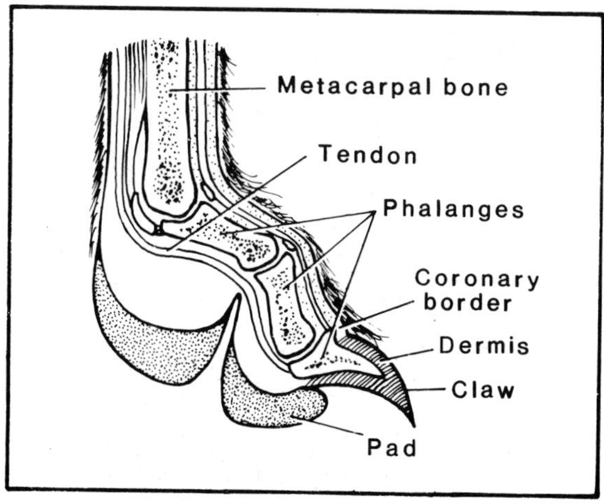

Fig. 7.13 **The claws.**

injections are given into the muscles (usually in the hind leg) underlying the skin, intravenous injections are given straight into the bloodstream (usually the vein running down the front of one of the forelegs is used). Intraperitoneal injections are given into the cavity between the abdominal wall and the abdominal organs.

The ear

The ear consists of four parts:
1. the ear flap;
2. the external ear canal;
3. the middle ear;
4. the internal ear.

1. **The ear flap** is held erect by a sheet of cartilage covered with skin.

2. **The external ear canal** is composed of a tube of cartilage and is lined with a specially developed skin called the integument, which produces a waxy material. The canal has a sharp bend at its lower end where the vertical part joins the horizontal part. The end of the horizontal part of the canal is sealed by the ear drum.

It is important that the external ear canal be kept clear of excessive amounts of wax and debris, otherwise infection may occur resulting in otitis externa (ear canker). The most common cause of ear disease in the cat is infestation with ear mites; they can be seen with an auroscope usually in the

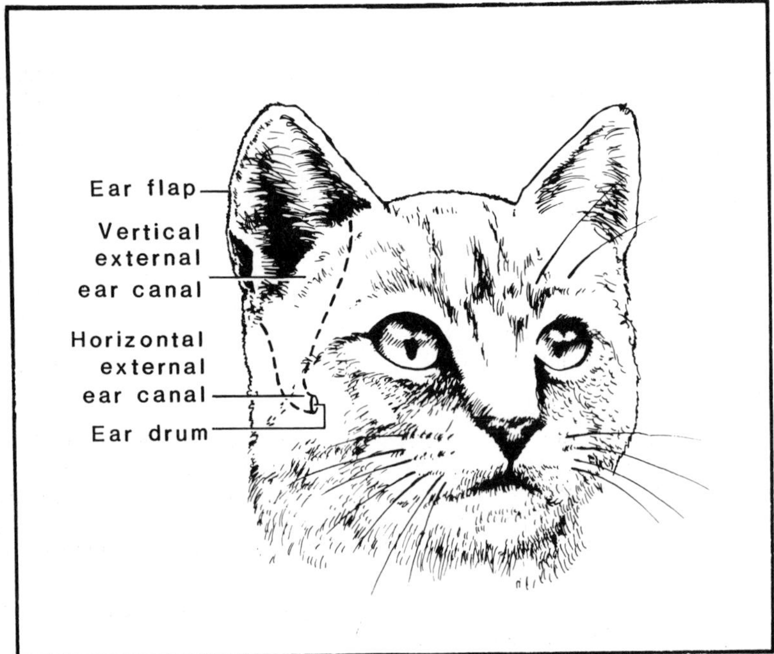

Fig. 7.14 **(a) The external ear.**

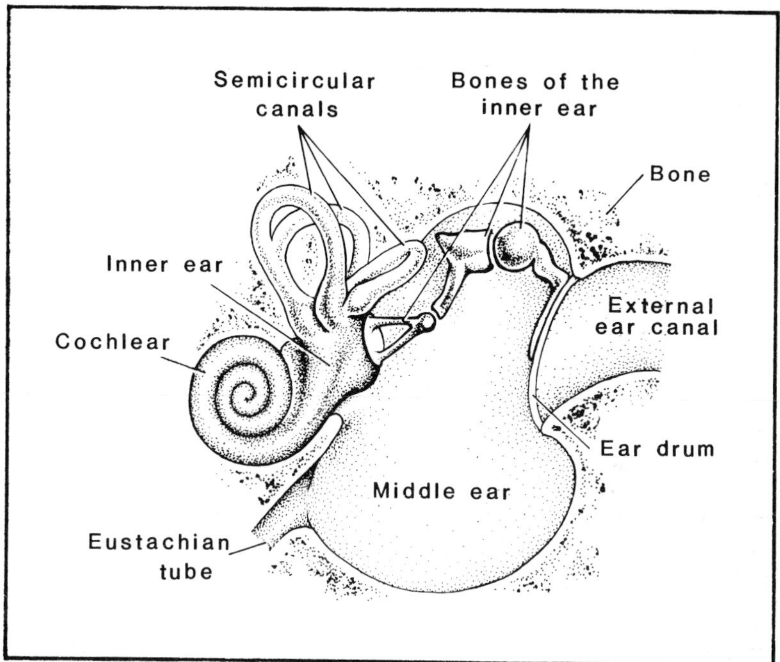

Fig. 7.14 **(b) The middle and inner ear.**

horizontal part of the canal. In chronic cases of otitis externa the lining of the ear becomes very thickened so that the canal is occluded and the ridges often rub together to form ulcers. By the time that has happened the only sure cure is to open the canal to the outside by carrying out an operation called an aural resection.

3. **The middle ear** is housed in a cavity in one of the bones which makes up the skull. It consists of a chamber that contains three small bones which connect the ear drum to a window at the opposite side. These bones transmit sound vibrations to the inner ear. Pressure differences between the middle and external ear are equalized by means of the eustachian tube, which leads to the back of the mouth and which is also situated in a cavity in a bone of the skull.

4. **The inner ear** consists of a number of sealed tubes which contain fluid. The cochlea picks up vibrations from the middle ear and is concerned with hearing. The semi-circular canals contain nerve endings which sense the fluid movement in the tubes that are set at right angles to each other. By monitoring the fluid movement the animal is able to keep its balance and orientate itself in space.

While disease of the external ear is common, middle and inner ear disease is rare, but is usually very serious when it does occur.

If external ear disease is not treated promptly and properly, it can lead to a serious problem that may need a surgical operation to correct.

The eye

Essentially the eye is a fluid-filled globe that is 'housed' in the orbit in the skull. Attached to the outside of the globe are a number of muscles which are able to move the eye upwards, downwards and from side to side.

The lens, pupil and the ciliary body divide the eye into two parts:

1. the anterior chamber which is filled with fluid called the aqueous humour;
2. the posterior chamber which is filled with a thick fluid called the vitreous humour.

The correct pressure within the eye is maintained by fluid being continually produced and drained away. If this mechanism goes wrong the pressure in the eye will rise, resulting in the eye increasing in size and the cornea becoming opaque – this is called glaucoma.

The outermost layer of the eye is tough and thick and is called the sclera. Over the front of the eye this layer takes the form of a transparent window called the cornea.

The lens is attached by a ligament to the ciliary body which is muscular. Contraction of this muscle alters the shape of the lens so that the animal can focus on objects at different distances.

The back of the eye is linked with the retina. Nerves which have light-sensitive endings in this layer transmit messages through the optic nerve to the brain, where they are 'decoded' into a 'picture' of what is being seen. The back of the eye of dogs and cats also contains a separate area called the tapetum which reflects light. The glowing effect of dogs' and cats' eyes at night is produced when a beam of light falls on to the tapetum in surrounding darkness and is reflected.

The front of the eye is protected by the upper and lower eyelids which when closed completely cover the eye. The place where the eyelids join is known as the canthus or the 'corner of the eye'. Cats have a third eyelid, the nictitating membrane or haw, which lies close to the surface of the eye in the inner corner of the eyelids. When the eye recedes into the skull, as can occur when the cat is out of condition and the fat behind the eye decreases in amount, or when the eye is pushed backwards into the head, the third eyelid will come across to protect the eye from possible damage. The third eyelid may also protrude temporarily in a cat that has been stressed, e.g. by a long car journey or being taken to a cat show. A gland which produces lubricating fluid (the Harderian gland) lies under the third eyelid. It may occasionally become enlarged and protrude from behind the third eyelid and cause a problem.

The skin on the outside of the eyelid is continued on the inside of the eyelid and over the cornea as a thin layer called the conjunctiva. Because the lids protrude over the eye the conjunctiva is bent back on itself to form a sac as it continues over the eye. The surface of the eye is lubricated by fluid (tears) produced by the lacrimal gland that drain into the conjunctival sac. Any excess tears are carried away in small ducts that are situated in the inner corner of the eye and which lead to the nose. If more tears than normal are produced, or if this duct becomes blocked, fluid runs down the side of the animal's face and may cause staining or inflammation of the skin. The head shape of some of the longhaired and flat faced breeds can cause interference with proper drainage of tear fluid so that there is overflow down the face. The upper and lower eyelashes protrude from the point where the skin on

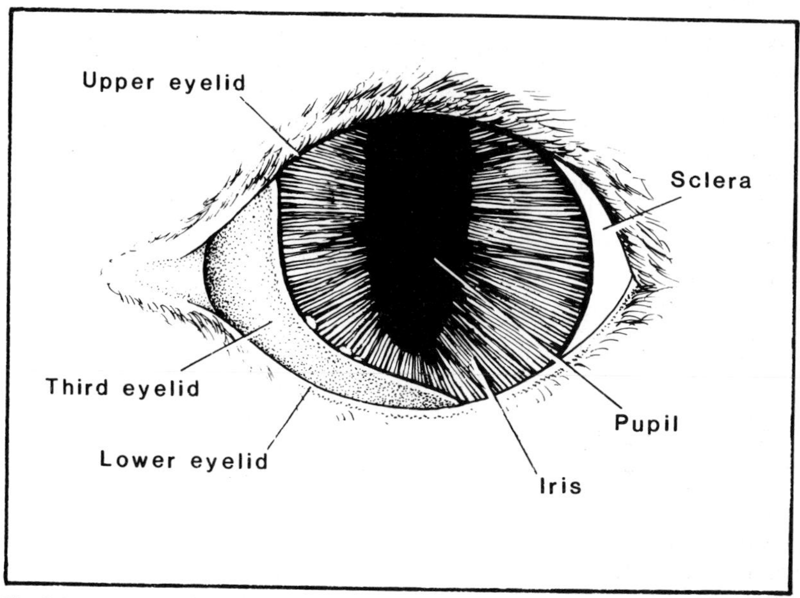

Fig. 7.15 (a) **External appearance of the eye.**

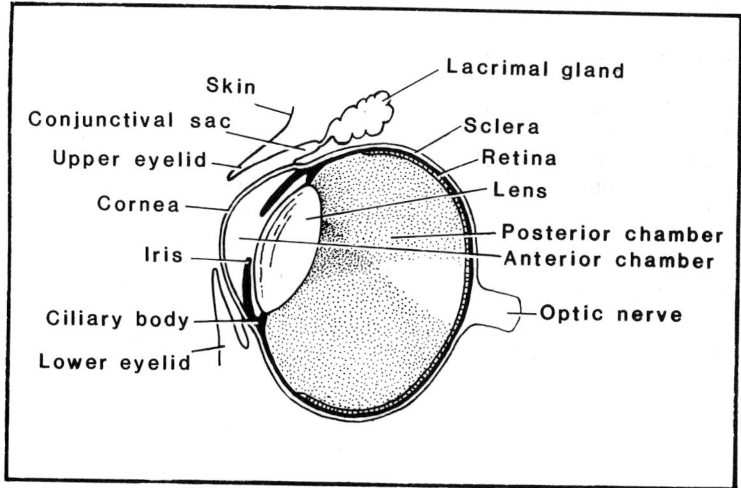

Fig. 7.15 (b) **Section through the eye.**

the outer side of the eyelids and the conjuctiva join. Sometimes there is an extra layer of lashes, distichiasis, which rub on the surface of the eye and cause a problem. In other cases the eyelids may turn inwards, again making the lashes rub on the surface of the eye causing inflammation – this is called entropion.

- If the cornea is damaged or the pressure in the eye increases it will become opaque.

- In young animals the lens is elastic. This elasticity decreases as animals age so focusing becomes more difficult.
- Sometimes the lens will be detached from its ligaments and fall either forward or backward. This is a lens luxation (dislocation) and can lead to glaucoma.
- Opacity of the lens is known as a cateract which may be partial or complete. Hereditary defects or a deficiency of an amino-acid, taurine, in the diet can affect the retina and reduce vision.
- Bacterial infection of the conjunctival sac leads to inflammation (conjunctivitis).

The internal organs

The inside of the body is divided into two parts by the diaphragm:
1. the thorax – containing two pleural cavities and a pericardial cavity;
2. the abomen – containing the peritoneal cavity.

The circulatory system

All the organs which make up the body need oxygen in order to function normally. This essential requirement is brought by the red cells in the blood, which in turn are carried around the body in a continuous tube called the circulatory system. The blood is propelled round the system by the action of the heart, which is in fact a muscular pump fitted with valves to ensure that the blood travels in the right direction. Problems can occur if the heart valves leak (incompetence) or do not open properly (stenosis). Sometimes drugs need to be given to strengthen the beat of the heart if the muscle becomes weakened by age or disease.

Essentially, blood which has circulated round the body and become exhausted of oxygen returns to the right atrium. It is passed through the

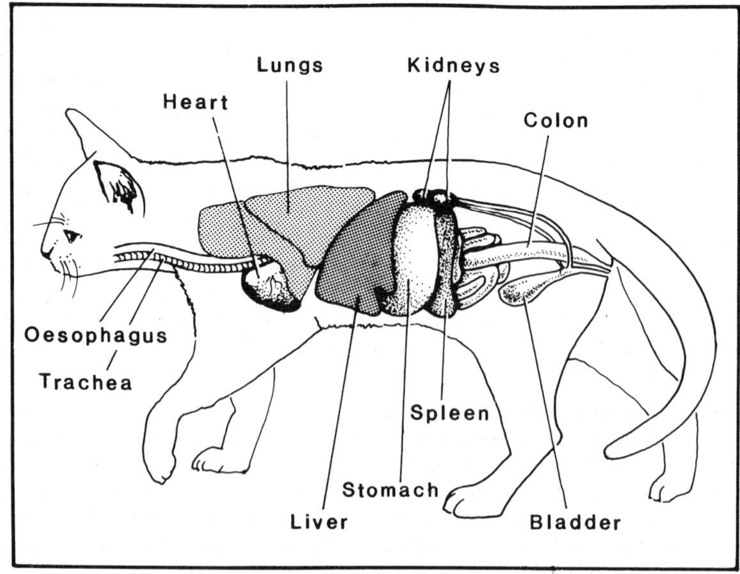

Fig. 7.16 **The internal organs.**

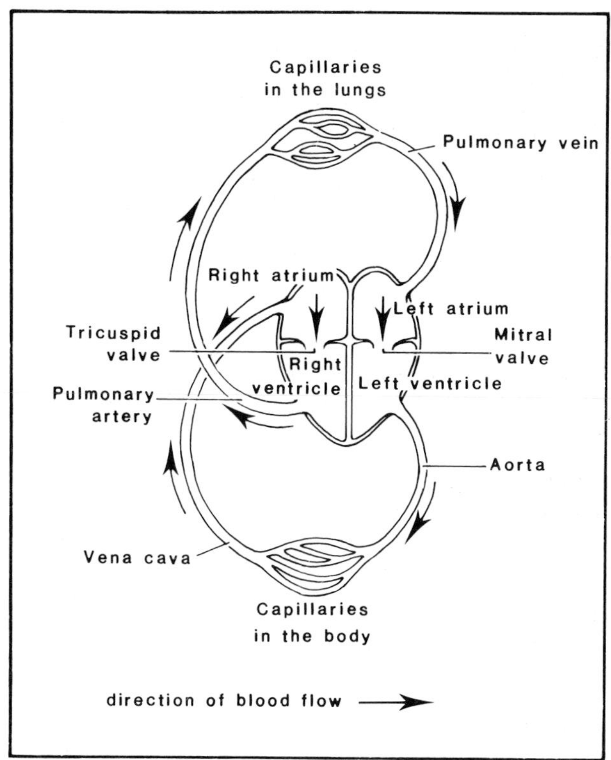

Fig. 7.17 **A schematic illustration of the circulatory system.**

tricuspid valve into the right ventricle which pumps it through the pulmonary artery to the lungs. As the blood passes through the small tubes in the lungs (the capillaries) it picks up oxygen. Oxygen-enriched blood returns from the lungs to the left atrium, is passed through the mitral valve to the left ventricle and then pumped via the aorta to be distributed to the capillaries throughout the body. A small amount of fluid from the blood and some cells leak out into the tissues to be gathered up in another series of channels called the lymphatic system, which in turn drains back into the blood system. This lymphatic system has a number of 'glands' or 'nodes' situated throughout its length. These glands, which sometimes become swollen in the case of infection in a tissue, act as filters and remove bacteria and other debris from the blood and they are also responsible for the production of some types of white blood cells and antibodies that protect the body against infection.

The spleen lies near the stomach in the abdomen. It is responsible for producing some of the elements that make up blood and also for removing old worn out red blood cells. It also acts as a storage area for blood and thus varies considerably in size according to the amount of blood required in the circulatory system at any particular time. The bone marrow – the cavity of the long bones – is filled with marrow which produces red blood cells and some types of white blood cells.

Blood contains:

- red blood cells – which carry oxygen;
- white blood cells – which can engulf bacteria and other foreign matter within the body, and produce antibodies to combat infection;
- blood platelets – important mediators of the clotting mechanism.

These components are carried in a fluid called plasma.

Clotting – if blood leaks from the system, fibrin filaments formed from one of the constituents in the plasma link together to form a web or net which traps the cells in the blood to form a clot. The clear fluid that remains is called serum.

Blood Tests – veterinary surgeons will sometimes take a blood sample to test for:

- The number of cells of each type in a standard volume of blood. The packed cell volume (PCV) – the amount of space taken up by the cells, when they are allowed to sediment, in comparison with the plasma.
- The erythrocyte sedimentation rate (ESR) – the speed with which the red blood cells sediment out when the blood is left to stand.
- The levels of various enzymes and other constituents normally found in blood.
- The levels of protective antibodies to various diseases for diagnostic purposes to identify the best time for vaccination or to check that vaccination has been effective.

Such tests help in the diagnosis of diseases and can also give a guide to the prognosis of a case.

The digestive system

In order to work, the body needs food to provide a source of energy to allow organs to grow and to replace worn out tissues. Food needs to be 'processed' by the digestive system in order to provide materials in a form that can be utilized. Essentially, the digestive system is a muscular tube, or tract, with openings at one end where food goes in and at the other end where waste material (excreta) comes out. A number of glands associated with the digestive system discharge the fluid they produce into the tube to facilitate the breakdown of food into essential elements. The procedure is as follows.

The digestive process

1. If the food is presented in chunks it is torn into small pieces and crushed by the teeth in the mouth, otherwise it is swallowed whole.
2. Saliva, produced by the salivary gland, helps to lubricate the food as it passes through the oesophagus into the stomach. The salivary juices also begin the digestive process.
3. The oesophagus is a simple tube which passes down the neck and enters the chest, passes over the heart and through the diaphragm into the stomach. Large objects swallowed inadvertently may become stuck in the oesophagus at the entrance to the chest at the base of the heart or where the oesophagus goes through the diaphragm, and may require surgical removal.
4. The entrance and exit to the stomach are guarded by a ring of muscle, and cardiac sphincter and the pyloric sphincter. The pyloric sphincter is responsible for regulating the passage of food from the stomach. The

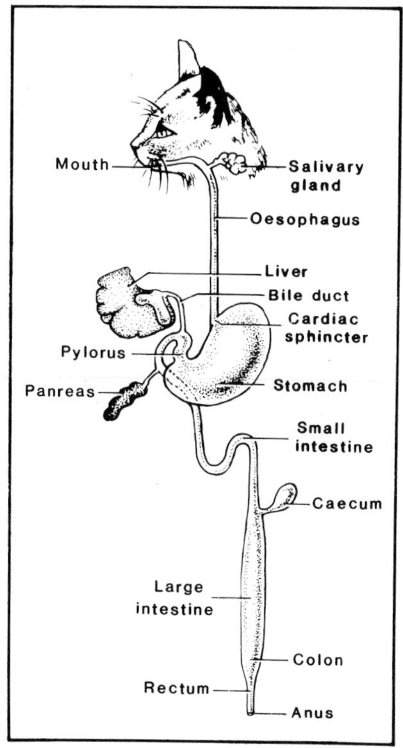

Fig. 7.18 **A schematic representation of the digestive tract.**

stomach wall produces digestive juices which help to process the food. Inflammation of the stomach is called gastritis.

5. Digestion continues in the small intestine aided by the bile and pancreatic juice. The useful products are absorbed through its wall into the blood stream.
6. The digestive process, aided by bacteria, and absorption of useful material, particularly fluids, continues in the large intestine.
7. The caecum is equivalent to the appendix in man.
8. The faeces (the motions or stools) are made up of waste material and are 'stored' in the rectum to be passed, usually twice a day.

The pancreas

The pancreas produces juices which help digestion, but it also manufactures the hormone insulin which circulates in the blood and is responsible for regulating the amount of available glucose in the body.

The liver

Besides producing bile, which helps digestion, the liver is also responsible for regulating the storage and usage of carbohydrate, the mobilization of body fat, the detoxification and excretion of toxic substances, and the synthesis of proteins that occur in the blood. It also helps to stabilize the body temperature.

Note

- The collective word viscera is used to describe all the abdominal organs together.
- Sometimes the rectum will protrude through the anus – this is called a rectal prolapse. It is nearly always a sequel to a severe and protracted attack of diarrhoea and requires veterinary attention and possible surgical correction.

The urinary system

The urinary system is responsible for removing much of the excess water and many waste products that accumulate in the body. The kidneys, which lie one on each side of the body near the spine, high up in the abdomen, filter these materials from their blood supply. Fluid leaves the kidney by the ureter which leads to the bladder. The urethra leads from the bladder to open either through the vulva in the female or the penis in the male. In the female the urethra is short, whereas in the male it is long and arches over the pelvis.

- Small crystals, or stones, may accumulate in the bladder and urethra leading to urinary obstruction. This condition occurs especially in male cats and is a serious problem requiring urgent veterinary attention.
- Nephritis is the word used to describe inflammation of the kidneys.

The respiratory system

The main function of the respiratory system is to bring about effective oxygenation of the blood but it also plays a role in heat regulation and the loss of excess water. Expansion of the chest, brought about by the movement of muscles in the chest wall and a downward movement of the diaphragm,

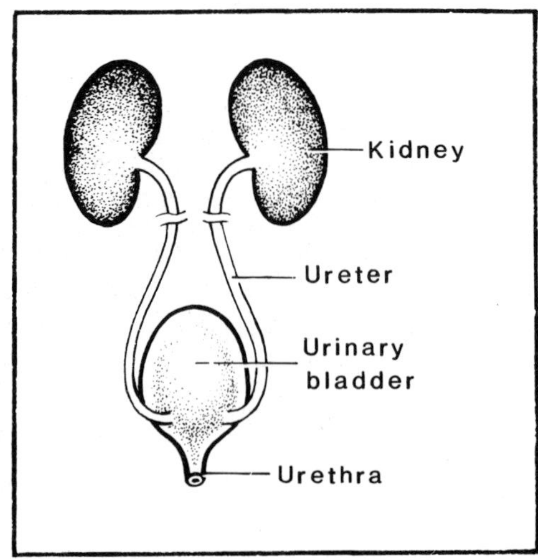

Fig. 7.19 **The urinary system.**

creates a negative pressure in the thorax which inflates the lungs and causes air to be drawn in through the nose and, during exercise, through the mouth. Air passes through the pharynx, which is common to the respiratory and digestive tracts, into the larynx and reaches the lungs via the trachea. Within the lungs, the trachea divides into two bronchi and these divide again like the branches of a tree to form bronchioles which end in air sacs, the alveoli. Blood circulating in the wall of the air sacs picks up oxygen as it passes through. The lungs are made up of a mass of grape-like air sacs supported in connective tissue.

- **The nasal chamber** is linked by scrolls of delicate bone covered with a sensitive lining. Its main function is to warm and filter air and to aid the sense of smell. The chamber is linked to sinuses which are cavities in the bones that make up the skull.
- **The pharynx** is common to the respiratory and digestive tracts. When the cat is eating, the trachea is closed by the epiglottis and the nasal cavity is sealed by the soft palate.
- **The larynx** consists of a tube made up of cartilage. Its function is to prevent food entering the trachea and to produce sound (vocalization) by vibration of the vocal chords it contains.
- **The trachea** is a straight tube held permanently open by C-shaped cartilages; the 'open' side of the cartilages is adjacent to the oesophagus and allows for the swallowing of boluses of food.
- The respiratory rate in a normal resting cat is 10 to 30 breaths per minute.

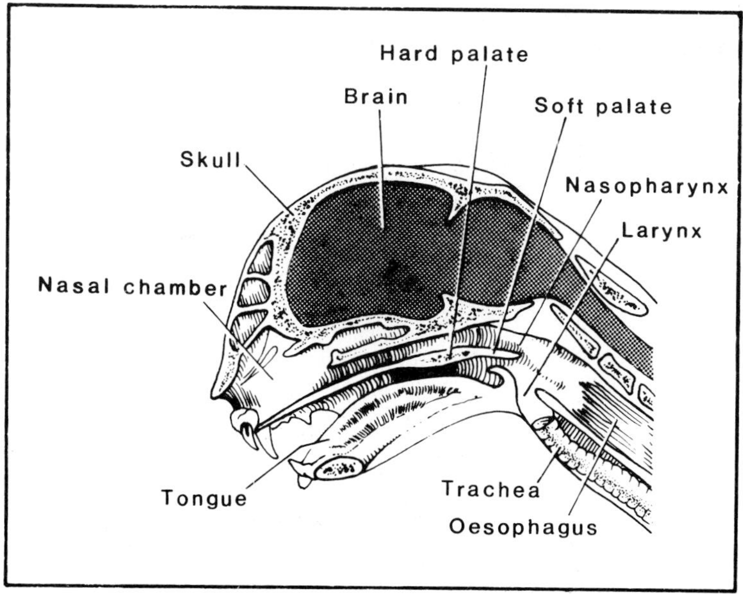

Fig. 7.20 **(a) Section through the head to show the larynx and pharynx.**

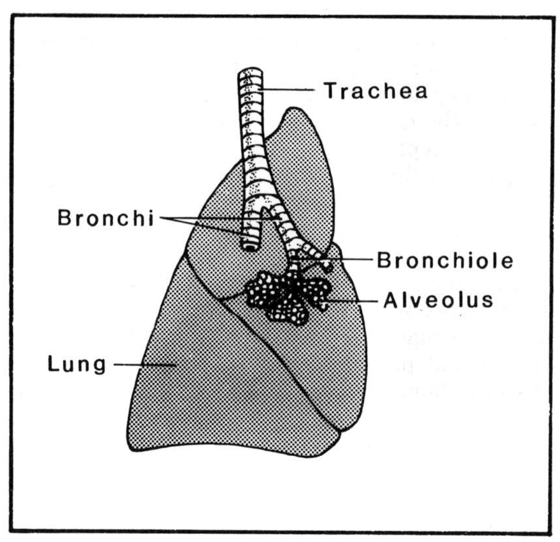

Fig. 7.20 **(b) The lungs.**

The genital system

The male

Male cats have two testicles in a pouch (the scrotum) just below the anus. The testicles produce spermatozoa which pass through tubules to a duct called the epididymis where they are stored. During mating the spermatozoa pass from the epididymis through another duct, the vas deferens, which joins the urethra (see also this chapter, The Urinary System). On the way the spermatozoa are mixed with fluid from the prostate and other glands to form the semen which is ejaculated from the erect penis through the urethra during coitus.

The testicles also produce the male sex hormone, testosterone, which is responsible for producing the secondary male characteristics. The testicles descend into the scrotum from the abdomen in normal kittens. In some animals, one or both testicles are permanently retained in the abdomen. The cat with only one testicle descended is known as a unilateral cryptorchid (monorchid) and as cryptorchid where neither is descended. Retained testicles are a hereditary problem, and although a monorchid cat is fertile, he should never be used for breeding as the fault may be transmitted to his offspring. Monorchidism is regarded as a major fault in showing.

A castrated cat is one in which the testicles have been completely removed surgically, usually to curb wandering, fighting, and spraying strong smelling urine. Neutered cats are infertile. The castrated male tends to beome less active and to put on weight; the diet should be adjusted accordingly.

The female

Female cats have two ovaries which are situated in the abdomen near the kidneys. When the cat is in season (calling) the ovaries produce eggs which, however, are not released unless the cat is mated; this is called non-spontaneous ovulation and contrasts with the other domestic mammals, e.g.

bitches, in which the eggs are released spontaneously during the heat period. The eggs are caught by the fimbriae and pass down the oviducts where they are fertilized by spermatozoa. The fertilized eggs then pass into the uterus where they develop into foetuses. The cat's uterus is made up of two long horns and the uterine body. It opens into the vagina by the cervix which is kept shut, except during oestrus and when giving birth. The female genital tract opens to the exterior through two lips which make up the vulva.

Between heats the uterine horns are no thicker than a piece of string, but when the cat is calling they increase in size to become rather thicker than a pencil. The pregnant uterus has a diameter of one to two inches and may contain as many as six or seven kittens.

Besides producing eggs, the ovaries manufacture the female sex hormones, oestrogen and progesterone. These are responsible for bringing about the secondary female sex characteristics and the development of the mammary glands (see also Chapter 7, The Hormonal System).

- During coitus, spermatozoa ejaculated from the male penis are deposited around the cervix. They pass through the uterus and into the oviducts where the eggs are fertilized.
- Spaying (ovariohysterectomy) involves the complete removal of the uterus and the ovaries of the cat. This is of course done under general anaesthesia and is a major operation.

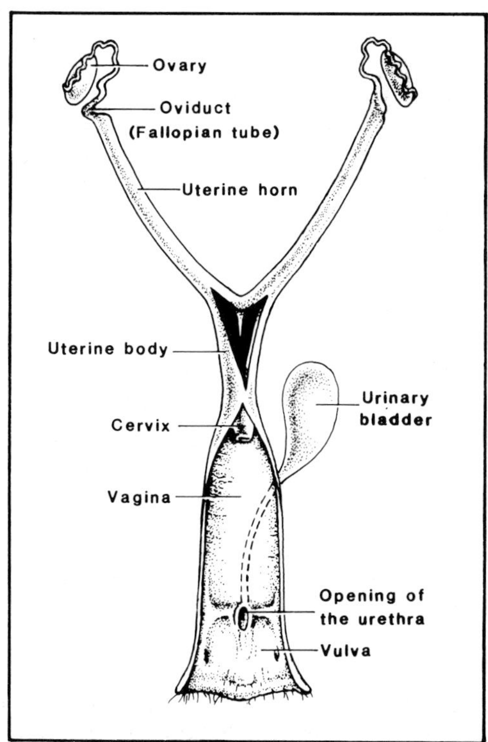

Fig. 7.21 **The genital organs of the queen.**

- Very occasionally the lining of the vagina will protrude through the vulva after kittening, this is called a vaginal prolapse and requires veterinary attention.

The nervous system

The function of the nervous system is to receive messages from outside the body and, after analysing them, to cause the animal to respond in an appropriate way.

The nervous system is essentially divided into two parts:

1. **The central nervous system**
   This consists of the brain and spinal cord, both of which are protected by bone – the skull in the case of the brain and the bony canal through the vertebrae in the case of the spinal cord.

2. **The peripheral nervous system**
   This consists of nerves which connect the central nervous system to the rest of the body.

If a cat sees a fly, messages are sent from the retinas of the eyes to the brain. Messages are then sent to the muscles of the limbs to cause the animal to spring accurately and at precisely the right moment onto its prey.

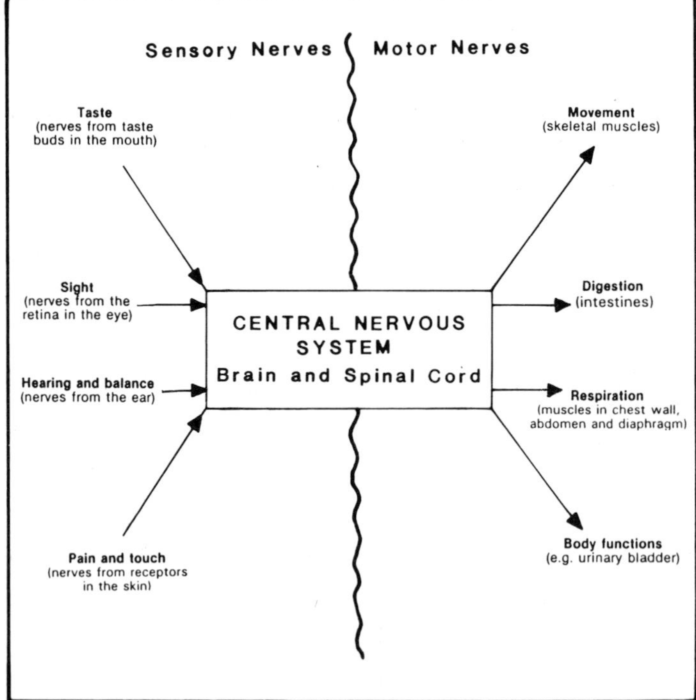

Fig. 7.22 **A diagrammatic illustration of how the central nervous system works.**

Nerve impulses are sent automatically from an organ when it is full, and the central nervous system responds, also automatically, to send a nerve impulse to the muscles in the organ to make them contract and empty. In some such cases, e.g. the urinary bladder, the brain can override the automatic response, as occurs in house-trained animals. In other cases, for example the filling and emptying of the stomach, the nervous impulses which cause contraction of the muscles and dilation of the sphincters are purely automatic and cannot be overriden consciously.

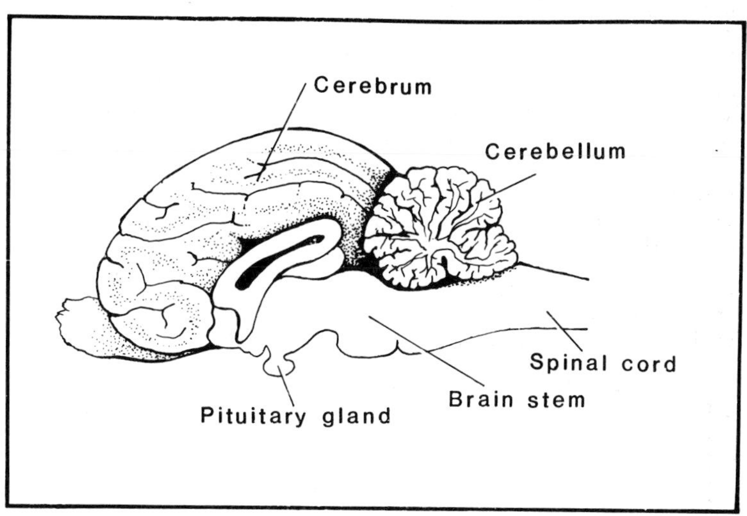

Fig. 7.23 **(a) The brain – longitudinal section (side view).**

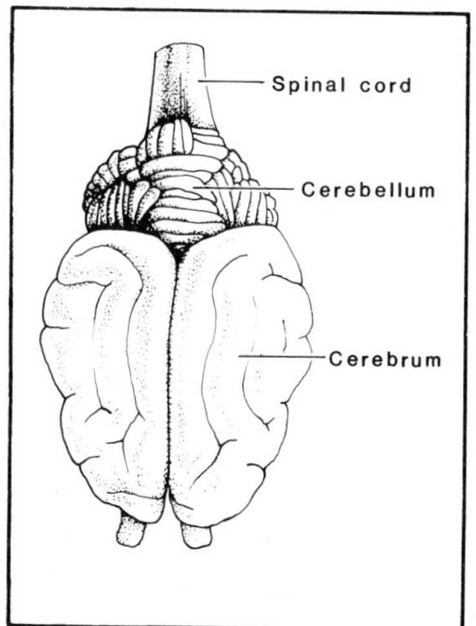

Fig. 7.23 **(b) The brain from above.**

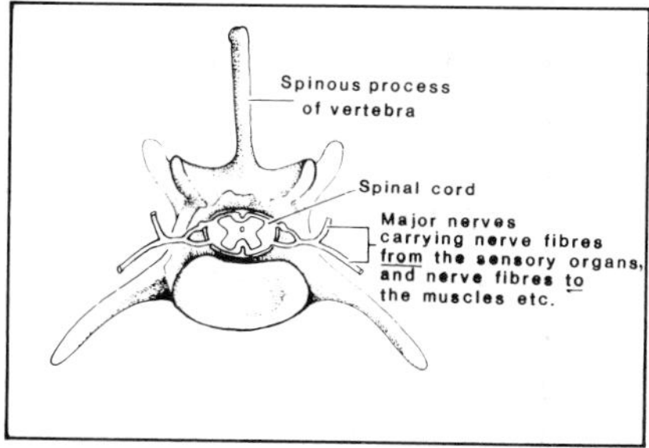

Fig. 7.23 **(c) The spinal cord (section through vertebral canal).**

The hormonal system

A number of glands called 'endocrine glands', situated in various parts of the body, produce hormones which are spread by the circulatory system throughout the body. They instruct the organ or body system they control to perform a specific function. Many organs which are under hormonal control receive messages from one hormone which makes them work more quickly, and from another which makes them work more slowly or stop. Thus the hormones control the body's activity very precisely.

Besides their effect on specific parts of the body, the hormones work together rather like the players in an orchestra, the whole being conducted by the hormones produced by the pituitary gland which is situated at the base of the brain. The amount of hormones present in the blood is being continually monitored by the body and adjusted to meet the animal's need at any particular time. Details relating to the production and function of the hormones are given in Table 7.2.

The oestrous cycle

All female animals have a cyclic pattern of reproductive behaviour which is known as the oestrous cycle. In scientific terms queens are described as being seasonally polyoestrus. This means that they have periods of a few days during which they will accept the male (oestrus) followed by a short period of sexual inactivity (di-oestrus). The sequence of events as illustrated by the small circle in Figure 7.24 is repeated until the end of the breeding season. The last period of sexual activity in the breeding season is followed by a longer period of sexual inactivity (anoestrus – the non-breeding season) which lasts until the first oestrus of the next breeding season. This is illustrated by the largest circle in Figure 7.24. Ovulation does not occur in cats spontaneously but is induced naturally by mating or artificially by hormone administration or stimulation of the cervix with a glass rod or the equivalent.

In artificial conditions this pattern may be upset and in controlled environments queens may never go through a period of anoestrus. In one survey of breeding queens in the UK it was found that nearly half did not have a non-breeding season.

Oestrus in the queen is usually referred to as 'calling' and during this phase the queen crouches, holds her tail to one side, vocalizes and shows frequent rolling and treading.

Generally, puberty is reached at nine and a half months of age (range four to 18 months). In one survey it was found that, on average, puberty occurred earlier in Burmese cats than other breeds.

The duration of the various stages of the oestrous cycle are not very well documented in the literature. Most reports show however that in the UK queens cycle between January and September with peaks of sexual activity in February, May, June and, occasionally, September. When anoestrus occurs it generally lasts from late-September until late-January. Cycles are 18–24 days long on average and, in the presence of the male, oestrus lasts four days (range three to six days) but is extended to five to 10 days if the queen is not mated. Ovulation occurs 27 hours (range 24 to 30 hours) after coitus.

The average duration of pregnancy is 63 days (range 61 to 69 days). After the birth of a litter the average interval before the next call is eight weeks

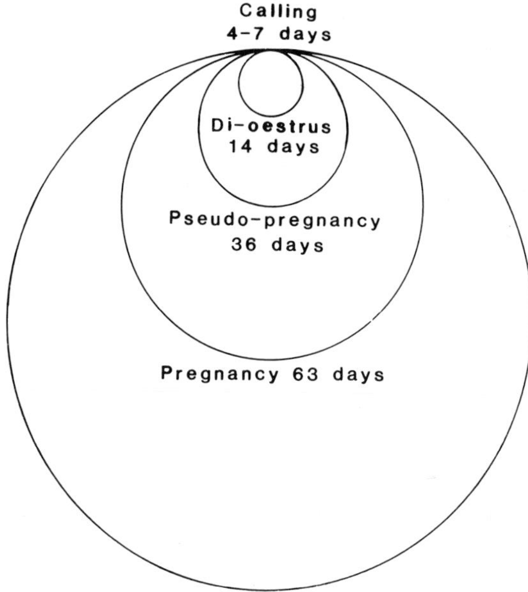

Fig. 7.24 **The oestrous cycle.**

(range one to 21 weeks). The interval may be dependent on the age at which the litters are weaned and, in cats with a non-breeding season (anoestrus), upon the time of year when the litter was born.

The average number of kittens born alive in all breeds is 4.5 (range 1 to 9). Approximately six per cent of kittens are likely to be still born, the incidence being highest in Persians possibly because the broad, flat face predisposes towards the problem. On average 87 per cent of kittens born alive are successfully reared.

There is evidence that pseudo-pregnancy can occur in cats after any non-fertile mating but it is difficult to be sure that conception and reabsorption of the foetuses has not occurred. If this happens the interval between calling is increased to about 36 days.

The physiology of the oestrous cycle

In the queen, as with other female animals, it seems that there is an inborn cyclic activity in the hypothalamus, a specific area in the brain which is in fundamental control of reproductive function. This part of the brain is, however, sensitive to both internal and environmental stimuli such as heat and light, particularly the length of daylight. It may also be stimulated, through pheromones, by the presence of toms and other queens. The oestrous cycle is therefore controlled by a complex interplay between the hypothalamus and the reproductive tract with the anterior pituitary, an endocrine gland situated at the base of the brain, acting as a central relay.

The sequence of events in simple terms is as follows. At the end of the periods of sexual inactivity, di-oestrus or anoestrus, the hypothalamus produces a releasing factor which stimulates the anterior pituitary to produce follicle stimulating hormone (FSH) which controls the development

Table 7.2. The endocrine glands and the hormones they produce

Gland	Situation	Hormone/s produced	Action
Thyroid	The gland lies alongside the trachea at the end nearest the mouth	Thyroid hormone	Controls the activity of the body tissues. Deficiency (hypothyroidism) results in poor growth in young animals. Older animals, lacking in the hormone, become sluggish, overweight, and have poor hair growth. Excess amounts of the hormones cause hyperactivity (hyperthyroidism)
Parathyroid	The two parathyroids are small glands situated alongside the thyroid	Parathyroid hormone	Controls the calcium stores in the body and is therefore important in the development of the skeleton
Adrenal	The two adrenal glands are small glands which lie near the kidneys	Adrenaline – produced by the centre of the gland (the medulla)	Prepares the animal for action and is excreted in quantity if the animal is frightened, needs to fight or run away
		Corticosteroids – produced by the outer layer of the gland (the cortex)	One group of these hormones controls the salt and water content of the body. The other hormones produced by the adrenal cortex enhances the animal's resistance to stress and infection. Excessive production of corticosteroids causes Cushing's syndrome. Addison's disease is caused when too little hormone is produced
Pancreas	Lies within a loop of the small intestine	Insulin	Controls the amount of glucose in the blood. Animals with sugar diabetes are lacking in the hormone
Testes	The two testes are situated in the scrotal sac	Testosterone	Responsible for the male characteristics of tomcats, particularly aggression, spraying behaviour and the smell of the urine
Ovaries	Contained in the abdomen near the kidneys	Oestrogens (*produced by the follicles – the developing eggs*)	Responsible for the female characteristics of female cats. Prepares the female tract for mating, and is responsible for 'calling' behaviour. This hormone also helps to bring about development of the mammary glands
		Progesterone (*produced by the corpora lutea – bodies which are formed in the ovaries in the space left when the eggs are released*)	Progesterone is responsible for preparing the uterus so that it can support the foetuses. It maintains pregnancy. It causes the mammary glands to develop so that they can eventually produce milk

Table 7.2. (cont.)

Gland	Situation	Hormone/s produced	Action
Pituitary	Situated at the base of the brain. The gland is divided into two parts, the anterior part which produces the first four hormones listed in the next column and the posterior part which produces the remaining two	1. Thyrotropic hormone	1. Controls the action of the thyroid
		2. Corticotropic hormone	2. Controls the action of the adrenal cortex
		3. Growth hormone	3. Controls the animals growth particularly up to puberty
		4. Gonadotropins:	4.
		(a) Follicle-stimulating hormone	(a) Promotes the ripening of eggs in the ovaries
		(b) Luteinizing hormone	(b) Causes ovulation
		(c) Prolactin	(c) Aids the formation and maintenance of the corpora lutea in the ovaries and stimulates the mammary glands so that they are ready to produce milk
		5. Anti-diuretic hormone	5. Acts on the kidney to prevent excessive excretion of urine
		6. Oxytocin	6. Makes the pregnant uterus contract at kittening and stimulates the release of milk from the mammary glands

of follicles (eggs) in the ovaries, which in turn secrete the sex hormone oestrogen. At low levels this latter hormone exerts a positive feedback on the anterior pituitary stimulating more FSH to be released resulting in further follicle growth and increased oestrogen levels. This process continues until the follicles are mature and ready to rupture. If the queen is not mated these follicles regress rapidly after about three days, the oestrogen levels in the blood decline abruptly and the queen enters di-oestrus. If, on the other hand, coitus occurs the anterior pituitary is triggered to release luteinizing hormone (LH) in a pulse which causes ovulation. The ruptured follicle is rapidly converted into a solid glandular body, the corpus luteum. The development of the corpora lutea is initiated in response to LH and is maintained by the luteotrophic factor(s). The corpora lutea secrete progesterone which prepares the uterus to receive the fertilized eggs, and maintains pregnancy if the mating was successful, or brings about pseudo-pregnancy if the mating was fertile.

Oestrus control

The need for oestrus control

The majority of pet queens are 'spayed' to prevent them calling and having kittens. However there is often a need to rest breeding queens between litters, to prevent indiscriminate siring and to control calling until they are fully mature. Because it is reversible, chemical control using progestogens, one of the active ingredients in the human contraceptive pill, largely meets this requirement. (Any compound which mimics the physiological effects in the body of the naturally occurring sex hormone progesterone is called a progestogen. Most of the substances are steroids.)

Types of product available

Two types of product are used to control calling in cats – tablets for oral administration, and modern injections with a medium duration of action which are given subcutaneously. The older *depot* injections are not now indicated for use in queens in the UK.

Method of administration

The products mentioned above can be used in three ways:

(a) *Suppression of calling* – a short course of tablets or a single injection is given at the onset of calling. The signs of calling will usually stop within two to three days and even if the cat is mated it should not become pregnant provided medication has been given for a few days, to allow it to work, before mating occurred.

(b) *Temporary postponement of calling* – a course of tablets is given lasting for two months if started in di-oestrus, or for 18 months, if started in anoestrus. Alternatively, a single injection can be given in di-oestrus or anoestrus.

(c) *Permanent postponement of calling* – for safety reasons, only the injectable products can be used for this purpose. Repeat injections are given in anoestrus induced by an injection given as in (a) or (b) above. The first dose of the permanent postponement course is given three months after the induction dose, the second after a further four months. Subsequent doses are given at five monthly intervals.

Return to calling after medication

The occurrence of the next call following oral medication may be variable because queens are seasonally polyoestrus and ovulation does not occur spontaneously. However, the next call after a suppression dose given in the breeding season will probably occur a few days later than normally expected, on average four weeks after the last tablet is given. Queens given a correctly timed postponement course will not call whilst they are receiving the tablets.

The majority of queens will call six and a half months after being injected for the suppression or temporary postponement of calling. Cats will return to calling on average seven months after the last injection of a permanent postponement regime. In either case the return to calling will be further delayed if the non-breeding season (anoestrus) intervenes.

Veterinary consultation

The control of oestrus in queens is a complex matter and it is therefore important to spend time discussing with your veterinary surgeon the methods that are available and to decide together what action is most appropriate in any given situation. Such matters as the reason why heat control is needed, the age and health status of the queen, and the likely hazards of medication or surgery will all need to be considered and a reasoned judgement made.

'What ifs' in relation to oestrus control

What if my queen is mis-mated?

Unfortunately, in contrast to bitches, there is little that can be done in queens to avert pregnancy immediately after mating. This is because the potent oestrogens are not safe for use in cats. However, it is sensible to consult your veterinary surgeon without delay since in some cases early oral medication is possible. It is possible also that he will advise that an injection to make the uterus contract and expel its contents be given about halfway through pregnancy. Alternatively, if you have no intention of breeding from your queen in the future, he may advise that she is spayed (he will remove the ovaries and the uterus containing the developing foetuses at one time), usually about three to six weeks before she is expected to kitten.

What if my queen is found to be pregnant unexpectedly?

It makes sense to consult your veterinary surgeon promptly so that you discuss with him what actions are appropriate in your particular case. In such situations you may decide that it is best to have your queen spayed. Such an operation can be carried out right up to a week or so before kittening is expected and will involve the removal of the ovaries and the uterus containing the developing kittens. If you are anxious to retain your queen's breeding capability and she is in kitten before mid-term then your veterinary surgeon may be able to given an injection to make the uterus contract and expel its contents. Alternatively in such a situation you could opt to let the pregnancy proceed and kittening to take place naturally but resolve to cull the litter down to a maximum to two kittens, which should be left to assuage the queen's maternal instinct and utilize the milk supply. It is not true that letting your queen have a 'mongrel' litter will ruin her ability to produce pure bred kittens in the future.

CHAPTER 8

SIGNS AND SYMPTOMS OF ILLNESS

Introduction

Early recognition and treatment of illness is important, not only to save pain and suffering, but also because treatment is likely to be more effective.

The object of this chapter is to help the owner to recognize, identify and to describe accurately the signs of pain and illness in their pet and to know when to seek veterinary advice. The observant owner will thus be able to supply an accurate and detailed history should veterinary treatment become necessary. An accurate history can be a crucial factor in helping the veterinary surgeon to arrive at a correct diagnosis and is therefore a prelude to effective treatment. Your veterinary surgeon may appreciate having the history in writing.

Observing cats for signs of illness

- Responsible owners will spend time observing the normal habits, reactions and detailed appearance of their cat when in full health, so that any alterations which may be indicative of the beginning of illness will be noticed quickly.

- Any small change in behaviour or any unusual physical signs should mean that the cat is kept under extra close scrutiny for a few hours, or a few days, until either more positive signs develop or the cat has returned to normal. To enable proper observation of defecation and urination during this time it may be necessary to restrict the cat temporarily to one or more rooms in the house, with access to a litter tray. A cat under observation for illness should of course not be taken to cat shows or to any other situation which may cause it stress.
- It may not be beneficial to seek veterinary advice in the very early stages of discomfort, as the vet will usually want some positive signs to develop to enable proper diagnosis prior to treatment. The discerning owner should know instinctively when this stage is reached.
- Cats, like humans, may have days when they feel 'off colour' for no obvious reason. If these episodes occur often with your cat, a note of days, times and surrounding circumstances should be made. Veterinary advice should then be sought in order to interpret the information collected in this way.
- Cats may show changes in behaviour in response to changes in their life-style or environment. For instance moving house, a new baby, changes in working hours, acquiring another pet, or new cats moving into the neighbourhood can produce behavioural changes in your pet which may sometimes be mistaken for signs of ill-health. It is important, therefore, to bear this in mind when observing your cat (see Chapter 4).

Signs and symptoms

Most feline illnesses are shown by a combination of signs and symptoms.

Signs of illness are objective evidence that something is wrong which is readily apparent to an observer, e.g. diarrhoea or sneezing.

Symptoms of illness are changes in sensation of bodily functions experienced by the patient, e.g. the pain caused by trying to put an injured foot to the ground. Although cats are at a disadvantage in being unable to describe their subjective symptoms, they are nevertheless able to indicate in a number of ways what they are experiencing, but it is necessary to learn how to interpret these indications correctly.

It is important for the owner to keep an open mind about the nature of an illness during the early stages. Not all cases of a particular illness show all the signs and symptoms associated with that illness. Furthermore, many signs are common to a number of different diseases. Jumping to the wrong conclusion too early may prevent help being sought at the right time and delay the start of proper treatment.

The significance of the various signs of illness shown by cats will be found under the section of this chapter headed 'What if my cat . . .?' Suffice to comment here on temperament and behaviour changes, and temperature taking.

Temperament and behaviour changes

Cats are creatures of habit. Any marked changes not associated with changes in the household or environment may be indicative of illness. However, allowances should be made for jealousy, resentment and pining, as

Table 8.1. Symptoms of pain in specific areas as indicated by tell-tale 'signs'

Area of pain	Signs that indicate pain is felt
Head pain (headache)	Half closed eyes coupled with pressing of the top of the head into furniture and garden objects. Unwillingness to move head freely, neck stiffness, sometimes gentle head shaking or vacant staring
Eye pain	Pawing and rubbing at eyes. Affected eye often half-closed and watering. Avoidance of strong light on affected side
Ear and mouth pain	It is not always easy to distinguish between the two as the nerve path-ways are very close. One ear may be carried low and the head tilted to the affected side. The cat may shake its head and paw at the affected ear. There may be drooling or excess saliva and reluctance to eat – especially with hard food
Throat pain	Gagging (retching), drooling, head and neck kept in an extended position, difficulty in swallowing shown by gulping and coughing
Abdominal pain	Continual glancing round at the site of pain and biting or licking at the area. Sitting in a 'hunched-up' position. Reluctance to move and complaining bitterly when handled. Vomiting, diarrhoea or constipation. Loss of appetite and condition
Limb and joint pain	Depending on the severity and site of the pain, limping will vary from hardly being noticeable to where the whole leg is carried off the ground. In cases of doubt the cat's movement should be watched carefully, paying particular attention to the head and pelvis. A nodding action of the head or rump will be seen when the sound fore or hind leg is put to the ground. Lameness associated with foot dragging can be indicative of nerve damage or a fractured bone in the leg. A cat with arthritic pain in the joints will walk stiffly with a hunched position. It may have difficulty getting up, jumping and, in severe cases, bending its head to eat or drink
Spinal pain	Sometimes a cat will appear lame when the actual site of the pain is in the spinal column. Other signs of back pain can be a resentment to touch or accidental knocks, reluctance to stretch or groom properly, difficulty in jumping, difficulty in normal defecation and urination, collapse of the hindquarters and incontinence
'Hind end' pain	Frequent and sudden turning round to look at the tail is a common response to 'hind end' discomfort due, for instance, to anal gland pain. Also, frequent licking under the tail and rubbing or dragging its anus along the floor (scooting) can indicate pain or discomfort in this region
General internal pain	Varied signs depending on the degree and location of the pain and also on the individual animal. However in general there may be depression, panting, increased pulse rate, and dilation (widening) of the pupils. An ungroomed appearance, inappetence and a tendency to hide may also be seen. Cats in pain are usually silent but may exhibit aggressive growling or hissing if approached. If the pain is severe the animal may howl and make attempts to escape if indoors

well as undue persecution by a dog, child or another cat, or the onset of calling or kittening in queens.

Temperature taking

The cat's normal temperature is considered to be 101.5°F (38.6°C); this figure is only an average and it may well fluctuate either above or below this in quite normal, healthy animals. Generally speaking it is not wise or helpful for an inexperienced owner to take their cat's temperature unless specifically requested to do so by their veterinary surgeon – it is not a procedure that is taken kindly to by most cats and thermometers can be broken in the rectum all too easily!

Pain

Pain is probably the most significant symptom of illness or injury and it is important to understand the way that cats indicate that they are suffering from pain in a particular area or organ. The tell-tale signs by which pain in various areas can be identified are noted in Table 8.1.

'What if my cat . . .?'

Introduction

This section seeks to answer the questions which worry cat owners when their pet shows signs which may indicate that it is ill. Each topic begins with the words 'What if my cat . . .?' and it is hoped that the details given will help owners to decide whether:

- the sign is normal and no action is required;
- some simple 'treatment' is needed;
- first aid action is indicated;
- veterinary help should be obtained and, if so, how urgently it is needed.

Use the Index of Diseases and Conditions, Figure 8.1 or the list on page 97, to identify the relevant number.

HISTORY TIP
Throughout the book there are highlighted *History tips*. These show information which will be important for the veterinary surgeon to know when making a diagnosis. Usually this information can only be supplied by the observant owner and so you have a very important function to perform in contributing towards the restoration of your pet to perfect health. The history which you supply can be crucial in making a correct diagnosis and rapid recovery.

Fig. 8.1 'What if my cat . . .?'

Use this diagram to identify the relevant 'what if' number. The 'what ifs' are also listed numerically on page 97.

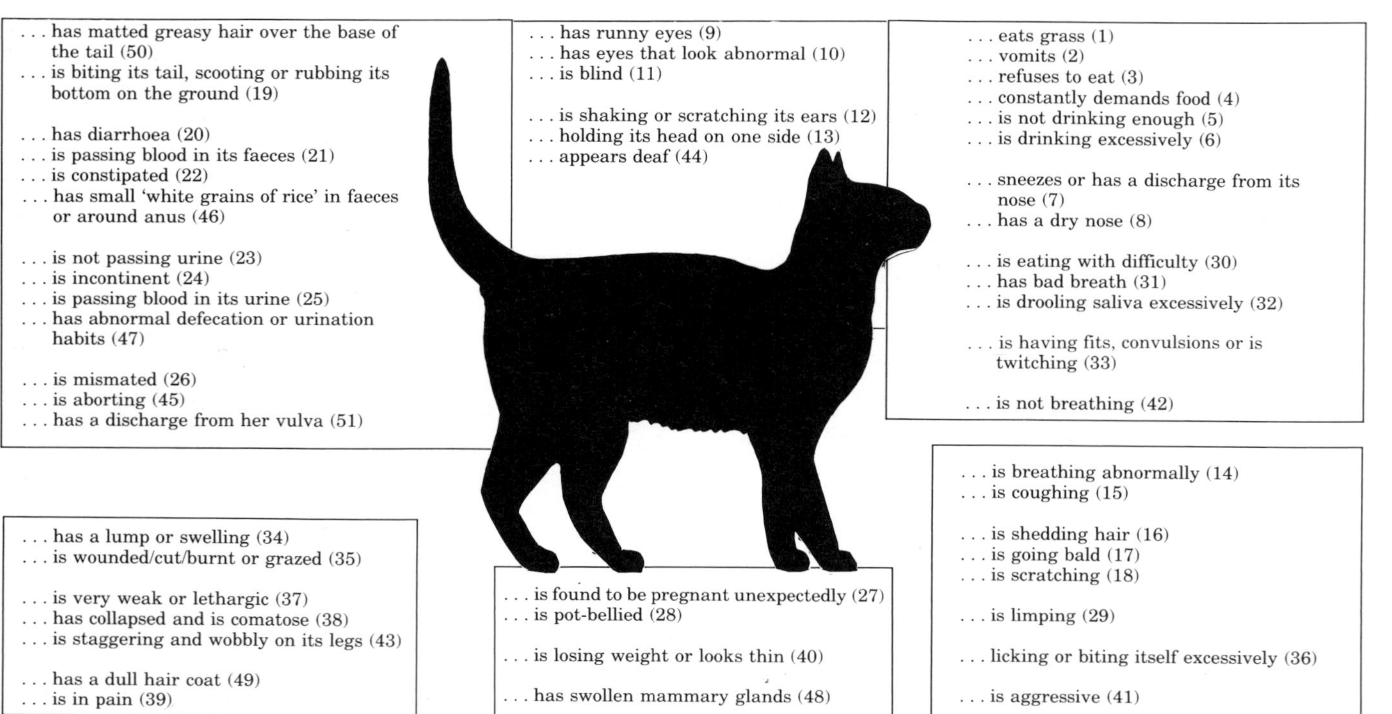

. . . has matted greasy hair over the base of the tail (50)
. . . is biting its tail, scooting or rubbing its bottom on the ground (19)
. . . has diarrhoea (20)
. . . is passing blood in its faeces (21)
. . . is constipated (22)
. . . has small 'white grains of rice' in faeces or around anus (46)
. . . is not passing urine (23)
. . . is incontinent (24)
. . . is passing blood in its urine (25)
. . . has abnormal defecation or urination habits (47)
. . . is mismated (26)
. . . is aborting (45)
. . . has a discharge from her vulva (51)
. . . has runny eyes (9)
. . . has eyes that look abnormal (10)
. . . is blind (11)
. . . is shaking or scratching its ears (12)
. . . holding its head on one side (13)
. . . appears deaf (44)
. . . eats grass (1)
. . . vomits (2)
. . . refuses to eat (3)
. . . constantly demands food (4)
. . . is not drinking enough (5)
. . . is drinking excessively (6)
. . . sneezes or has a discharge from its nose (7)
. . . has a dry nose (8)
. . . is eating with difficulty (30)
. . . has bad breath (31)
. . . is drooling saliva excessively (32)
. . . is having fits, convulsions or is twitching (33)
. . . is not breathing (42)
. . . has a lump or swelling (34)
. . . is wounded/cut/burnt or grazed (35)
. . . is very weak or lethargic (37)
. . . has collapsed and is comatose (38)
. . . is staggering and wobbly on its legs (43)
. . . has a dull hair coat (49)
. . . is in pain (39)
. . . is found to be pregnant unexpectedly (27)
. . . is pot-bellied (28)
. . . is losing weight or looks thin (40)
. . . has swollen mammary glands (48)
. . . is breathing abnormally (14)
. . . is coughing (15)
. . . is shedding hair (16)
. . . is going bald (17)
. . . is scratching (18)
. . . is limping (29)
. . . licking or biting itself excessively (36)
. . . is aggressive (41)

'What if my cat . . .?'

1. eats grass
2. vomits
3. refuses to eat
4. constantly demands food
5. is not drinking enough
6. is drinking excessively
7. sneezes or has a discharge from its nose
8. has a dry nose
9. has runny eyes
10. has eyes that look abnormal
11. is blind
12. is shaking or scratching its ears
13. is holding its head on one side
14. is breathing abnormally
15. is coughing
16. is shedding hair
17. is going bald
18. is scratching
19. is biting its tail, scooting or rubbing its bottom on the ground
20. has diarrhoea
21. is passing blood in its faeces
22. is constipated
23. is not passing urine
24. is incontinent
25. is passing blood in its urine
26. is mismated
27. is found to be pregnant unexpectedly
28. is pot-bellied
29. is limping
30. is eating with difficulty
31. has bad breath
32. is drooling saliva excessively
33. is having fits, convulsions or is twitching
34. has a lump or swelling
35. is wounded/cut/burnt/grazed
36. is licking or biting itself excessively
37. is weak and lethargic
38. has collapsed and is comatose
39. is in pain
40. is losing weight or is looking thin
41. is aggressive
42. is not breathing
43. is staggering and wobbly on its legs
44. appears deaf
45. is aborting
46. has small white 'grains of rice' in faeces or around anus
47. has abnormal defecation or urination habits
48. has swollen mammary glands
49. has a dull coat
50. has matted, greasy hair over the base of the tail
51. has a discharge from her vulva

1. What if my cat eats grass?

Many cats will eat certain kinds of grass from time to time. Although we don't really know why they do this it is probably for one of two major reasons:

- Grass acts as a very good source of roughage.
- Eating a lot of coarse grass will often induce the cat to vomit. This may help in situations where the stomach is overfull, excess digestive juices have accumulated, or where a hairball or other indigestible matter is partly blocking the stomach. In this way the cat is using the grass as a natural emetic.

Therefore, although probably not essential, it seems to do the cat no harm to eat grass provided the grass has not been sprayed with a toxic chemical.

Some owners even provide trays or pots of growing grass for housebound cats – particularly if they start showing signs of eating the houseplants! (See also Chapter 4.)

However, if grass eating is accompanied by prolonged or persistent vomiting, and particularly if the vomit contains blood, veterinary advice should be sought quickly.

2. What if my cat vomits?

Occasional incidents of vomiting in cats are to be expected and are generally unimportant.

- Vomiting is part of the natural defence mechanism in the body, enabling the stomach to get rid of an excess of food or undigestible or decayed matter before it passes further into the digestive system and causes harm. Cats will sometimes eat grass to induce vomiting and thus assist the natural defence mechanism (see 'What if' No. 1).
- Prolonged or persistent vomiting, particularly if the vomit contains blood, requires immediate veterinary attention.

There are two main types of vomiting in cats, true vomiting and regurgitation.

True vomiting

This involves the use of the muscles of the abdomen, chest or diaphragm (i.e. heaving) in order to eject the contents of the stomach. Often the cat will appear anxious with increased salivation and swallowing just before vomiting and may emit a cry or groan as it vomits.

The main danger of repeated or continuous vomiting is dehydration (loss of body fluids), so that the volume of circulating blood is decreased and the cat rapidly goes into a state of shock. Dehydration can be recognized by picking up a fold of skin on the cat's back between your thumb and forefinger. If the fold remains 'tented' when you release it, dehydration is present.

It is wrong to allow a vomiting cat to drink water too rapidly, as this can lead to further vomiting and set up a vicious circle. However it is also dangerous to withhold water completely. Instead, small amounts should be offered every half-hour.

In cases of persistent vomiting where the cat is not eating, it may be helpful to dissolve one heaped tablespoon of glucose (*not* ordinary household sugar) in one pint of previously boiled water which has been left to cool. This solution should be offered in small quantities in order to supply the cat with the energy and fluid it requires. This is an emergency measure for use where prompt veterinary advice cannot be obtained.

HISTORY TIP

If the vomit contains identifiable food, it may be helpful to record the time it has been in the stomach. Note particularly whether the vomit consists of small food particles with a quantity of frothy saliva or large quantities of recently drunk water plus yellow bile and stomach fluids. Note also if there is evidence of hair (fur) or roundworms (white, string-like objects) in the vomit.

Finally it is important to make a record of how much water is given and when. Note how long it is retained.

Regurgitation

Although this may initially appear similar to true vomiting there are differences. Regurgitation is a more passive action used to bring up sausage-shaped boluses of something recently eaten. The food is usually brought up fairly sluggishly in contrast to the more dramatic act of true vomiting. The affected cat, or other cats, may re-eat the regurgitated food.

Although regurgitation can be simply due to the cat eating too quickly (in which case small portions should be fed, a little at a time) it can be a sign of oesophageal disease or blockage. Persistent regurgitation in any cat therefore warrants prompt veterinary advice.

> **HISTORY TIP**
> Note how much of the food given is being regurgitated and also the time in relation to feeding.

The significance of true vomiting

Vomiting is a feature of some of the more serious diseases and conditions in the cat, particularly feline infectious enteritis, the Key-Gaskell syndrome (feline dysautonomia), feline infectious anaemia and feline leukaemia. In these diseases vomiting will usually be accompanied by other signs such as loss of appetite, and sometimes diarrhoea. Veterinary help is needed at once in these cases and must never be delayed in any situation where:

- the cat is listless, physically depressed or in pain;
- blood is seen in the vomit;
- profuse diarrhoea accompanies the vomiting;
- the vomiting is persistent or frequent.

Vomiting may also be caused by eating unsuitable or decaying material. This will often result in gastritis, an inflammation of the lining of the stomach, resulting in vomiting in an attempt to rid the body of the offending substance. As a general rule cats are much less likely to ingest harmful substances than, for instance, dogs, due principally to their fastidious feeding habits. However, certain irritant materials can be ingested whilst the cat is grooming itself, if the cat's fur has accidentally or deliberately been contaminated with such substances. Whatever the reason, the ingestion of irritant or toxic substances may be accompanied by drooling from the mouth and possibly signs of abdominal pain. Veterinary help is needed urgently.

> **HISTORY TIP**
> If the cat is known to have eaten a poisonous substance, e.g. a garden chemical or slug bait, take the original container with you to the veterinary surgeon, as the manufacturer's analysis may be helpful in tracing an antidote to the poison.

Intestinal obstructions can sometimes occur in cats as a result of swallowing foreign bodies such as string, sewing needles threaded with cotton or nylon, coins etc., and be the cause of vomiting. This is more common in kittens than adult cats and arises as a sequel to the cat's natural habit of exploring unusual objects with its mouth. Small blunt objects may well pass through the digestive system and cause no problem, however on occasion complete or partial obstructions can occur. Obstructions can also occur due to twists in the bowel or the telescoping of one part of the bowel into another, again particularly in kittens, often as a result of acute intestinal infections or heavy worm burdens. The signs depend on whether the blockage is partial or complete and also on where the obstruction is. In general, however, the cat will be listless and depressed, be disinclined to move and adopt a 'hunched-up' posture, may vomit and become dehydrated and will probabably have a tense, painful abdomen.

If you suspect that your cat has swallowed some object and is showing any of the signs described, it is important to consult a veterinary surgeon immediately as surgery may be required and it is better done before the cat becomes exhausted by frequent attempts to vomit.

Hairballs are a common cause of vomiting especially in longhaired breeds and during periods of heavy moulting (spring and summer). The hair may accumulate in solid masses in the stomach which can rub against the lining and cause irritation leading to vomiting. Alternatively the cat may eat grass in an attempt to induce vomiting to bring up a hairball (see 'What if' No. 1). The occasional ejection of a hairball in this way is a normal and quite natural occurrence and should not be a cause for concern. However, since hairballs sometimes pass further down the gut and cause problems there, it is wise to groom your cat frequently to remove dead hairs from its coat. It is also advisable to dose the cat regularly with liquid paraffin (half a teaspoonful once or twice weekly) during the moulting period if it is prone to vomiting hairballs.

Projectile vomiting is the term used to describe a particular kind of vomiting action in which food is ejected with force, sometimes over a distance of up to a foot. It is usually seen in young cats soon after weaning and is often associated with some malfunction or narrowing of the pylorus (the exit valve from the stomach). Siamese cats seem to be more prone to this than other breeds. Affected animals will appear poorly grown, although they are often bright and have a good appetite. Seek veterinary help immediately as surgical or medical treatment may be possible.

HISTORY TIP
An estimate of how much food is retained, as well as an indication of how long after feeding the vomiting occurs, is helpful. In addition, daily weighing of the kitten will enable close monitoring of growth and weight gain.

Travel sickness does occur in cats although most cats will travel without vomiting – although they may yowl! However, some more highly-strung individuals may become nauseated, and drool and vomit when travelling in a car. Covering the cat basket and avoiding feeding before travelling helps to prevent cats vomiting, as does gradual acclimatization to travelling by short, frequent trips. If these measures are not successful then your veterinary surgeon can supply a mild sedative for long trips. It is not desirable to give medication intended for travel sickness in humans except on veterinary advice.

3. What if my cat refuses to eat?

Whilst inappetence may be the first sign of a major illness, it is also not uncommon for a healthy, well-fed cat to refuse to eat occasionally, often for the reasons listed below.

Common reasons for healthy cats refusing food

- Inappetence may be due to environmental stresses such as change of ownership, change of location, travelling, strangers or other animals present at feeding time, or the effects of hot, humid weather.
- Toms will often refuse food when there is a queen on call nearby. Similarly queens on call will often forget about food until they calm down.
- Refusal of the food you provide for your pet may be due to the cat obtaining food from elsewhere – either eating scraps put out for the birds or from rubbish bins, or from someone locally who feeds your cat when it goes visiting.
- Cats have a highly sensitive sense of smell and are often very fussy about eating food which, although to us may still appear fresh, has started to 'go-off' or 'spoil'.
- Queens may refuse to eat just prior to kittening and also for up to 12 hours afterwards.

Persistent refusual of food, especially if accompanied by other signs of illness, needs careful monitoring. The cat should not be force-fed but can be tempted with a variety of foods. Should none of the above explanations apply, seek veterinary help if the cat's appetite is markedly reduced for three or four days, or if it refuses to eat at all for more than 24 hours.

HISTORY TIP

Note particularly:

- How long it is since the cat's appetite was normal.
- Whether the cat refuses all foods, or will eat only certain types.
- Whether the cat is capable of chewing and swallowing by offering small pieces of a favourite titbit.
- Whether or not the cat is drinking normally.
- Whether the cat, as far as you can tell, is passing normal motions at the usual frequency.
- If vomiting has occurred. If so, record the frequency and type.

4. What if my cat constantly demands food?

Unlike dogs, most cats tend to self-regulate their food intake and very few therefore eat to excess provided they are fed on a properly balanced feline diet. Since cats prefer to feed by means of frequent, small meals throughout the day, most cases of cats 'constantly demanding' food can be rectified by adopting ad-lib feeding of dry or semi-moist food. However, when changing to an ad-lib regimen it is wise to keep an eye on how much the cat consumes each day and to weigh your pet regularly, because unfortunately *some* cats may become overweight. In this case you will obviously have to return to a more strict control of the amount of food given.

A cat that is frantically hungry and never satisfied, or shows a sudden unexplained increase in appetite, particularly where body weight starts to be lost, should be investigated by your veterinary surgeon. Although such cases are rare, it is possible that some metabolic disorder, or an impairment of digestion or absorption, could account for this clinical picture.

HISTORY TIP
Note how long the condition has been apparent. If possible obtain a sample of the cat's faeces. Note whether the cat is also drinking excessively and, if she is an unspayed female, when she was last on call. Note any changes in general behaviour and also when the cat was last wormed and what preparation was used.

5. What if my cat is not drinking enough?

Cats normally produce a concentrated urine and therefore excrete their metabolic waste products with only minimal loss of body water. This in turn means that less water is required to be consumed to make good the loss. In fact, with cats fed on a moist diet such as tinned or home cooked meat it is possible that *all* of the daily water requirement can be met from the food alone (such foods can contain around 75 per cent water). Thus if your cat is not fed on a dry or semi-moist diet, is not vomiting, does not have diarrhoea, or is not otherwise ill, then it is quite possible that you may not observe your pet drinking at all!

It is, however, recommended that a bowl of clean fresh water be readily available for each and every cat irrespective of the type of diet. This is particularly important when a dry or semi-moist diet is fed since, in contrast to the moist canned foods, the dry diets may only contain 8 per cent water. Even in this case it is still possible that a perfectly healthy cat may not *appear* to be drinking since it is common for many cats to drink from gutters, puddles, baths, etc., despite being provided with fresh, clean water by the owner. If your cat has this habit take care that the puddles do not contain the residue of toxic chemicals or disinfectant.

From the above it is clear that an otherwise healthy cat which appears not to be drinking enough is seldom a cause for concern. If, however, your cat is suffering from diarrhoea, is not eating for some reason or is otherwise 'off colour' then you may have to persuade it to drink fluids.

The only occasions when water should be withheld from your cat are:

- on the advice of a veterinary surgeon for a few hours before an anaesthetic is administered, since this will reduce the risk of complications due to vomiting during the operation;
- if your cat is vomiting frequently – in this case it may become very thirsty due to the loss of fluids and rapidly drink large amounts of water in order to make good the loss. This in turn may further irritate the lining of an already inflamed stomach and cause the animal to vomit again. In this situation only small amounts of water should be given every half-hour or so to ensure that a vicious cycle of drinking followed by vomiting does not occur.

6. What if my cat is drinking excessively?

It is always useful for owners to have a note of how much their cat drinks normally. Any departure from normal which is not brought about by outside circumstances will then give rise to special observation to see if it has significance with regard to illness.

Common reasons for increased thirst in healthy animals

- Polydipsia (excessive drinking) can occur in hot weather or after eating salty food.
- Lactating queens may consume an increased amount of fluids.

Fairly sudden increases in drinking in other circumstances is a significant sign of illness which should always receive veterinary attention.

HISTORY TIP

Make an estimate of how much the cat drinks by measuring the contents of the water bowl and by taking into account any other water to which the cat has access. Excessive drinking may be associated with diabetes or kidney disease and it will therefore be useful to try to obtain a fresh urine sample to take with you when consulting your veterinary surgeon. Although this is not the simplest of tasks, it can often be done by encouraging your cat to use a litter tray in which only a very small amount of newspaper or cotton wool has been placed. The urine left in the bottom of the tray can then be collected, or squeezed out of the cotton wool, into a clean, dry jar and taken to the surgery for analysis without delay. Only a small quantity is required.

In addition, be prepared to tell the veterinary surgeon about any change in behaviour and let him know what medicines, if any, the cat is being given or has recently received.

7. What if my cat sneezes or has a discharge from its nose?

Although the occasional sneeze or short bout of sneezing is normal and can occur due to nasal irritation from dust, aerosol sprays, powders etc., more frequent sneezing either singly or in bouts, and sneezing accompanied by nasal discharge, should be a case for increased observation and concern.

Some possible causes of sneezing and nasal discharge in cats are:

- Upper respiratory tract disease caused by a viral infection.
- Bacterial or fungal infection of the nasal cavity or sinuses.
- Nasal tumours.
- Cleft palate or nasal injury following trauma to the head (e.g. from a road traffic accident).

Of these possible causes, by far the most common is viral upper respiratory tract disease (also known as cat 'flu). Whatever the cause, any cat showing persistent sneezing and nasal discharge should be examined by a veterinary surgeon without delay. Since the cat may well be running a temperature and feeling generally 'off colour' it should be kept indoors in a warm, well-ventilated room whilst waiting to be taken for a veterinary examination. On no account should any proprietary human cold or 'flu remedies be given as these may contain drugs which can be harmful to cats.

> **HISTORY TIP**
> Be prepared to provide the following information during the consultation:
> - How long the sneezing has been noticed.
> - The dates and types of any vaccines your cat has received in the past (if possible take the cat's vaccination certificate with you).
> - Whether your cat has been in contact with any unfamiliar cats recently, e.g. at shows, boarding catteries etc.
> - The character of any nasal discharge which has been present i.e. whether it has been clear and watery, or thick and purulent, and also whether any blood has been noted at any stage.
> - Details of any other signs of illness such as loss of appetite, discharge from the eyes, drooling saliva, general depression, etc.
>
> **N.B.** Do not take a sneezing cat into the waiting room at the veterinary surgery, as it may well be infectious. Telephone for a special appointment or leave the cat in your car and ask the receptionist's advice for the correct procedure.

8. What if my cat has a dry nose?

Most normal healthy cats have a wet nose. This moisture comes from two sources:

(a) It is mainly produced by glands in the lining of the nasal cavity. This secretion appears at the corners of the nostrils and then spreads across the surface of the nasal skin.

(b) The surface skin can also be moistened as a result of the cat licking its nose.

It is important to realize that a dry nose is not necessarily a sign that your cat is unwell. A cat that has been lying in front of a fire or has just woken up may well have a dry nose! However if the dryness is persistent and is accompanied by more specific signs of ill-health such as lack of appetite or listlessness then it is wise to seek veterinary advice. In many cases of illness a dry nose can occur as a result of:

- Dehydration resulting in a reduced production of normal nasal secretions.
- Increased body temperature resulting in increased evaporation of moisture from the nose.
- A reduction in the cat's normal grooming behaviour including licking its nose.

> **HISTORY TIP**
> Look for any signs of ill health in a cat with a persistently dry nose as this will aid your veterinary surgeon in arriving at a correct diagnosis of the underlying problem.

9. What if my cat has runny eyes?

A clear eye discharge is a normal feature in some breeds of cat and usually occurs because the nasolacrimal ducts which drain the fluid from the eye surface into the nose are unable to function efficiently. This situation occurs particularly in breeds with flattened faces, such as Persians, and may result in crescent shaped tear stains. In white coated cats these will cause a ginger discoloration of the fur in this area.

In other cats the tear ducts may occasionally become blocked or narrowed, or conversely there may be excessive tear production due to chronic irritation of the eyeball. Certain ocular defects such as misdirected eyelashes or turning in of the eyelids (entropion) can be the root cause of this chronic irritation. Some of these defects are inherited and some are acquired. Thus, although surgical correction is often possible, your veterinary surgeon may advise that the cat is not used for breeding or showing.

Although a clear ocular discharge can also occur as a result of a smoky or dusty atmosphere, this will usually only give a temporary discharge and the eye will soon return to normal once the environmental cause is corrected. As a general rule therefore, any cases of an unusual persistent clear discharge should be examined by a veterinary surgeon to identify any underlying cause and so that appropriate treatment can be given if necessary.

On the other hand, a thick, cloudy discharge may well indicate a bacterial or viral infection. With viral infections such as feline influenza, a clear discharge will initially be seen which will soon change to a more cloudy, white discharge as the disease progresses. As there are a number of infectious agents which can produce similar signs in this respect, it is important that veterinary advice is sought as soon as possible in any cases where a cloudy discharge is apparent. Meanwhile, the cat should be kept isolated indoors. To avoid the discharge matting the fur and possibly irritating the skin, the area around the eyes may be bathed gently with cotton wool soaked in warm water.

Finally, any cases of runny eyes where pain is also present should be examined by a veterinary surgeon urgently, whatever the appearance of the discharge.

HISTORY TIP

Note how long the discharge has been present, and whether it was initially present in one eye and now occurs in both eyes. Note also whether the discharge was initially clear or cloudy and whether you have noticed any signs which would suggest eye pain.

Since runny eyes can be a sign of more generalized respiratory diseases, such as feline influenza, note whether the cat has been sneezing and whether it appears off colour, i.e. not eating, listless, unwilling to go outside, etc.

10. What if my cat has eyes that look abnormal?

An accurate study of the normal eye helps the owner to appreciate any changes quickly. The following conditions which cause cats' eyes to look abnormal will be noticeable to an observant owner.

Dislocated eyeball (eye protruding from its socket) – Due to trauma. This is an emergency. Take care to prevent the cat damaging the eye further during transport to the surgery.

Bulging or prominent eyeball – Can occur as a result of injury, infection, glaucoma, or (rarely) a tumour.

Swelling of the eyelids – This can commonly occur due to infection of the eyelid skin following scratches acquired in a fight. Alternatively, severe conjunctivitis, which may occur in cases of cat 'flu, may cause swelling of the eyelids. More rarely, a tumour can also result in swelling of the lids.

Eye appears blue or cloudy – This occurs as a result of inflammation and swelling of the cornea – the transparent 'window' at the front of the eye. Again, this can be due to a number of causes such as injury, infection, allergy, glaucoma or tumour.

Pupil appears white or cloudy – As distinct from the previous sign, in this case the cornea is unaffected and the white area is seen in the central pupil area deeper in the eye. This indicates a cataract, or opacity of the lens. Causes of cataracts range from injury, through inflammation of the eye to diabetes mellitus.

Change in colour of the eye – A change of colour of the iris can occur in cases of inflammation within the eye itself, bleeding within the eye, or tumour formation.

An opaque patch on the surface of the eye – Possible causes are: *a film over part of the cornea* caused by inflammation (keratitis) or by a failure of tear production (dry eyes); *a corneal ulcer* as a result of either injury or infection.

Corneal necrosis or sequestrum is a condition seen only in cats and more often in Colour-point, Siamese and Persian breeds. In this condition an irregular shaped, flat, dark brown or black area is seen on the surface of the cornea.

Prominent third eyelid ('skin' over the eye) – In this case a 'skin', which is actually the third eyelid, will be seen partially covering the inner part of the eye, usually both eyes are affected.

A prominent third eyelid is usually just a sign that there is either a specific eye disease, or more commonly that there is a generalized condition causing the cat to be off colour or run-down.

A red lump protruding at the inner corner of the eye ('cherry eye') – This is caused by a gland on the inner surface of the third eyelid becoming swollen and bulging out of the corner of the eye.

Dilated (enlarged) pupils in daylight – Normally the pupils will get smaller (constrict) in light and only enlarge in dark or dull conditions. Persistently enlarged pupils can occur as a result of eye conditions such as a glaucoma, cataract, retinal degeneration, infections of the eye, tumours of the eye or brain, certain cases of poisoning, or more generalized disease conditions such as the Key-Gaskell syndrome (feline dysautonomia).

Abnormal eye movement (nystagmus) – A condition where the eye makes involuntary side-to-side or up-and-down movements. There is a hereditary nystagmus affecting some strains of Siamese cat. Most cases in adults cats will occur, however, as a result of disease of the inner ear affecting the balancing organs, or head trauma. In these cases the head may also be held at an abnormal angle. Nystagmus may also occur in some cases of poisoning.

It is important with any of the eye abnormalities mentioned above, to seek veterinary attention without delay as many of the conditions, if not treated, can lead to total blindness.

HISTORY TIP
Try to pinpoint the first time you noticed any change in the eyes and whether at that time there was pain and irritation.

11. What if my cat is blind?

Cats that become partially or completely blind can manage very well on familiar territory by using scent and hearing, provided they are given a certain amount of consideration and unexpected hazards are not left in their way.

Loss of sight should not be a reason for having a well-loved cat destroyed when it is otherwise healthy. Sudden blindness in a younger or middle-aged cat needs immediate veterinary help. Prompt veterinary advice in this way may mean that effective treatment is possible.

HISTORY TIP
Note when the condition was first apparent. Check whether blindness is total or partial. Observe whether the pupils respond, by constricting, to a torch light shone into each eye in turn. If the pupil fails to constrict it is probable that the cat is blind in the affected eye. Young kittens in a litter can be tested by moving a hand in front of them. A kitten with good eyesight will follow the hand, a kitten with poor vision will not.

Inherited eye defects

Compared to dogs, cats suffer from relatively few inherited eye defects. However some are recognized:

Progressive retinal atrophy

Progressive destruction of the light sensitive tissue at the back of the eye.

Sign Failing sight in both eyes leading to total blindness. Usually starts in young to middle-aged cats. No treatment is possible.

Breeds affected Abyssinian, Siamese*, Persian*.
(*Hereditary link is suspected, though not proven.)

Corneal necrosis sequestrum

Sign A flat, dark brown or black area on the surface of the cornea. Usually in one eye only but can be present in both. Can affect cats of any age. Surgical removal may be indicated.

Breeds affected Persian, Siamese, Colour-point.

Corneal dystrophy

A condition affecting the normal growth and development of the cornea.

Signs Appears at about four months of age. Initially seen as a cloudy area in the centre of the cornea affecting both eyes. No treatment is possible.

Breed affected Stump-tailed Manx.

Epiphora
Tears coming from the eyes.

Signs Wet streaks down the face due to overflow of tears from the inner eye. In cats with light-coloured coats, a reddish-brown discoloration of the hair in this area may be seen. Occurs as a result of the large, prominent eyes and flattened face affecting normal tear drainage via the naso-lacrimal ducts.

Breed affected Persian.

Entropion
'Rolling in' of the eyelid.

Signs Irritation of the cornea due to the hairs and lashes from the in-turned lid. Results in excessive tear production and partial or complete closure of the lids on the affected side. Cat may show signs of eye pain. Surgical correction is often required.

Breeds affected Hereditary link is suspected in longhaired breeds, but has not been proven.

Strabismus
Squint.

Signs Convergent strabismus (eyes coming together) is seen as an inherited condition. This condition is becoming less common due to selective breeding. Treatment is not possible.

Breed affected Siamese.

Nystagmus
Involuntary movements of the eyes.

Signs Both eyes show intermittent, short, side-to-side movements – usually fairly rapid. Vision is usually not affected.

Breed affected Siamese.

12. What if my cat is shaking or scratching its ears?

It is important to be familiar with the appearance of your cat's normal, clean ear, so that when you make a routine inspection, you will be aware if any changes are taking place. A small amount of light-brown, waxy secretion is normal and necessary to the health of the ear but there should be no unpleasant smell.

Many cats will occasionally scratch their ears, but frequent or violent episodes of scratching are signs that something is wrong.

Signs of ear disease
- Repeated scratching and head shaking.
- Head held with the painful side downward.
- Dark, reddish-brown wax in the ear.
- An unpleasant smell from the ear.
- Inflammation – heat, swelling and pain in the canal and flap.

Treatment

Any disease of the ears must be properly diagnosed and treated without delay, as a simple condition may develop rapidly into a more complex situation which may become difficult and expensive to treat. In addition the acute pain caused by ear disease may make the cat irritable and inclined to become aggressive when the ears are touched.

No attempt should be made to treat ear disease with proprietary remedies which may be inappropriate or of no benefit for the particular condition affecting your cat. Always seek veterinary advice early as delay could mean that the disease will spread to affect deeper structures within the ear, or require surgery to cure the condition if it has become chronic.

Possible causes of ear disease – *Otitis Externa (Canker)*

- **Earmites** – Tiny mites living within the ear can cause acute irritation which makes the cat scratch or rub the ear, thereby damaging the tissue. Cats appear to be very tolerant of the presence of these mites and it is usually only when large numbers are present that they show signs of irritation. Treatment requires the use of products that contain an ingredient which will kill the mites. Ear mites are readily passed on to dogs in the household.
- **Foreign bodies** – Although the open ear canals and fastidious habits of cats make the risk of problems due to foreign bodies much lower than in dogs, grass seeds and awns can on occasion lodge in the ear. Typically, cats that have a foreign body in the ear suddenly scratch violently, shake and often hold their head to one side. Do not attempt to remove the foreign body. Take the cat at once to the veterinary surgery, where treatment can be carried out, if necessary, under a local or general anaesthetic depending on how difficult the object is to remove and on how distressed the patient is.
- **Infections due to bacteria or yeasts** – Most of these infections are secondary to some other irritating cause. They will tend to cause intense irritation and a discharge with an offensive smell. Specific antibacterial and/or antifungal medication from the veterinary surgeon is needed.
- **Allergy or an extension of skin disease** – Since the lining of the ear canal is merely modified skin it is possible that a more generalized dermatological problem can manifest itself to the owner as an ear condition. Diagnosis and treatment by a veterinary surgeon is obviously required when these causes are involved.

HISTORY TIP

Tell your veterinary surgeon if you have other cats in the home or if your cat has close contact with other cats in the neighbourhood.

It will help if you can indicate clearly whether the signs of irritation were suddenly apparent, or whether they gradually became worse over a few days.

13. What if my cat is holding its head to one side?

This sign usually indicates that the cat has an ear problem but it may also be associated with trauma to the head, infection or tumour of the brain. Sometimes there is no apparent cause. Veterinary attention should be quickly sought whatever the underlying cause since many of these cases will resolve provided prompt treatment is given following accurate diagnosis. Some causes of this sign are described below.

Aural haematoma
A blood filled swelling on the ear flap.

Signs A hot and irritating swelling of the ear flap increasing slowly in size over a period of two to three days usually accompanied and preceded by signs of ear irritation (see 'What if' no. 12).

Possible causes Otitis externa, where the constant scratching and head shaking will rupture blood vessels within the ear flap. Also can occur as a result of trauma, e.g. being scratched or bitten on the ear during a fight.

Otitis externa
Inflammation and irritation of the ear canal.

Signs See 'What if' no. 12.

Possible causes See 'What if' no. 12.

Otitis interna
Inflammation of the balance and sound receptors.

Signs Head tilted downwards on affected side. Circling towards the affected side. Nystagmus (involuntary eye movements). Deafness on affected side.

Possible causes Infection, either following infection of middle ear or via bloodstream.

Damage to the area of the brain controlling balance

Signs Unsteady gait circling towards the affected side, nystagmus (involuntary eye movements), loss of some of the balance reflexes.

Possible causes Present at birth with a possible hereditary factor in some litters of Siamese and Burmese kittens and possibly other breeds. Many of these will recover of their own accord as they get older.

Trauma following e.g. road traffic accident.

Epilepsy (fits).

Infection of the brain with bacteria, viruses, fungi or protozoa.

Thiamine (vitamin B_1) deficiency. Rare if cat fed on commercial 'balanced' diets. Can be seen in cats fed substantially or entirely on raw fish.

Tumours of the brain.

Ototoxicity
Toxic damage to the inner ear.

Signs Deafness, head tilt, circling, nystagmus (involuntary eye movements).

Possible causes Can be caused by a number of drugs given at high doses and/or over long periods e.g. the antibiotic dihydrostreptomycin.

Idiopathic feline vestibular syndrome

Signs Sudden onset, one side affected, mimics otitis interna. Seen especially during the summer months.

Possible causes Cause unknown. Fairly common in adult cats. Almost all cases recover completely within 10 days.

> **HISTORY TIP**
> Has there been any recent injury involving the ear flaps? Have regular checks of the cat's ears indicated any signs of otitis externa? Has there been any unusual behaviour or accident within the recent past? What diet is the cat normally fed on?

14. What if my cat is breathing abnormally?

Cats breathe through the nose when at rest. Panting is less common in cats than in dogs and open mouthed breathing usually indicates distress, because the cat is either very hot or frightened, has a serious lung disease, or is in pain.

Abnormal breathing in cats can be associated with some important emergency situations.

- **Heat stroke** – Immediate Action: Cool the cat's body temperature by any means possible – cold water, ice, dunking in a stream, even surrounding it with packs of frozen food. Subsequent Action: Beware of cooling the cat too much and lowering the body temperature too far. Ten minutes application of cold should be enough. Take the cat for a veterinary check even if it appears fully recovered.
- **Airway obstructions** – See page 171.
- **Electric shock** – Immediate Action: Switch off the electricity. If this is not possible, do not touch the cat with your hands, but move it away with a wooden handled broom. Subsequent Action: Pull the tongue forward in the mouth to allow the cat to breathe. Push down rhythmically on the ribs at about five second intervals to induce breathing. If this fails then mouth to nose resuscitation may be tried. Keep up artificial respiration while transporting the cat to the veterinary surgery.
- **Chest injury**

Signs Sudden onset, distress, cuts and bruises, shock, weakness, pain.

Causes Falls, road traffic accidents, mauled by dog, blow or kick to chest, penetration by objects e.g. airgun pellets, arrow etc.

Action Gentle transport to veterinary surgery. Care is needed in handling a distressed cat since it may be unpredictably aggressive, and personal injury could result.

Other types of abnormal breathing are:

Snorting or 'snuffling' when breathing through nose

Possible causes Indicates partial blockage of the nasal passages with fluid or mucus. Cat may have to 'mouth breathe' during moderate exercise to compensate. Mucus or fluid can result from infection e.g. in chronic rhinitis/sinusitis or nasal tumour.

Action Examination by veterinary surgeon to determine cause and advise on possible treatment.

Panting and rapid breathing

A cat normally breathes at the rate of 25–30 breaths per minute at rest. After exercise this rises to 60–90. Rapid breathing and panting may indicate something is wrong.

Possible causes Blocked nostrils (see above). Overheating – has the cat been left in a very hot environment with no opportunity to escape? Injury – has the cat been in an accident? Fright – is the cat frightened for any reason e.g. transport in a car to a veterinary surgery? Respiratory disease – has the cat signs of respiratory disease such as fever, sneezing, runny eyes, or coughing? Pain – is the cat showing signs of pain anywhere in the body? (See Table 8.1 page 94.) Poisoning with certain poisons.

Action Veterinary consultation.

Shallow and rapid breathing

The inspired breath is not deep enough to expand the rib cage fully. Signs of distress and collapse are often present.

Possible causes Pain on taking a deeper breath due to pneumonia, pleurisy or fluid or air in the chest cavity. Damage to ribs, chest wall or diaphragm due to road traffic accident, fall or fight. Poisoning with certain poisons.

Action Careful removal to veterinary surgery.

Dyspnoea (difficult or laboured breathing)

The cat may indicate that it is having difficulty breathing by crouching down with the elbows held out away from the chest.

Possible causes Usually a sign of serious lung disease e.g. severe pneumonia, fluid or air in the chest cavity or a tumour in the chest.

Action Careful removal to veterinary surgery.

HISTORY TIP

In all cases of abnormal breathing, it is helpful to know if the onset of the signs has been gradual (over some weeks) or is a more sudden occurrence. Does the abnormal breathing only occur when the cat is moving about or when resting as well? Has the cat been involved in any accident or trauma?

NOTE

With any breathing problem it is better to seek veterinary advice early rather than regret not having done so later.

15. What if my cat is coughing?

Coughing is relatively uncommon in cats. However where it does occur it can be caused by a number of different agents both infectious and non-infectious and thus veterinary examination will usually be required. Possible causes of coughing include:

Inhaled irritants
For example, dust, aerosol spray, cigarette smoke, dry coat shampoos.

Signs Rapid and exaggerated breathing, watering eyes, possibly also sneezing.

Action Remove possible irritants. If cat does not show improvement fairly quickly telephone veterinary surgeon for advice.

Allergic bronchitis
Some cats develop an allergy to sprays, cat litter etc.

Signs Sudden onset of bouts of dry coughing. Exaggerated breathing.

Action Seek veterinary attention immediately. Prompt treatment will usually result in a dramatic improvement.

Feline Influenza
Cat 'flu, a common viral respiratory infection of cats.

Signs Eye and nasal discharges, sneezing, fever, depression, off food.

Action Veterinary consultation.

Pneumonia
Can occur as a complication to cat 'flu or following inhalation of food or medicines when force-feeding or dosing an animal.

Signs Fever, depression, off food, breathing difficulties (dyspnoea).

Action Urgent veterinary treatment required.

Lungworm Infection
Cats can pick up lungworms from eating rodents, birds etc.

Signs Many cats have small numbers of lungworm which cause no real clinical signs. However occasionally heavy infestations are found and can cause coughing.

Action A veterinary diagnosis will involve examination of a fresh faeces sample for typical lungworm larvae. This infection can be treated with specific anti-parasitic drugs.

HISTORY TIP
Do not take a coughing cat into the vet's waiting room as some coughs can be contagious. Telephone for a special appointment or leave the cat in your car and ask the receptionist's advice on what to do next. Take with you your cat's vaccination certificate.

16. What if my cat is shedding hair?

All cats shed dead hair from their coats. This shedding tends to occur all year, especially in the longhaired breeds, although most shedding and new growth of hair occurs in late spring and early summer. It is recommended that cats are groomed on a regular basis to help remove these dead hairs and avoid problems such as furballs, which are caused by a result of large amounts of hair accumulating in the stomach and intestine. In general, longhaired cats need daily grooming while shorthaired varieties can be groomed once or twice a week.

The following are other causes of hair loss.

Post-kittening and lactation

In some queens the cause of hair loss in these cases is because the hair growth cycle is suspended during pregnancy therefore more hair is lost at one time. Treatment is by worming, to remove any internal parasites that may be present, and early weaning, which will help reduce hair loss and speed recovery to normal. Consult your veterinary surgeon about the possible need for vitamin supplementation.

Post-infection/chronic infections

Diseases that affect the digestive system so that nutrients cannot be absorbed properly can cause hair loss. Frequently the coat may not grow normally for weeks or months after such an illness. Hair loss is often associated with chronic debilitating diseases. Consult a veterinary surgeon about diet and the need for vitamin and mineral supplementation.

Old age

A generalized hair loss can be expected in extreme old age.

Poor diet

Cats which have acute digestive problems, allergies, or which have been kept on a poor or unsuitable diet may show a sparse, harsh, dry coat. This will improve when the cause is remedied.

> **HISTORY TIP**
> A photograph of the cat when in full coat may be of help to the veterinary surgeon when estimating the amount of hair loss.

17. What if my cat is going bald?

Hair loss can be a secondary feature of some skin conditions causing itching (pruritus) or irritation. In this case the cat will lick, bite or scratch at the offending area(s), damaging the surrounding skin and hair and causing local hair loss around the lesion. If the problem is primarily one of excessive scratching, see 'What if' no. 18; if the cat is biting or licking, see 'What if' no. 36.

However hair loss, or alopecia, can also occur without any obvious signs of irritation. The following are some of the possible causes.

Ringworm

Signs An enlarging, bald or partially bald patch of skin, often circular in shape. The exposed skin is usually dry but not itchy.

Cause A fungal infection of the surface skin and hairs. The name 'ringworm' is misleading as the condition is not caused by a worm.

Action The cat should be taken to the veterinary surgeon for diagnosis at an early stage. Treatment with antifungal drugs can help cure the condition but *care should be taken in handling infected cats as ringworm is a disease which can be passed to man* (a *zoonosis*). Ringworm is one of the conditions looked for at the veterinary examination before a cat can be admitted to a cat show.

Feline endocrine alopecia

Signs Areas of symmetrical hair loss on either side of the body. Usually the underlying skin is normal in appearance and no itching is present. This condition is only seen in neutered cats (either castrated males or spayed females).

Cause Unknown, but possibly the result of an hormonal imbalance.

Action Treatment needs to be discussed with your veterinary surgeon since the condition is sometimes difficult to treat successfully. However a number of cats have responded to hormone treatment, which in some cases has to be on a continuous basis to avoid the problem recurring.

Hair loss as a sign of ill health or stress

This type of hair loss occurs due to a shortening of the period in the hair growth cycle during which new hair normally grows. As a result more hair is shed than is usually the case and areas of partial baldness may be seen.

Signs Increased shedding of hair, sometimes associated with dry skin and sometimes with greasy skin.

Cause An underlying condition such as kidney, liver or chronic intestinal disease or stress of pregnancy or lactation.

Action If due to pregnancy or lactation then consult your veterinary surgeon about vitamin supplementation, worming and possible early weaning. If due to an underlying disease condition then the veterinary surgeon will advise on possible treatment.

18. What if my cat is scratching?

Cats, like humans, scratch because they itch. The nerve endings which transmit the itch sensation lie close to the surface of the skin. When the cat scratches the nerve receptors are damaged and no longer react. The mild pain which results is better tolerated than an irritation. A cat's claws and vigorous scratching action can cause considerable damage and open the way for bacteria to invade the broken skin, complicating the condition seriously.

Persistent scratching should not be allowed to continue. The main causes are usually irritation due to earmites (see 'What if' no. 12) or fleas. In the case of fleas the irritation arises either as a direct result of the flea bites themselves, or indirectly as a result of an allergy developed not uncommonly to flea excreta or flea saliva which is inoculated in small amounts when the flea bites. This allergy gives rise to a skin condition known as feline miliary dermatitis (Miliary Eczema) where a number of raised scabby spots are seen, mainly along the cat's back. The skin is very itchy and some loss of hair from scratching, biting and licking the affected area will probably occur.

Sometimes the cause is easily detected and can be treated simply but if scratching persists, seek veterinary help. It is often cheaper in the long run to buy an effective anti-parasitic treatment from the veterinary surgery. Also, it may well be necessary to use additional medication to clear up the condition – this will almost certainly be the case with miliary dermatitis where anti-allergic or hormone tablets or injections are widely used. When treating a case of parasite infection it is important to consider treatment of other animals within the household with an appropriate remedy, and also to take action to eradicate parasites from the cat's bed and the rest of the house.

Other causes of scratching include inflammatory conditions of the skin caused principally by contact or food allergies, bacterial infections or, occasionally, neuroses.

HISTORY TIP
It will be helpful if you can be as specific about the scratching behaviour as possible. Does the cat scratch at only one area of its body or more generally? Is the scratching more intense at any particular time of day, in any particular surroundings, or when the cat is hot or cold? Is the scratching getting progressively more frequent and intense?

19. What if my cat is biting its tail, scooting or rubbing its bottom on the ground?

This behaviour is sometimes seen in cats and is usually due to anal gland problems.

The anal glands, situated on either side of the anus, should empty every time faeces are passed, depositing their contents on the faeces as a scent marker. Occasionally they may be evacuated when the cat is frightened.

In anal glands which become overfull through not being emptied regularly, as may occur in cases of constipation or diarrhoea, the secretion may dry out and become difficult to pass. This condition, called anal gland impaction, causes irritation and the cat will respond by biting or scooting. A veterinary surgeon will be able to manually express the contents and, provided the underlying cause has cleared up and no infection is present, the cat should return to normal.

Anal glands which become overfull and are not expressed may become infected, form an abscess and burst, causing a malodorous wound. This situation is more serious and requires intensive veterinary treatment in order to clear up the infection present. Sometimes it may be necessary to operate and surgically remove chronically infected anal glands.

Other conditions which may cause a cat to bite or rub its hind end include:

Matted hair around anus following bouts of diarrhoea – See 'What if' no. 20 for information relating to diarrhoea in the cat.

Matted hair should be gently and carefully clipped away. The sore area can be gently washed with baby soap and water, rinsed and dried. A human nappy rash cream can be applied to soothe and protect the skin.

Tapeworm infestation – In cases of tapeworm infestation of the intestine, the segments of the worm may cause some slight irritation as they wriggle out of the anus and around the surrounding skin. See 'What if' no. 46.

Stud tail – A condition due to over-production of a greasy discharge from an area of specialized glands on the upper surface of the base of the tail. This occurs mainly in uncastrated males (hence the name) and appears as oily, matted hair in this region. See 'What if' no. 50.

> **HISTORY TIP**
> Try to observe how often scooting occurs. Is it a major behaviour pattern throughout the cat's day, or does it only occur after defecation?

20. What if my cat has diarrhoea?

Diarrhoea is defined as the passing of liquid faeces. It is always worthwhile taking note of the frequency with which your cat passes faeces, and if possible their consistency, type and amount, so that you are aware of any changes from normal. It should be remembered that cats usually pass motions which are softer and less well-formed than, for example, those of dogs. Faeces of the consistency of putty are considered quite normal. However if a change is seen, close observation should be kept on the cat for other signs of disease, as diarrhoea can be a common indication of many illnesses, some relatively trivial, but some of a serious nature.

Colour of normal faeces

The colour of faeces is affected by the type of food being consumed. The faeces will be pale when white meat is fed, dark if raw meat is given, and may have a reddish tinge when the cat has eaten commercially prepared food.

Digested blood from the stomach or small intestine produces a black stool. There may be streaks of fresh blood on the faeces in conditions where the lower bowel is damaged. Where any more than a small fleck of blood is seen, the veterinary surgeon should be consulted immediately as this sign can be associated with diseases such as feline infectious enteritis and feline leukaemia; it may also occur in some cases of poisoning.

Diarrhoea

Diarrhoea is most frequently caused by digestive problems. The bowel looseness is likely to cease when the food which started the problem is withdrawn or if dietary changes are made gradually.

First aid treatment

- Withhold food for 24 hours (8–12 hours in the case of kittens) to rest the intestines.
- Water must always be freely supplied; diarrhoea cannot be 'dried up' by withholding water.
- Begin feeding again using cooked egg-whites, or white fish, with plain boiled rice, fed in small quantities, if the cat will accept it. The total for the first day should be no more than half the normal ration.
- Confine the cat indoors while following this first aid regimen. This will avoid scavenging during the enforced fast, and allow you to keep a closer eye on the animal and on its motions. N.B. Remember to provide a litter tray!

If diarrhoea persists, or if there are other signs of illness, contact your veterinary surgeon without delay, since it may be caused by bacterial or viral infection, or may on occasion be associated with severe endoparasitic infestation. Diarrhoea merits even earlier veterinary attention in young kittens as they quickly become dehydrated.

HISTORY TIP

When giving the history of the case it is important to try to distinguish between types of loose stool.

Is the cat passing:

- a greater number of stools than normal?
- a normal number of stools but very loose or accompanied by quantities of fluid?
- stools containing jelly-like mucus?
- blood-streaked or bloody stools – how much blood and what colour (i.e. bright red or black)?

It is also useful to note whether the cat is eating and still has a good appetite, whether it is seen to strain a lot trying to pass faeces and whether it is also vomiting.

NOTE

It can be helpful to take to the veterinary surgeon a small quantity of freshly passed faeces for examination. Pack the sample in a small, carefully washed yoghurt pot or similar container and label with your name and the date.

To be able to provide this information and also the sample for your veterinary surgeon, it will probably be necessary to confine the cat indoors with a litter tray.

Other causes of diarrhoea may be:

- Overfeeding in young kittens.
- Feeding liver or offal in large amounts.
- Too much milk – some cats may react to even very small quantities of milk because of an intolerance of milk sugar (lactose) or to milk proteins.
- Unfamiliar foods, which are consequently not digested properly.
- Scavenging.
- Decaying or putrid food – although cats, due to their fastidious eating habits and keen sense of smell are unlikely to eat food which is 'off'.
- An underlying disease elsewhere in the body, such as kidney, liver or pancreatic disease.

NOTE

Queens that eat large numbers of afterbirths when kittening may temporarily have diarrhoea.

It is worth noting that diarrhoea can be associated with stress, particularly in cats with a nervous temperament. A new cat in the neighbourhood, thunderstorms, overexcitement or moving house have been known to cause diarrhoea in cats.

A peaceful, less demanding life without stressful episodes may be all that is required to effect a cure.

21. What if my cat is passing blood in its faeces?

Occasional, very slight streaks of fresh blood on the outside of the stool are likely to come from a small broken blood vessel around the anus and are unimportant provided the cat is otherwise well. However, if even this small amount of blood is seen persistently, veterinary advice should be sought. Any quantity of blood greater than a small fleck is a reason to seek veterinary advice urgently, even if the cat is otherwise well.

HISTORY TIP
Be prepared to estimate the quantity of blood passed, its frequency and colour, fresh red or dark digested blood. Note also the colour and consistency of the faeces. It can be helpful if a typical sample of blood-stained faeces is taken to the veterinary surgery.

22. What if my cat is constipated?

Constipation (difficulty and pain caused by trying to pass hard lumps of faeces) is the most frequent sign of a large intestine problem in cats. Constipation can result from the simple causes listed below and may be cured by the administration of small doses of liquid paraffin (½–1 teaspoonful twice daily is usually sufficient) and some other simple actions, making a visit to the veterinary surgery unnecessary. However if constipation continues and/or the cat is obviously in pain, then veterinary attention should be sought.

Some common causes of constipation are:

Eating bones or garden bone meal – Bones are very constipating. Some cats eat bones, but if these individuals show signs of constipation then this should be prevented. If you spread bone meal as a fertilizer around plants in the garden take care that your cat is not eating it.

Hair in the intestine – The ingestion of large amounts of hair following self-grooming during particular periods of hair loss such as spring/summer, or during illness, can lead to the formation of hard, coarse faeces wound up with masses of hair. This can be prevented by grooming the cat and occasionally dosing with liquid paraffin (see 'What if' no. 2).

Lack of exercise – An overweight lazy 'indoor' cat is more likely to suffer from constipation than an active 'outdoor' cat. In addition the confinement indoors for an extended period of a cat that is normally allowed to roam (for instance after moving house) may lead to constipation as these cats may be reluctant to use litter trays.

Other causes of constipation include:

Disease affecting the normal motility of the large intestine particularly the condition called The Key-Gaskell syndrome (feline dysautonomia). In this condition there is a degeneration of the nerves controlling a number of internal organs, including the lower intestine. The normal muscular contractions which move the contents along and eventually cause the faeces to be expelled from the anus are affected and thus the cat becomes constipated. Usually other signs will be present in this condition, and veterinary diagnosis and treatment is essential.

Old age. Constipation, associated with a generally reduced muscular tone and contractibility of the large intestine in older or debilitated cats is not uncommon. The precise cause is often impossible to determine. Veterinary advice should be sought as soon as possible since a number of treatments are available which may be of assistance in such cases.

Physical injury or trauma to the pelvis are often seen in road traffic accident cases. The pelvis may become narrowed as a result and this can lead to constipation. Veterinary advice should be obtained on the management of such individuals.

FIRST AID TIP
Where constipation is caused by the simple causes listed, such as inappropriate feeding, confinement in the house, etc., medicinal liquid paraffin may be given at the dose of ½–1 teaspoonful twice daily by mouth. Giving too great a quantity is not harmful, but the excess may leak from the anus and may soil the cat's bed. It is important when dosing with any liquid medicine that it is not forced down the throat if the cat starts struggling. This can lead to some being inhaled and may cause respiratory problems. It is far better to trickle it in a little at a time, whilst at the same time calming the cat by stroking and making soothing noises.

NOTE
One of the signs of constipation, that of frequent attempts to pass motions without success and straining during the attempt, is also a sign of cystitis (inflammation of the bladder) or a blocked bladder. It is important to check and see whether the cat is passing urine normally. If in any doubt as to whether cystitis or blocked bladder is present, the cat should be taken to the veterinary surgeon as a matter of urgency (see 'What if' nos 23 and 25).

23. What if my cat is not passing urine, or is straining to pass small amounts frequently?

It is important to distinguish between straining to pass urine and constipation; the posture adopted by cats for both acts can appear similar. Not passing urine may be a voluntary decision on the cat's part, for instance if it is confined indoors for some reason, despite having access to a litter tray, or if it is moved into a new unfamiliar environment, the cat may fail to pass either urine or faeces for as long as 24 hours.

In other circumstances, failure to pass urine or difficulty in doing so, is always a serious emergency and must certainly not be neglected if it continues for more than 24 hours. Be prepared to consult your veterinary surgeon earlier if other signs of illness are present. The pain of a full bladder which cannot be emptied is agonizing.

HISTORY TIP
Normal urine is yellow and clear, but certain drugs can alter the colour. Check with your veterinary surgeon if you notice any change in colour or smell of the cat's urine when on medication. It is useful for the veterinary surgeon to have a fresh urine sample available in any cases of possible urinary problems. For instructions on how to obtain a sample, see History Tip 'What if' no. 6.

Feline urological syndrome (FUS) is a fairly common condition, of neutered male cats in particular, where a sandy type of material forms in the bladder and can block the relatively narrow urethra (the tube leading from the bladder to the outside, along which urine passes). Initial signs of a problem may be due to cystitis (caused by irritation of the bladder by the sandy material) or a partial blockage. In this case the cat will be seen to spend a lot of time on its toilet area, will strain often (this can be mistaken for constipation), may twitch its tail and may also spend a lot of time licking his penis or the area under its tail.

If the cat is not treated at this stage then a complete blockage may occur. This is an emergency and immediate veterinary treatment must be given to avoid permanent damage or even death of the animal.

Treatment of a blocked bladder usually involves the passing of a fine tube (catheter) under general anaesthesia. In severe or recurring cases it may be necessary to operate to eliminate the dangerous bottleneck in the urethra where blockages occur. It is obviously far better to try to prevent this condition occurring in the first place. A number of measures can be taken to help ensure this in cats which are prone to problems with FUS:

- If the cat is fed a dry diet change to a moist or semi-moist feed.
- An important component of this sandy material which causes the problem is magnesium. High magnesium diets should therefore be avoided. Your vet will advise and may prescribe a special diet for your cat to help cure and prevent the condition.
- Encourage the cat to drink more liquids.
- Make sure that the cat has plenty of opportunity to pass urine frequently. Where possible allow your cat access to the outside.

24. What if my cat is incontinent?

True incontinence can be defined as the dripping or dribbling of urine without the cat being aware of it. A distinction must thus be made between abnormal urination behaviour, and true incontinence.

Abnormal urination can occur as a result of:

- **A nervous-type behaviour** in the case of a new arrival, or unfamiliar surroundings. This behaviour usually corrects itself once the cat has settled and discovered the litter tray or been allowed access to the outside. Cleaning the 'accident spot' with a strong solution of biological detergent should help prevent the cat continuing to use that area as a toilet.
- **Territory marking** (spraying) is particularly seen in entire toms, although it can occur in neutered toms and both spayed and entire females. Castration or spaying may help minimize the problem, as will cleaning any affected areas in the house with strong detergent solution. If the problem persists, your veterinary surgeon may be able to help with advice on behavioural therapy and possibly medication in the form of tablets or injections.
- **Senility or extreme old age** can result in abnormal urination in some cats which have been housebound all their lives. This may be because of difficulty in getting about. More litter trays placed about the house may solve the problem in this case. However some cats will still soil indoors and, if the cause is not a kidney or bladder infection which can be treated, it may be a problem the owner has to put up with.
- **Increased urine production** as a result of a disease such as diabetes or a chronic kidney disorder can result in the cat producing greater volumes of urine and thus having to urinate more frequently. A cat which has

started to urinate more copiously and more frequently will also need to drink more water. In almost all cases of increased urine production the cat will need to drink to replace the loss and water must be freely available at all times. Restricting water will *not* help reduce the amount of urine.

Any cat showing such signs must be taken as soon as possible for veterinary examination.

- **Cystitis** can result in abnormal urination. The cat may be seen to urinate more frequently and sometimes in unusual places such as in the bath or sink. Usually only small quantities of urine are passed and sometimes blood may be seen in the urine (see 'What if' no. 25). If cystitis is suspected the cat must be taken to a veterinary surgeon at the earliest opportunity for examination and treatment.

True incontinence can be seen as a result of:

- **Congenital anatomical abnormalities** of the urethra or the vertebral column/pelvis. Such problems will be present from birth and will thus be first noticed in young cats and kittens. A veterinary examination will be required to determine the nature of the abnormality.
- **Paralysis** of the nerves controlling bladder function following fractures of the base of the spine as can sometimes occur in road traffic accidents. The diagnosis and management of such cases must be under the direction of your veterinary surgeon.
- **Disease or degeneration** of the nerves controlling bladder function can be seen in some cases of The Key-Gaskell Syndrome (feline dysautonomia). Faecal incontinence or constipation may also be seen in such cases and veterinary advice must be sought if this condition is suspected.

HISTORY TIP

It is helpful to know whether the cat has true incontinence (urine dribbling away all the time) or merely abnormal urination behaviour (is able to hold and release urine at intervals although not in the 'proper' places). Can you relate any external circumstances to episodes of abnormal urination or incontinence?

A fresh urine sample may be useful in such cases. For instructions on how to obtain a sample, see History Tip 'What if' no. 6.

25. What if my cat is passing blood in its urine?

It is not unusual for a newly-kittened queen to have a blood-stained discharge from the vulva which may blend with the urine. In any other circumstances blood in the urine is a serious sign, so a veterinary surgeon should be consulted as soon as possible. It is helpful and will save time if you can take a fresh urine sample with you (for instructions, see History Tip, 'What if' no. 6).

HISTORY TIP

1. Note whether blood is present in the urine each time the cat urinates.
2. Try to observe if blood is present in the first or last amounts of urine to be passed, or whether it is generally mixed with the urine.
3. Check whether the cat is having difficulty passing the urine, and whether urination is accompanied by pain before, during, or after urine is passed.

Blood in the urine may be associated with the following conditions: feline urological syndrome (FUS) (see 'What if' no. 23), bacterial cystitis, warfarin poisoning.

Other possible causes include growths and tumours in the urinary or genital tract (these are rare); injury to the urinary or genital tracts following trauma – most frequently following a road traffic accident; and stones (calculi) in the bladder (also rare in cats).

26. What if my cat is mismated?

See Chapter 7, 'What ifs' in relation to oestrus control.

27. What if my cat is found to be pregnant unexpectedly?

See Chapter 7, 'What ifs' in relation to oestrus control.

28. What if my cat is pot-bellied?

It is normal for young kittens to show considerable abdominal distension after eating, but if the expansion is gross, consideration should be given to spreading the food intake over more but smaller meals.

A pot-bellied kitten which is thin on the shoulders and hindquarters, with a poor coat, is probably suffering from an overburden of worms, see section on Endoparasites, Chapter 9.

Other causes of a pot-bellied appearance which are not due to overfeeding are pregnancy, pyometra (pus in the uterus), hormonal disorders (rare), and some other major disorders which can be accompanied by fluid accumulation in the abdomen, such as liver or kidney disease, heart disease or feline infectious peritonitis (see Chapter 9). If in doubt seek veterinary attention.

> **HISTORY TIP**
> Take a fresh faeces sample with you to the surgery if you suspect the condition is due to worms in a kitten or young cat.

29. What if my cat is limping?

Cats limp because of pain or a 'mechanical' problem in the leg. It is not always easy to find out which leg is causing pain but it helps to watch the cat moving across in front of you, as well as coming towards and going away from you.

A cat may often take the weight off the injured leg when standing still and, when moving, may nod or drop the head as the weight goes on to the sound foreleg. Similarly the hindquarters will be dropped when the sound hind leg is placed on the ground. If a cat is holding its leg off the ground the problem is mostly likely to be in the foot. If it places its foot gently to the ground or drags the leg, the injury is likely to be higher up.

Very often an acute limp is easily diagnosed and can be cured by first aid. Look at the foot to detect impaled thorns, splinters of wood, balls of tar, stone chippings, or other such objects which can cause limping in cats.

Gently examine the rest of the leg for signs of injury, such as swelling deformity, pain, loss of function or a break in the skin. In most cases it is sensible to seek veterinary advice promptly, but if the cat is otherwise well, is eating and the pain is not severe, then such an action can be delayed for 24 hours. It will be helpful to your veterinary surgeon if you have already managed to identify the painful area or located some injury. Other causes of limping may be:

Arthritis

Cause Inflammation of a joint which may be caused by infection, a previous injury or 'wear and tear' degeneration.

Signs Chronic pain, difficulty in rising, reluctance to jump and general reluctance to walk which may ease after some movements are made.

Action Many new products are available to veterinary surgeons which can ease the pain, but continual medication may be needed.

Bone fractures

Cause Usually the result of road traffic accidents or falls.

Signs Severe pain of sudden onset; inability to put weight on the leg which may be visibly deformed.

Action Contact a veterinary surgeon quickly for diagnosis and fixation of the fracture. Repair is usually good. See Chapter 10 for advice on care and transport to the surgery.

Dislocations

Cause The displacement through accidental injury of one or more bones which form a joint.

Signs Sudden onset of pain; limb function is reduced and may be noticeably different in length from the sound leg.

Action Veterinary consultation at once as there may be internal bleeding or an associated fracture. Generally, correction of a dislocation is more likely to be successful if it is carried out without delay.

Infected bites

Cause Bite wounds obtained during hunting (e.g. rats) or fighting. Infection develops at the base of the puncture wound and causes swelling and pain of the area. If involving a joint, infected bites can result in an infectious arthritis.

Signs Swelling and extreme tenderness of a particular area of the leg. The inital bite wound may not have been noticed since the amount of bleeding from such wounds is usually small. The puncture wound can often be identified by feeling carefully for a few matted hairs that can be easily plucked out attached to a small scab.

Action Veterinary consultation for treatment and possibly antibiotic medication.

Sprains

Cause Damage to a ligament or tendon by being overstretched or torn through wrenching or twisting.

Signs Sudden pain occurring while running, climbing or fighting, followed by inability to use the leg; swelling, and tenderness when the area is touched.

Action Put a cold compress on the leg to reduce the swelling and pain. A prompt veterinary consultation is necessary to assess the extent of the damage and commence treatment.

30. What if my cat is eating with difficulty?

Difficulty in eating is often a sign that pain is present in the mouth when the cat feeds. Other signs of mouth pain include drooling of saliva and pawing at the mouth. One of the more common causes of oral discomfort and gum disease in cats is tartar or plaque building up on the teeth. Tartar is formed gradually by a combination of bacterial action and chemicals in the saliva, leading to a hard coating over the teeth and gums. It causes an inflammation of the gums (gingivitis) forcing the gums to recede and allowing pockets of infection to establish. This in turn leads to more serious tooth and gum infections and eventually to loss of teeth if untreated.

The condition can be prevented to some extent by the feeding of a certain amount of hard 'dry diet' to provide the teeth and gums with some natural exercise.

Treatment when tartar has become established involves dental scaling by a veterinary surgeon and the extraction of any loose or diseased teeth at the same time.

Further causes of difficulty in eating include:

Foreign body lodged in mouth

Signs Sudden onset of gagging, retching, drooling or foaming at the mouth; pawing and rubbing at the mouth.

Cause Typically a piece of bone, fish hook, needle, a piece of cotton wound round the teeth or an elastic band caught round the base of the tongue.

Action It is best not to persist in trying to remove the obstruction if it does not come away readily, but to take the cat to the veterinary surgery. A sedative or anaesthetic may be needed while the obstruction is removed.

Mouth ulcers

Signs Drooling, pawing at mouth, red, ulcerated areas visible on tongue and palate. If due to respiratory virus infection then most cats will also show signs of cat 'flu (sneezing, nose and eye discharges, fever, loss of appetite). If due to kidney failure the breath will often smell of ammonia.

Cause The most common causes of mouth ulcers in the cat are infections with the respiratory viruses (the cause of cat 'flu) or chronic kidney failure as seen in a number of older cats.

Action Veterinary consultation for either cat 'flu or kidney failure. In the case of possible cat 'flu remember the disease is highly contagious and so leave the cat in the car while you wait for a consultation to avoid infecting other cats in the waiting room.

Neoplasia (growths and tumours in the mouth)

Signs Visible swellings on the tongue, palate or gum; often ulcerated. Offensive breath.

Action Veterinary consultation as soon as possible to determine whether removal possibly by cryosurgery (freezing the tumour tissue) is indicated.

Rodent ulcer

Signs Slowly enlarging ulcer usually seen on the upper lip just to one side of the midline.

Cause Unknown, however constant licking by the cat's rasp-like tongue may well enlarge the lesion.

Action Treatment by a veterinary surgeon will be required. This may well involve general anaesthesia on one or more occasions to freeze or chemically cauterize the ulcer as well as the administration of drugs to reduce the inflammation. Hormone tablets or injections are sometimes effective.

Other possible causes of difficulty in eating can be trauma or injury to the mouth, teeth or jaw. A fractured lower jaw can occur in cats which jump from too great a height due to the chin striking the ground on landing. Also, burns of the mouth following ingestion of caustic substances on the coat whilst grooming, or due to biting through a 'live' electric flex, may cause extreme oral discomfort for a period and tend to inhibit normal eating behaviour.

31. What if my cat has bad breath?

Mild cases of halitosis (bad breath) are often associated with what the cat eats. For example, a fish-flavoured diet will give a characteristic fishy smell. Scavenging from rubbish bins may also render the breath unpleasant.

Where the odour is persistent and very noticeable, it is wise to have the cat examined by a veterinary surgeon. Other possible causes of bad breath include:

Periodontal disease

Cause Inflammation of the gums (gingivitis) associated with the accumulation of tartar deposit. This is by far the most common cause of loss of teeth in cats.

Comment Common in older cats.

Action Regular visits to the veterinary surgeon for scaling can be enormously useful for the cat's health and comfort. Feeding hard, crunchy food as part of the diet can help prevent the condition occurring.

Foreign body lodged in mouth

See 'What if' no. 30.

Non-specific gingivitis and stomatitis (inflammation of the gums and lining of the mouth)

Cause Unknown, possibly bacterial infection in some cases.

Comment A number of cases of gingivitis and stomatitis occur that are not associated with the accumulation of tartar.

Action A number of possible treatments have been used in such cases. Consult your veterinary surgeon as soon as signs are noticed as early treatment is likely to be more successful.

Other possible causes

Bad breath may be associated with kidney disease and liver disease.

32. What if my cat is drooling saliva excessively?

Drooling or hypersalivation is a normal response when anticipating food or when frightened. It is often also one sign of non-specific mouth pain.

Possible causes of this include:

Mouth ulcers
See 'What if' no. 30.

Periodontal disease
See 'What if' no. 31.

Non-specific gingivitis or stomatitis
See 'What if' no. 31.

Foreign body lodged in mouth
See 'What if' no. 30.

Other possible causes of hypersalivation include poisoning with certain garden chemicals such as insecticides or slug bait (metaldehyde), ingestion of irritant substances on the fur during grooming, electrical burns in the mouth caused by biting or chewing 'live' electric flex, or associated with nausea, for example in cases of travel sickness.

Any cat showing unexplained hypersalivation, particularly if it is also 'off colour', must be taken as soon as possible to a veterinary surgeon for examination.

33. What if my cat is having fits, convulsions or is twitching?

It is normal for young kittens to twitch frequently when resting and older cats may twitch and make other movements during their sleep while dreaming. These twitching episodes are very different from a true fit or convulsion. A fit is a convulsive seizure, occurring usually while the cat is relaxed or asleep. The first fit which an owner observes often occurs in a young cat. A fit usually begins with a period of behavioural abnormality (aura) where the cat may appear disorientated or frightened, may sit in unusual postures, cry out or become aggressive. This is followed by a period of rigidity (tonic phase) which is in turn followed by shaking and spasms of the muscles, progressing to involuntary paddling with the paws (clonic phase). There may be involuntary passing of faeces and urine and the cat may temporarily lose consciousness. The fit may last for only a minute or two and the cat may recover quickly and appear perfectly normal. In other cases the fit may be more prolonged and the cat may appear dazed and disorientated for some time after the convulsions have stopped.

In severe episodes, one fit may lead quickly to several more. Although it is not likely that the cat will harm humans or itself while in a fit, it is wise to be cautious. The type of first aid treatment administered during human fits is inappropriate for cats, and no attempt should be made to force anything into the cat's mouth. While the fit lasts, do not touch the cat, but remove anything lying nearby which could cause it injury and gently move the cat by using a blanket if it is lying in a dangerous place such as the top of the stairs or by a fire. Turn off radios and the television and keep the room dark and quiet.

> **HISTORY TIP**
> Make a note of the progress and duration of the fit and the circumstances which preceded it. Unless the cat is suffering from a prolonged episode of fitting *there is little point in asking the veterinary surgeon to make an urgent visit to the cat*, as it will almost certainly be normal by the time help is obtained. Once the cat is out of the fit, report the occurrence to the veterinary surgeon on the telephone. It will probably be wise not to attempt to make a surgery call the same day as the cat is best kept quiet for some hours following a fit.

Kittens may react to severe pain, especially of an abdominal nature, by having convulsions. Veterinary diagnosis and treatment of the underlying cause will be needed.

Epilepsy, often showing for the first time in young cats, does occur, but this condition can in many cases be controlled by medication, allowing the cat to lead a relatively normal life. Since fits may sometimes be associated with brain tumours, dietary deficiencies, previous traumas, inherited conditions such as hydrocephalus (water on the brain), feline infectious peritonitis, toxoplasmosis, kidney disease, and poisoning, always seek veterinary attention as an accurate diagnosis of the cause is essential before any medication is given.

Rabies

In other countries, a cat having a fit would have to be considered a possible rabies case, but this is extremely unlikely to be the case in Britain, unless the cat has only recently been released from a quarantine kennel, or has been bitten by a dog or cat which has been illegally smuggled into this country. If you have any suspicion that this may be so, tell your veterinary surgeon so that he can immediately report the matter to the Ministry of Agriculture, Fisheries and Food, Rabies Division. Even if your fears may be unfounded, where this deadly disease is concerned it is better to err on the safe side.

> **HISTORY TIP**
> It will be helpful to the veterinary surgeon if you can recall any traumatic incident in the cat's life, e.g. a fall, or being hit by a car, which may have caused brain damage not perceived at the time.

34. What if my cat has a lump or swelling?

Any lumps or swellings which do not disappear within a few days should be investigated by a veterinary surgeon. This is particularly important for the early recognition of abscesses and to identify tumours early in their development.

Types of swelling include:

Abscess

Causes Swelling beneath the skin caused by bacterial infection. Often the result of a bite or puncture wound.

Signs Pain, heat and swelling develop over a few days probably with subsequent bursting and discharge of pus. Abcesses may occur anywhere on the body but are often found around the side of the face or the base of the tail and especially in tom cats due to fighting.

Action Contact the veterinary surgeon as the condition may need surgical drainage and medication with antibiotics.

Ulcers

Cause Various.

Signs A red, eroded area occurring on any part of the body.

Action Seek veterinary advice without delay.

Haematoma (blood filled swelling)

Cause The result of an injury to blood vessels under the skin. The ear flap is a common site. See also 'What if' nos 12 and 13.

Signs A soft swelling and distortion of the area – sometimes painful, but not usually so, to the touch.

Action Consult your veterinary surgeon as surgical treatment may be required. A post-operative haematoma may require a support bandage which the veterinary surgeon will show you how to put on.

Tender area at an injection site

Cause A local irritant reaction to a component in the injection.

Signs Pain and swelling and possible heat. If the injection has been given into a leg muscle, possibly lameness.

Action Further treatment is seldom required unless the cat is in a lot of pain, but the matter should be reported to the veterinary surgeon.

Stings and insect bites

Signs Sudden swelling which may be severe and dangerous if the face and mouth are affected.

Action If sting is visible, pull it out with tweezers. Apply meat tenderizer to area. Observe amount of swelling. Keep cat indoors and quiet. Veterinary attention is needed if swelling is acute in mouth and throat. If the cat seems in great pain your veterinary surgeon may be able to give you extra advice over the phone.

Ticks

Signs Usually no discomfort is shown by the cat. A smooth white or grey 'growth' or 'cyst-like' swelling, the size of a pea, is seen. More than one tick may be present on the cat and the areas most commonly affected are the head, neck and limbs.

Action Do not attempt to pull the tick out as this will probably result in the head being left *in situ* under the skin and may cause a local reaction. Instead take the cat to the veterinary surgeon who will probably 'anaesthetize' the tick to make it release its grip before removing it. If your cat is prone to acquiring ticks then ask the veterinary surgeon about insecticide preparations, some of which can be used at intervals to prevent tick infestation.

Bruising after injury

Signs Pain and heat in the affected area which may also be grazed and bleeding.

Action Seek veterinary advice if pain is severe.

Lumps and Swellings may also be associated with urticaria (hives) and possibly tumours.

> **HISTORY TIP**
> In the case of non-urgent lumps and swellings, make a note in the cat's record to remind you when the swelling was first noticed, where it is, and the size (diameter). It is also a good idea to compare it in size and shape with a common object, e.g. a coffee bean, a coin etc. Subsequent measurements will provide vital information on the rate of enlargement, a possible crucial factor in deciding whether surgery will be necessary.

35. What if my cat is wounded/cut/burnt/grazed?

There are some common situations when the owner can help their cat by giving first aid treatment, but all these conditions need to be checked by a veterinarian as soon as possible.

Burns and scalds

Cause These are usually by liquids being spilt over the cat in the kitchen and sparks from logs or open fires, or from sleeping in hot ashes on the hearth.

Action The immediate treatment is to bathe the area with a lot of cold water to reduce the heat to the skin. Cut away debris and matted hair if it is not too painful to the cat. Get the cat to the veterinary surgery at once if it is in a lot of pain, but certainly within 12 hours.

Wounds

Cause Fight wounds are the most common and very often they become infected. This is because, when they are caused by claws or teeth, the wounds are invariably quite deep but only have a small opening on the surface, which soon closes, leaving infection trapped deep down. Such wounds need careful treatment by a veterinary surgeon, often involving the administration of antibiotics. Traffic accidents also account for many injuries which break the skin.

Action There is seldom much bleeding unless a large blood vessel is severed, but grit and dirt frequently contaminate wounds. A small cut can be washed out with clean water containing a little weak disinfectant. Cut the hair away from the edge of the wound very carefully. If the wound is large, painful or heavily contaminated, a veterinary consultation is essential. Otherwise, gentle bathing at least three times a day and the application of soothing ointment must be carried out diligently. If you have any doubts about the severity of a wound or, if during healing, the edges are inflamed and sore and the surrounding area is hot to the touch, seek veterinary advice without delay.

36. What if my cat is licking itself excessively?

Licking is part of the normal grooming procedure in cats to clean dirt off the coat or paws, to clean a wound, or to remove excess secretions. Many cats will also lick their companion animals in displays of mutual grooming which is recognized as a sign of affection between individuals. However, grooming in cats can be more than just a matter of personal cleanliness – many cats will indulge in frantic displays of grooming in response to fright or indecision as a kind of displacement activity!

If the cat is seen to be licking excessively at one area of the body, check for some unsuspected injury, insect sting, or thorn embedded in the flesh. Continual licking can cause additional damage to the skin and so should be investigated. Excessive licking may be indicative of:

Ectoparasite infestation

Cause Infestations of the skin or coat with fleas, lice or mites.

Signs Scratching, licking or biting at the skin excessively. Crusty nodules may be present on the skin in some cases.

Action Various insecticidal preparations made especially for cats are available to treat mild cases. In addition, other cats or dogs in the household should be treated and action taken to eradicate parasites from the cat's bed and the rest of the house. If a heavy infestation is present with associated skin and coat damage due to self trauma, then veterinary advice should be sought prior to such treatment.

Miliary dermatitis

Cause An allergic reaction to flea bites or flea excreta.

Signs Severe irritation, licking, scratching and biting with associated loss of hair and crusty nodules, usually along the skin on the back.

Action Veterinary advice should be sought since anti-allergic medication may be indicated in addition to rigorous flea control both on the cat and in the environment. Hormone tablets or injections are often used to treat this condition.

Neurodermatitis

Cause Stress factors, particularly in 'highly strung' breeds such as Siamese, Burmese or Abyssinian.

Signs Excessive licking, cleaning or hair pulling, leading to some loss and damage of hair with no apparent underlying cause.

Action A thorough veterinary diagnosis will be required since many cases are found to have a physical cause at the root of the problem, i.e. fleas, mites, foreign bodies imbedded in the skin etc. In true cases of neurodermatitis where no underlying cause is found then the cause of the stress must be identified and removed.

Tranquillizers or hormones may be used judiciously by the veterinary surgeon in some of these cases.

In addition to these conditions, excessive licking around the anus or base of the tail can be a sign of anal gland problems, tapeworm infestation or stud tail (see 'What if' no. 19). Excessive licking of the penis in males can be a sign of problems due to feline urological syndrome (see 'What if' no. 23).

37. What if my cat is weak and lethargic?

Cats sleep a great deal more than other animals – on average 16 hours a day! This, combined with the fact that they prefer the hours of twilight and darkness for many of their activities, may make them seem lethargic. However, a normal cat should be fully alert and active when awake and capable of responding immediately to the slightest change in its environment. A decrease in this general level of alertness and activity may signify weakness or lethargy due to illness. In this case there will usually be other more prominent and specific signs, but if you feel your cat is less active than it should be, it is always wise to seek veterinary attention.

Lethargy and obesity can be associated and be a consequence of each other – see Chapter 6.

Other causes of lethargy include: kidney disease; anaemia; heart disease; feline leukaemia; diabetes mellitus; poisoning with certain poisons; and various tumours. (See Index of Diseases and Conditions.)

38. What if my cat has collapsed and is comatose?

Cats in the terminal stages of any serious illness, or in extreme old age may collapse.

Any disease or condition which makes breathing difficult may cause a cat to collapse temporarily. Heat stroke, which may occur if the cat is confined in a stationary car, or in a very sunny room, can cause collapse – see 'What if' no. 14.

When a cat which has been previously healthy collapses suddenly, ensure that the mouth and nose are clear of discharges and obstructions, keep the cat warm, and seek veterinary advice urgently.

Some more specific causes of collapse include:

Shock (following road accident, or serious haemorrhage)

Signs Cold, limp, lifeless, with rapid shallow breathing. Lips, gums and eye rims (conjunctivae) very pale.

Action Seek nearest veterinary surgeon immediately. Give nothing by mouth, cover the cat loosely and keep warm.

Trauma to the head (following road accident)

Signs Bleeding from nose or ears. Breathing may be irregular. Other signs of injury elsewhere on the body will usually provide a clue that the cat has been involved in a road traffic accident.

Action Move the animal as little as possible to avoid further injury. Transport cat gently and swiftly to the nearest veterinary surgery on a rigid board, and cover loosely to keep warm.

Hypothermia (following exposure to intense cold)

Action Apply *gentle* warmth, keep the cat loosely covered until you reach the veterinary surgery. Give warm milk if the cat is able to swallow, do *not* give brandy or other spirits.

Collapse may also be associated with the following conditions: poisoning, particularly where metaldehyde (slug bait), alphachloralose (some types of mouse poison) or ethylene glycol (antifreeze) are involved; epilepsy; heart disease; kidney disease; diabetes mellitus; electric shock. (See Index of Diseases and Conditions.)

HISTORY TIP
Be prepared to tell the veterinary surgeon the exact circumstances surrounding the collapse, i.e. what the cat was doing just beforehand, any trauma which occurred, and the time it took for the cat to return to normal.

39. What if my cat is in pain?

As a general rule most cats are stoical about pain and although they may be badly injured or very ill they will give little, if any, indication of the site of the pain.

If a minor accident, such as stepping on a paw, appears to have caused pain which has not subsided within a few hours, seek veterinary advice. Occasionally the pain may appear generalized and difficult to locate. If pain is persistent, always seek veterinary diagnosis. Cats may show signs of pain before other signs become apparent.

Where the location of the pain is obvious, e.g. in mouth, ear, abdomen or from an abscess, consult the relevant 'What if'.

Other causes of severe pain may be: arthritis; cystitis/feline urological syndrome; feline infectious enteritis (panleucopenia); poisoning. (See Index of Diseases and Conditions.)

40. What if my cat is losing weight or is looking thin?

Unlike most dogs, many cats will refuse to eat if stressed. In some cases this can persist to cause a quite alarming loss of weight and condition. Environmental stresses, such as moving house, change of owner, boarding, or a new cat or dog in the house, may all cause loss of appetite in some cats. Where no other obvious reason or sign of disease is present, this form of self-starvation should be treated by attempting to restore the former environmental conditions as far as possible to remove stress. In this respect the cat's normal feeding regimen should be maintained by feeding at the usual place, by the person who normally feeds it and from its usual feed bowl. Although it may be impossible to return every aspect of the cat's life-style to 'normal', most cats will respond to this strategy and can be encouraged to eat again.

Queens can lose weight when feeding a large litter as they may not be able to process enough food through their bodies to maintain their own weight as well as producing enough milk for the kittens. They will usually recover quite quickly if they are allowed free access to high quality food after weaning. Worming two or three times at four weekly intervals after the kittens are weaned may help the queen regain her normal condition. If there is any doubt whether the cat is being fed sufficient food of good nutritional quality, consult Chapter 6 and/or seek veterinary help.

Where an adequate diet is provided and none of the above circumstances apply, but the cat still loses weight, this is an indication that disease may be present – particularly in elderly cats where certain chronic conditions can cause an accelerated weight loss on top of the usual, more gradual loss of weight due to old age. In any situation of this type, professional help should be sought, since the cause of the weight loss may be obscure and can be associated with many major disorders.

> **HISTORY TIP**
> Before going to the surgery, list the cat's menu giving quantities of all the food eaten and milk drunk. If you are using commercially formulated food take a package or label with you, so that the veterinary surgeon can see the manufacturer's analysis of the contents.

41. What if my cat is aggressive?

Aggression in cats is always dangerous as it can be a cumulative habit. A cat with aggressive tendencies can inflict quite severe damage and become increasingly fierce, unless the cause can be found and some strategy used to correct this fault. See Chapter 4.

42. What if my cat is not breathing?

Lay the animal flat on its side, open its mouth, pull the tongue forward and check that there is nothing obstructing the throat. See Chapter 10. Contact the veterinary surgeon urgently and take the cat to the surgery quickly if it is possible to do so.

43. What if my cat is staggering and wobbly on its legs?

Hind leg weakness can be expected during the recovery period from an anaesthetic, or during convalescence, and in very old cats.

During the recovery stage from a fit, the gait may be uncertain and wobbly. In any other circumstances, lack of a firm and steady hind leg movement is abnormal and, as this sign may be associated with serious conditions, veterinary help should be sought promptly.

Possible causes of unsteady gait include:

Vestibular syndrome

Infection or disorder of the balance organs situated in the inner ear which produces signs of circling movements, tilted head and nystagmus (involuntary eye movements). See 'What if' no. 13.

Trauma

Injury to the back or hip is common in cases of road traffic accident.

Signs Depending on the location and severity of damage, the cat may show signs ranging from mild hind leg lameness to complete paralysis. Usually there will be other visible signs of injury which will confirm a diagnosis of road traffic accident.

Action The cat should be transported as quickly and gently as possible to a veterinary surgery for full examination and treatment.

Iliac thrombosis

A 'cutting off' of the blood supply to the hind limbs because of a blood clot lodging in the major artery.

Signs Usually the cat's hind legs will become partially or completely paralysed. They will feel cold to the touch and no pulse will be felt in the groin. The cat may have a history of heart disease.

Action The cat must receive urgent veterinary attention as prompt medical or surgical treatment can in some cases determine how much hind limb function returns.

Hypervitaminosis A

A syndrome occurring in the cat caused by a diet which contains high levels of vitamin A being consumed over long periods. Due to the fact that raw liver is rich in vitamin A and is often also a favourite food, this syndrome is often seen in cats fed wholly or largely on raw liver.

Signs High levels of vitamin A over long periods cause excess bone to be deposited around the bones and joints, particularly in the limbs and spine. This results in stiffness and pain on movement and also 'pinching' of the spinal nerves in some cases causing signs of partial paralysis of the fore or hind limbs.

Action Veterinary examination will be required to confirm a diagnosis of hypervitaminosis A. Where an excess of liver is to blame this should obviously be excluded from the diet.

Thiamine deficiency

A dietary deficiency in thiamine (vitamin B1) can be caused by overfeeding with raw fish. This is because raw fish meat contains an enzyme which breaks down thiamine before it can be absorbed in the gut. Cases can also occur when feeding a 'home cooked' diet unless a source of vitamin B1 is added afterwards since high temperatures will destroy the natural vitamin present in the food.

Signs Inappetence, unsteady gait and tucked in chin which may progress in severe cases to convulsions (fits) and semi-coma.

Action The observant owner should be able to spot the early signs of abnormalities of gait and posture. In such early cases, prompt veterinary diagnosis and treatment should be able to reverse the clinical signs. Obviously the diet will also have to be altered to make sure sufficient vitamin B1 is available.

Signs of unsteady gait can also occur in cases of poisoning – particularly with insecticidal preparations, tumours of the brain and spinal column, and in diseases such as feline infectious peritonitis or the Key-Gaskell syndrome. In young kittens, infection with feline enteritis virus (panleucopaenia) of the pregnant queen, or of the kitten itself soon after birth, may cause damage to the brain resulting in unsteadiness. Also congenital cases of vestibular syndrome (see earlier), and some rare inherited enzyme deficiencies (lysosomal storage diseases) can produce various nervous signs including unsteadiness.

HISTORY TIP

If the cat is used to wearing a harness and lead then take this along to the consultation as it may assist the veterinary surgeon to see the cat moving around. Make a note of whether the staggering gait is consistently bad or whether the cat is better at certain times of the day. Be prepared to tell the veterinary surgeon about the onset of staggering – was it sudden or progressive? Also list what food the cat is fed.

44. What if my cat appears deaf?

With the exception of Siamese and Burmese cats, congenital deafness is often seen in blue-eyed, white-coated cats. Some white-coated cats are known as odd-eyed and have one blue and one orange eye. In these cases the cat may be deaf in just one ear. This congenital deafness is permanent and untreatable. Deafness in kittens does not become apparent until about four to five weeks of age, and breeders should test each kitten individually at this time. Deafness may not be recognized in situations where affected kittens can copy the actions of other litter members.

A general reduction in hearing sensitivity may occur in elderly cats as with dogs and humans. Other possible causes of deafness include:

Trauma

Damage to the delicate mechanisms in the middle- and inner-ear can sometimes occur on one or both sides in victims of road traffic accidents. In these cases there may also be signs of damage to the balance organs (see 'What ifs' nos 13 and 43). In any case of a road traffic accident or other serious injury, urgent veterinary attention should always be sought.

Vestibular syndrome

Deafness can occur in cases of infection or disorder of the balance organs in the inner ear. Signs of circling, tilted head and nystagmus (involuntary eye movements) will probably be present in these cases. See 'What if' no. 13.

Drug toxicity

The cat is very sensitive to the toxic effects of certain antibiotics – some of which, such as dihydrostreptomycin, can cause deafness when given over long periods. In such cases the deafness is usually irreversible.

Deafness in cats does not necessarily mean that the animal has to be destroyed. Many deaf cats are able to lead a near-normal life, but are obviously at an increased risk of being involved in road traffic accidents, so they may have to be kept indoors.

HISTORY TIP

Test the cat with an ultrasonic (silent) whistle and low frequency sounds to see if it can hear anything. Be prepared to say when you first noticed signs of deafness and whether you can associate this sign with any trauma or ear disease which may have since cleared up. In the quiet of your own home before going to the surgery, test the cat's response to loud and soft noises, both close to and far away, and in each ear. Tell the veterinary surgeon the results and your conclusions.

45. What if my queen is aborting?

Feline pregnancy can last from under 60 to over 70 days, so an early kittening is not necessarily an abortion. Although abortion is obviously a sign of pregnancy failure, most cases of pregnancy failure in queens result in resorption of the embryos rather than abortion.

Where an abortion does occur in a breeding cattery it is always a good idea to have the queen, and any dead foetuses which can be salvaged, tested for the presence of any infection which may affect other queens. Since the queen will often eat the expelled foetuses, it is not always possible to know when an abortion has occurred.

Causes of abortion may be infections with either bacteria, viruses (such as feline leukaemia virus) or possibly chlamydia (the cause of feline pneumonitis). Hormonal imbalance is not thought to be a common cause of abortion in queens.

Abortion may also on occasion be associated with accidental injury to pregnant queens and also with fighting between queens.

HISTORY TIP
It is important to be able to tell the veterinary surgeon the day of mating, whether one or more matings took place and within what space of time, whether the normal 'post-coital' reactions occurred, whether the pregnancy was normal before the abortion occurred, whether previous pregnancies have been normal.

46. What if my cat has small white 'grains of rice' in its faeces or around the anus?

The cause of this is almost certainly tapeworm infestation of the small intestine. The white, mobile 'grains of rice' are segments of tapeworm which are shed in the faeces and also from the rectum independently of bowel movements; this is why they may be seen in the hair around the anus or in the cat's bedding. The commonest species of tapeworm found in cats has a life cycle which usually involves the flea. Flea larvae, which are found commonly in the cat's bedding will ingest the tapeworm eggs released from the segments. A certain amount of development of the tapeworm egg takes place inside the flea so that when an adult flea is accidentally swallowed by the cat during grooming, a new tapeworm can develop and establish in the small intestine thus completing the life cycle.

Treatment of tapeworm infestation of cats will involve flea control in addition to worming with a preparation effective against tapeworms (see Chapter 9, Endoparasites).

47. What if my cat has abnormal defecation or urination habits?

Cats that urinate or defecate in inappropriate locations on more than just the odd occasion may be doing so for a number of reasons. There may be an underlying medical problem such as diarrhoea (see 'What if' no. 20) or cystitis/feline urological syndrome (see 'What if' nos 23 and 25), in which case treatment of the condition will usually be all that is necessary to clear up the problem.

Other possible causes are: stress; litter or environmental preference; infrequent cleaning of litter trays; preference for urinating or defecating at a particular location; learned behaviour as a result of having been allowed to persist in abnormal urination or defecation for some time; inappropriate site for litter tray; lack of privacy; other cats using the tray. For further information see Chapter 4.

48. What if my cat has swollen mammary glands?

It is normal for queens to show a reddening and enlargement of the nipples some three to four weeks after ovulation. This change is sometimes referred to as 'pinking up' and although it is often assumed that this is an accurate indication of pregnancy, it is in fact due to the hormone progesterone which is also produced in queens during *false* pregnancy. Apart from this and the normal mammary enlargement which occurs just before giving birth, any signs of enlargement or swelling of one or more glands should be a cause of concern and will necessitate a visit to the veterinary surgeon.

Some other causes of swollen mammary glands are:

Tumours

This is a not uncommon site for tumour formation especially in older cats. Unfortunately these can be malignant, and if left will spread via the bloodstream to the lungs. Any swelling in a gland which is discovered during routine examination of your cat, must therefore be seen by a veterinary surgeon as soon as possible. If it is a tumour, your veterinary surgeon may wish to X-ray the cat's chest to make sure that the lungs are clear before operating.

Mastitis

This is seen occasionally during lactation as one or more hot, swollen and painful glands. Very often the queen is off her food and running a high temperature. This is a serious condition both for the queen and her kittens. The queen should be taken at once to the veterinary surgeon who will probably prescribe antibiotics and advise poulticing the gland to draw off the milk. The kittens must be removed at once from the queen to prevent the spread of infection and also to avoid them drinking infected milk.

Mammary hypertrophy

This is a relatively uncommon condition seen occasionally in pregnant queens, or in cats of either sex during certain types of hormonal therapy. In this condition usually all the glands are involved with a very marked enlargement. If the condition is linked to hormone treatment then stopping the treatment will usually cure the condition. However it is important that veterinary opinion is sought since some cases of mammary tumours can be mistaken for mammary hypertrophy.

> **HISTORY TIP**
> Be prepared to tell your veterinary surgeon when the queen was last on call, and also if she was receiving any medication when the signs were first noticed.

49. What if my cat has a dull coat?

A healthy cat presents a sleek, well-groomed appearance with a clean, glossy coat. A dull, unkempt appearance in an animal which has previously exhibited signs of a healthy coat is a cause for some concern. On its own this sign should act as a warning to the observant owner to keep a close eye on the behaviour of their pet over the next few days.

Some causes for a dull coat are:

Dietary

Cause Fatty acid deficiency or vitamin deficencies can sometimes produce a non-specific dullness of the coat. Also hypervitaminosis A (*excess* vitamin A) can produce a dull ungroomed appearance due to new bone formation around joints making grooming behaviour difficult and painful (see 'What if' no. 43).

Action Check diet for possible vitamin deficiency (or excess in the case of vitamin A). If necessary seek professional advice from your veterinary surgeon. In cases of vitamin deficiency provide a vitamin supplement. In cases of fatty acid deficiency add equal amounts (½–1 teaspoonful) of vegetable oil and lard to the cat's feed each day until the coat texture improves. Other, specific products are available from your veterinary surgeon which may prove more effective.

Reduced grooming

Causes Noxious substances on the coat, such as oil or grease; heavily soiled coat; pain on stretching and twisting to groom as in cases of hypervitaminosis A (see 'What if' no. 43) or arthritis; general depression seen in illnesses such as cat 'flu; painful lesion on tongue as seen in some cases of cat 'flu.

Action If the reason is grease or oil on the hair then the cat can be gently sponged clean with lukewarm water and baby shampoo. In the cases of illness or pain on stretching to groom then veterinary advice should be sought.

In addition to the above causes, a dull coat can also be seen in more serious diseases such as renal disease, hepatic disease and diabetes. In these cases other signs of ill-health will normally be apparent which will provide clues as to the underlying problem. Any cat which is looking depressed, listless, off their food or otherwise ill in addition to having a dull coat should be examined at once by a veterinary surgeon.

HISTORY TIP

Be prepared to indicate how long the coat has been looking dull, whether the cat is eating normally, and to list the diet. Observe the cat to check whether grooming behaviour is normal or absent. Keep a close watch for any other signs of ill-health such as sneezing, depression, diarrhoea or vomiting.

50. What if my cat has matted, greasy hair over the base of the tail?

If these signs are confined to the top surface of the tail then the most likely cause is a condition known as 'stud tail'.

This is caused by an accumulation of the normal greasy secretion from the large number of glands present in the skin in this region. Although this condition is more commonly seen in entire males (hence the name) it can also be seen in entire females and neuters.

It is thought that in some cases keeping the cat indoors inhibits normal grooming behaviour and predisposes to this condition. Therefore the tail should be initially washed thoroughly with mild shampoo, and then kept clean by daily combing and cleaning with surgical spirit. The cat will usually manage to keep the area well-groomed after this, provided it is allowed increased access to fresh air.

51. What if my queen has a discharge from her vulva?

Although a vulval discharge is not generally associated with oestrus in the queen, occasionally a scant mucoid discharge may be observed at this time. This is normal and should be no cause for concern. Also normal is a discharge from the vulva following kittening. Initially this is a copious, thick, reddish fluid but over the next few days this generally clears to a yellowish, or clear, mucoid discharge. Again there should be no cause for concern provided:

- there is no strong smell to the discharge;
- the discharge does not become greenish or dark-red in colour;
- the discharge does not remain persistent and copious;
- the queen is not off her food, listless, or otherwise unwell.

Any of these signs may suggest an infection of the womb (metritis) caused possibly by a retained kitten or placenta, or by infection following contamination of the vagina at the time of delivery. Metritis is a serious condition and urgent veterinary treatment is needed.

Another possible cause of vulval discharge is:

Pyometra

An accumulation of toxic waste material in the uterus, not associated with pregnancy.

Cause Possibly infection superimposed on changes within the uterus brought about by hormone imbalance.

Signs Vulval discharge, loss of appetite, depression, swollen abdomen, increased thirst, possibly also vomiting.

Action If an owner suspects that their queen is suffering from this condition it is most important to seek veterinary advice without delay, since an emergency operation involving surgical removal of the uterus and ovaries may be needed to save the animal. However some cases can respond to medical treatment.

HISTORY TIP

In cases of possible pyometra your veterinary surgeon will want to know the dates when the queen was last in call.

CHAPTER 9
DISEASES AFFECTING CATS

The major infectious diseases

The most important infectious diseases of cats are:
- feline leukaemia virus
- feline T-lymphotropic lentivirus
- feline panleucopaenia (or infectious enteritis)
- feline infectious peritonitis
- feline respiratory disease complex (feline herpesvirus, calicivirus, *Chlamydia psittaci*)
- feline infectious anaemia
- ringworm

Feline leukaemia virus (FeLV)

Cause An immunosuppressive viral infection.

Transmission The virus can be transmitted in the saliva of an infected cat, from the uterus to embryos in a pregnant cat, or in the queen's milk.

Incubation period From exposure to clinical disease is often a long time, sometimes up to three years.

Outcome of infection

Once infected with FeLV, there are three possible outcomes: (i) total recovery, with elimination of the virus and the development of immunity; (ii) persistent infection, with the virus circulating in the blood (viraemia); (iii) apparent recovery, but with virus lying dormant (latent) in the bone marrow, and which can be reactivated at a later date.

Most cats that are exposed to FeLV will recover, but this depends on the age at which the cat is infected with the virus, and the dose of virus to which it has been exposed. All the kittens of persistently viraemic mothers are born with a permanent infection, and kittens under eight weeks old are also very susceptible. If the cat is exposed to a large dose of virus, it is more likely to become persistently viraemic.

Signs

Initially a high temperature, lethargy, lack of appetite, and occasionally enlarged lymph nodes.

If persistent viraemia is established, then the cat is at risk of developing a FeLV-related disease. The clinical signs associated with infection are varied, depending on which organ or body system the virus is replicating in. The majority of FeLV-related diseases involve the blood cells. Thus, diseases are encountered which are characterized by proliferation of cells, such as malignant tumours (lymphosarcoma) of the bowel, lymph nodes and other organs, and leukaemia, as well as conditions in which cells populations are depleted, such as anaemia and immunosuppression. Continuous immunosuppression will predispose the cat to other diseases, such as bladder infections and other infectious diseases.

Action

Veterinary attention. The diagnosis will probably be assisted by laboratory tests.

Laboratory diagnosis

A blood sample from the suspect case can be tested for the presence of the virus.

Control and prevention in multi-cat households

The persistently viraemic cat is a continual source of FeLV infection in a multi-cat household. To eliminate the virus from such a household, these cats must be identified (by a blood test) and removed. Your veterinary surgeon will be able to advise a programme which has been devised by researchers at Glasgow University.

Control and prevention in single-cat households

A single cat in a dwelling where outside access is not allowed need not be destroyed. However, in the case of a single cat which is allowed outside, and which therefore may be in contact with other cats, the decision whether or not to destroy the cat should be taken following consultation with a veterinary surgeon.

Feline T-lymphotropic lentivirus (FTLV)

Cause	A recently isolated immunosuppressive virus, belonging to the same family as FeLV (i.e. retroviruses). It multiplies in the T-lymphocytes (a white blood cell).
Transmission	As yet, little is known about the transmission of this virus between cats, but it is present in the cat's saliva, and it is suspected that transmission between cats is via a bite. However, FTLV is not thought to be very contagious.
Incubation period	Not yet known, but probably takes weeks or even months before clinical signs are seen following infection.
Outcome of infection	Once clinical signs of disease develop, it is very unlikely that the cat will recover. Some infected cats can appear perfectly healthy, others will have bouts of mild disease, but these cases may also deteriorate in time. It is not known if infection with this virus always causes disease.
Signs	There are no specific signs of disease associated with FTLV infection. This is because the virus causes immunosuppression, which allows other different infections to become established. However, the disease is associated with chronic, long-term illness, and clinical signs include weight loss, persistent fever, chronic stomatitis (inflammation of the stomach) and gingivitis (inflammation and ulcers in the mouth and gums), chronic diarrhoea, skin lesions, upper respiratory disease, neurological signs, enlarged lymph nodes, and changes in the number of white blood cells.
Action	Veterinary attention. Regretfully it is often necessary to painlessly destroy confirmed cases because of the severity of the disease.
Laboratory diagnosis	Diagnosis can only be established by the examination of a blood sample taken from the suspect case. Isolation of the virus from blood lymphocytes is expensive, time consuming and can only be carried out in some laboratories. A test to detect virus antibodies in the blood has been developed recently, and this test will make it easier to establish if a cat has been infected with the virus.
Control and prevention	With so little known about transmission of this virus it is not possible to advise on control of infection. However, if a new cat is to be introduced into a multi-cat household, it may be worth considering having a blood sample from the cat tested for evidence of infection to FTLV.
Disinfection	See FeLV.
Comment	There is no specific treatment for this disease, and once clinical signs become apparent the prognosis is poor. There is no association between FTLV in cats, and AIDS in man.

Feline panleucopaenia (feline infectious enteritis, feline parvovirus infection)

Cause	A small but very tough virus.
Incubation period	Two to 10 days.
Transmission	Virus is shed in large quantities from infected cats in their saliva, urine, faeces and vomit. It can also be transmitted across the placenta, in pregnant females. Clinically recovered cats may continue to excrete virus. The virus is very tough, and will also persist in the environment for up to one year, and can be carried from cat to cat on clothing, footwear and so on.
Signs	Lethargy, high temperature, lack of appetite, apparent thirst but refusal to drink. Vomiting, abdominal pain, occasionally diarrhoea, dehydration. In young kittens born to infected mothers, signs are first noticed at two to three weeks old. Affected kittens are unco-ordinated, and unable to walk normally.
Action	Immediate veterinary consultation.
Prevention	Consult your veterinary surgeon about vaccination to protect against this disease, and do not neglect regular boosters. If your cat is suspected of having this disease, keep it away from other cats; also, all members of the household should avoid other cats, as the virus can be carried on shoes and clothing.
Disinfection	This is an extremely tough virus to kill. Sodium hypochlorite (domestic bleach) and formaldehyde are the only effective common disinfectants. Domestic bleach is best used diluted 1 in 32, with some washing-up liquid added. Where a cat has died from the disease, it would be wise to disinfect the environment thoroughly, and wait at least six months before introducing another cat. Some modern disinfectants with specific activity against parvoviruses, which are effective in the presence of organic material and which have a persistent action, have recently become available. Your veterinary surgeon will advise whether they are more suitable in your particular situation.
Comment	This disease is not as common as it used to be, due to the effectiveness of the vaccines that have been developed to combat the disease.

Feline infectious peritonitis (FIP, feline coronavirus infection)

Cause	A feline coronavirus affecting a variety of tissues and organs and causing a sporadic, usually fatal, disease.
Incubation period	Variable, from days to months.
Transmission	Not yet clear. The route of infection is presumed to be by

ingestion. The virus may also be transmitted across the placenta, to developing kittens.

Signs At first, lethargy, raised temperature, poor appetite and progressive debility. After this stage, there are two clinical presentations:

(i) ***Wet (effusive, typical or peritoneal) form***
The cat develops an enlarged abdomen, due to the formation of abdominal fluid (ascites) or the cat may find breathing difficult, if the fluid forms in the chest. There is usually no pain.

(ii) ***Dry (non-effusive, atypical or extra-peritoneal) form***
A variety of organs may be affected with this form, and excessive fluid formation does not occur. The clinical signs reflect the organs involved. Often, it is the nervous system (giving rise to disorientation, incoordination, paralysis or fits) or the eye.

Action Veterinary consultation, possibly diagnosis will be confirmed with laboratory tests.

Disinfection of the environment This virus is readily killed, and the disinfectants described for feline panleucopaenia can be used.

Comment There is no effective treatment. No vaccine is currently available in the British Isles.

Feline respiratory disease (cat 'flu)

Most cases of infectious respiratory disease in cats are caused by one of two viruses: feline viral rhinotracheitis (FVR) virus and feline calicivirus (FCV). In addition, other organisms may be involved, such as *Chlamydia psittaci*, mycoplasmas and bacteria. The clinical signs that the various organisms produce differ somewhat, although the infected cat looks as though it has a severe cold. Usually a cat with upper respiratory disease is infected with only one of these organisms at a time, but combined infections can occur, especially when groups of cats are kept together. In these cases, your veterinary surgeon may need to carry out further diagnostic tests to establish which organisms are involved, and to give the appropriate treatment. Unfortunately, many cats that have recovered from the viral diseases do not totally eliminate the virus from their bodies, and become 'carriers' of the virus.

(i) Feline rhinotracheitis virus infection

Cause A feline herpesvirus (FHV–1), of a similar group of viruses that cause cold sores in man.

Incubation period One to 14 days, depending on the amount of virus that the cat has been exposed to.

Transmission The virus is excreted in the saliva and nasal discharges of infected cats, therefore if an infected cat sneezes, cats can become infected by breathing in infectious airborne viruses. The virus can also be spread on human hands, between handling cats, although the virus will not survive longer than one day in the environment. Most household disinfectants will kill the virus. Most recovered cats become 'carriers' of the virus, and will excrete the virus into their saliva when they are stressed, e.g. staying at a boarding cattery, moving home, or when feeding kittens. Usually, these cats are well themselves, but are infectious to other cats.

Signs Depression, poor appetite, raised temperature, sneezing, reddened eyes that may have a clear discharge, runny nose, and occasionally lots of saliva. Young kittens are usually the worst affected, although fatalities do not usually occur if the kittens are treated and nursed well. Signs generally improve within three weeks, but in some cats the damage caused by the virus is so severe that it can lead to permanent or recurrent bouts of 'flu. These cats may have noisy breathing, sneezing and a runny nose, and are often described as 'snufflers'.

Action Consult the veterinary surgeon, keep the cat away from other cats, especially when in the waiting room. Cancel attendance at any gathering of cats (e.g. shows) for six weeks.

Prevention Keep your cat away from any cat which has 'flu-like signs. Consult your veterinary surgeon about a vaccination course to protect against both FVR and FCV, and do not neglect annual boosters.

(ii) Feline calicivirus infection

Cause A small virus, that will survive for a week or so in a damp environment. Many different strains of this virus exist; some cause such a mild infection that it may go unnoticed, whilst others can cause severe respiratory disease.

Incubation period One to 10 days.

Transmission Similar to that described for FVR. Again, a 'carrier' state exists, in that some cats that have recovered from an infection may carry on harbouring the virus, whilst appearing healthy themselves.

Signs The large number of strains can produce a spectrum of severity of disease. In general, similar to those described for FVR, but in addition ulcers may form in the mouth, nose and on the tongue. These may begin as blisters on the tongue which rupture, and make eating painful and difficult.

Action As for FVR.

Prevention As for FVR.

(iii) Feline chlamydial infection

Cause — A small organism called *Chlamydia psittaci*, which has properties similar to bacteria and viruses, but which is classified as a bacterium.

Incubation period — Four to six days.

Transmission — The organism is shed in large quantities in the eye discharges of recently infected cats.

Signs — Reddened eyes (conjunctivitis), with moderately thick (mucopurulent) eye discharge. Occasionally swollen third eyelids and reluctance to open eyelids fully. May have mild nasal discharge and occasional sneeze. The cat's temperature is usually normal and it will continue to eat as usual.

Action — Consult your veterinary surgeon.

Prevention — Keep your cat away from any cat that has reddened eyes or eye discharge.

Comment — *Chlamydia psittaci* can infect the genital and gastrointestinal tracts of cats. It may contribute to reproductive failure in queens.

Feline infectious anaemia (FIA)

Cause — A disease of red blood cells caused by a very small parasite belonging to the family Rickettsia, called *Haemobartonella felis* (sometimes called *Eperythrozoon felis*).

Incubation period — Two to 50 days.

Transmission — Thought to be by blood-sucking parasites, e.g. a flea, transferring blood from an infected cat. Infection across the placenta from mother to kittens may also occur.

Signs — Infection may not be obvious. When clinical disease does occur, the signs are due to anaemia (depletion of red blood cells). The cat is lethargic, and loses weight, and will have pale mucous membranes. The spleen may be enlarged.

Action — Veterinary consultation.

Prevention — As the flea is implicated in transmission of the disease, it is wise to control the flea population on the cat and in the environment.

Comment — Many recovered cats are carriers of this parasite.

Ringworm (dermatophytosis)

Cause — Ringworm is the common name given to skin infections caused by the fungi microsporum and trichophyton.

Transmission — Direct contact with an infected animal or indirect contact with infectious material in the environment or on grooming implements. Material has been shown to survive on hairs in the environment for over a year. Recovered cats can be carriers of ringworm, and long-haired breeds are often symptomless carriers.

Signs — The classical 'ringworm' lesion is a rapidly growing, circular patch of total or partial hair loss around an area of broken hairs. These lesions may be in one area, or over the whole body. The head and legs are commonly affected, but large areas of the trunk may also be involved. The affected skin is usually dry, and often not irritating to the cat.

Action — Consult your veterinary surgeon, where a diagnosis of ringworm infection will probably be confirmed by laboratory tests. All the cat's coat may need to be clipped off and the cat may need to be bathed and given oral medication.

Disinfection of the environment — Bleach is rapidly effective.

Comment — Human cases of ringworm can arise from an animal source, and the cat is no exception. Show regulations are particularly severe about suspected or actual cases of ringworm and exhibitors whose cats have this disease may be unable to attend shows for some time after the last case has cleared up.

Endoparasites

Endoparasites are parasites which live inside the body as opposed to on its surface. Cats that are allowed to roam freely may catch prey, and as a consequence may acquire parasites from this source. The most common parasites that infect cats are:

- *Toxocara cati* – a roundworm
- *Toxascaris leonina* – another type of roundworm
- *Dipylidium caninum* – a tapeworm
- *Taenia taeniaeformis* – another type of tapeworm
- *Aelurostrongylus abstrusus* – a lungworm
- *Toxoplasma gondii* – a protozoan parasite

Toxocara cati

Description — A white roundworm (ascarid) three to six inches long and pointed at both ends which infects young kittens most frequently. Adult worms may be vomited or passed out in faeces of kittens.

Life cycle — Adult roundworms live in the small intestine, and lay eggs, which pass out in the cat's faeces. These eggs embryonate in a few days, i.e. an infective stage larva develops inside the egg. When these embryonated eggs are eaten by other cats, the larvae emerge and migrate around the cat's body, through the liver and lungs, and eventually return to the small intestine. Here, they mature to adult worms, and start to lay eggs themselves about six weeks after infection. However, roundworm larvae can lie dormant in the mammary tissues of the queen; the release of hormones during pregnancy can activate the larvae. These are shed in the queen's milk and are consequently ingested by the kittens. Again, a liver-lung migration of the larvae will occur, with the larvae returning to the small intestine to develop into egg-laying adults. Cats can also become infected if they eat earthworms, beetles, rodents or birds that have ingested roundworm eggs.

Signs Clinical disease due to roundworm in cats is confined mainly to young kittens, which acquire a heavy infection while suckling. Such kittens may have diarrhoea, a poor coat, and an accumulation of gas in the intestines, which gives a characteristic pot-bellied appearance.

Action Suitable roundworm treatment should be obtained from the veterinary surgeon, at the correct does for adults and kittens. Queens should be dosed when pregnant and lactating, and kittens should be dosed every three weeks from 4–16 weeks old. Free-roaming cats should be treated routinely twice a year.

Soil contaminated by faeces containing roundworm eggs is likely to be a permanent source of infection, with eggs surviving for several years. The destruction of eggs in cages, pens and on concrete runs is best achieved by vigorous scrubbing with large quantities of boiling water and detergent, or by steam sterilization.

Risk to humans There is a disease of humans, called visceral larval migrans, which is acquired by the accidental ingestion by humans of the eggs of the roundworms of the dog and possibly the cat. Eggs that have been eaten can hatch into larvae in the human gut, but will not develop into adult worms. Instead the very small larvae will travel around the body and become embedded in the body tissues, usually causing no problems at all. Very rarely, the larvae may settle in the eye, and in some cases where this has happened there has been impairment of vision.

The more important source of infection for man is the dog roundworm, and there is only a suggestion that the cat roundworm is also implicated. Furthermore the opportunity for human infection to occur from cats is less than for dogs, because cats out-of-doors bury their faeces and would not generally use public areas. Sensible precautions to take when keeping cats indoors include careful daily disposal of cat litter, insisting children wash their hands after playing with kittens, and continue with a worming programme as described earlier.

Comment Wormers purchased over the counter are not likely to be as effective as those provided by your veterinary surgeon. With many modern wormers, you are unlikely to see any live worms passed, as they are digested within the cat, and pass out unnoticed in the faeces. Do not discontinue worming because you see no worms passed.

Toxocara cati cannot cause threadworm infection in children, since the condition is due to another species of worm that does not infect cats.

Toxascaris leonina

Description A white roundworm (ascarid), very similar in appearance to *Toxocara cati*, but much less common.

Life cycle The life cycle of this roundworm is more simple than that of *T.cati*. Infection occurs by the ingestion of infective eggs. The eggs hatch in the intestine of the cat, and the hatched larvae develop into adult worms. They do not migrate, as is the case with *T.cati*. Thus, infection of kittens via the milk does not occur, and infection is unlikely to be seen in cats under six months old. However, infection can still be obtained from eating mice, voles and so on that have accidentally ingested the roundworm eggs.

Action Worming methods indicated for the elimination of *Toxocara cati* are effective, and similar precautions should be taken.

Dipylidium caninum

Description This worm is a segmented tapeworm which lives in the small intestine of cats. Despite its name, it is common in cats. It can measure up to 20 inches, but most are half this length. The worm has a small head which attaches to the wall of the intestine and a long, segmented body which contains maturing eggs in each segment. It is rare to see a complete tapeworm in faeces, but individual segments, loaded with ripe eggs, may be noticed, and these resemble cucumber seeds. When these segments have dried, they resemble grains of rice, and may be noticed around the anus or on the cat's coat or bedding.

Life cycle Fleas are a necessary part of the life cycle of *Dipylidium caninum*. Flea larvae swallow the eggs in tapeworm segments which have been shed by cats. These eggs mature as the flea develops, so that adult fleas are infectious for cats. When a cat is grooming and eats a flea, the worm larvae are released in the intestine, where they will mature into adult tapeworms.

Signs Most tapeworm infections are symptomless but severe infection may cause abdominal pain, and an increase in food intake. The shedding of segments may cause anal irritation and excessive attention in this region.

Action Your veterinary surgeon will prescribe a specific remedy for this tapeworm. Apparent failure to treat successfully is nearly always due to reinfection, which is certain to occur if flea treatment is not commenced.

Precaution	Maintain a regular campaign against fleas on the cat and around the home.
Transmission to man	This worm can infect humans, so an effective control programme as described above is essential.

Taenia taeniaeformis

Description	A segmented tapeworm, larger and stouter than *Dipylidium caninum*, but not as common.
Life cycle	Adult tapeworms live in the intestines of the cat. Segments containing maturing eggs are released and pass in the cat's faeces, similar to those for *Dipylidium caninum*. However, the intermediate host is not the flea, but rats, mice and voles that ingest the eggs. A small cyst forms in the liver of the rodent, and cats then become infected if they eat the infectious rodent, and start passing segments in about three weeks after eating the rodent.
Signs	As for *Dipylidium caninum*.
Action	Worming methods indicated for *Dipylidium caninum* are also effective. There is no transmission to man.

Aelurostrongylus abstrusus

Description	This is a small, slender worm, about two to three inches long, that lives embedded in the air passages of the lungs.
Life cycle	The adult worms in the lungs lay eggs, which hatch into larvae. These larvae are coughed up and swallowed, and pass out in the cat's faeces intact. The larvae in the faeces are eaten by the intermediate host which, for this parasite, is the slug or snail. Further development of the larva occurs, until the slug or snail is eaten by a cat. Once inside the intestine of the cat, the larva travels to the cat's lungs via the blood stream. That a cat should eat a snail or slug seems very unlikely, but if the infected snail or slug is eaten by another creature, e.g. a bird, then the cat can become infected by in turn eating the bird.
Signs	Usually, infection goes unnoticed. However, if there are a lot of worms, the cat may have respiratory disease, particularly coughing.
Action	Your veterinary surgeon will prescribe a specific remedy. There are no special precautions to take, and there is no transmission to man.

Toxoplasma gondii

Description	A very small parasite of cats that lives in the cells lining the intestines. It uses most mammals, including man, as an intermediate host.
Life cycle	The parasite replicates in the intestines of the cat, and non-infectious oocysts (eggs) are passed out in the faeces.

Table 9.1. Other endoparasites that occur in cats

Types of parasite	Scientific name	Description/life cycle	Signs in cats	Comments
Hookworm	Ancylostoma tubaeforme (also Ancylostoma braziliense, and uncinaria stenocephala)	A small roundworm which lives in the small intestine, that feeds on blood. Eggs are passed in the faeces, and develop into larvae. The larvae can then infect cats by being swallowed, or by penetrating the skin	Adult worms in the intestine can cause weakness, anaemia, and occasionally diarrhoea with blood flecks. When larvae penetrate the skin, they may cause a dermatitis	Not seen in cats native to the UK, common in Australia and Southern United States. Infection can be cured by strict hygiene measures and regular worming with an appropriate product
Whipworm	Trichuris serrata (also Trichuris campanula)	A worm with a thin front end and bulbous rear end. Lives in the caecum of the cat. Infection is by ingestion of larvae which develop within the egg, which is shed in the faeces	Mostly no signs, may cause diarrhoea	Not seen in UK, rare in Australia and North America
Nematode	Capillaria aerophila	A fine, slender worm, 10–12 inches long, that lives in the air passages in the lungs and trachea. After the eggs are layed, they are coughed up and swallowed, to pass in the faeces	In severe infections, causes a chronic cough and wheezing	Very rare in UK
	Capillaria feliscati (or Capillaria plica)	Small, hair-like worm. Lives in the bladder, and occasionally the kidneys. Eggs are passed in the urine	Usually no signs	Very rare in UK
	Ollulanus tricuspis	Very small roundworm, less than 1.0 mm long, found coiled on the stomach lining under a layer of mucus. Infection passes from cat to cat via infective larvae in the vomit	Generally do not cause signs of disease	Very rare in UK
Heartworm	Dirofilaria immitis	Adult worms live in the right-sided chamber of the heart, which release very small larvae into the blood stream. Mosquitoes spread infection by sucking the infected blood and passing it on to other cats	Fatigue, breathlessness, abdominal fluid (ascites), anaemia, chronic cough, sudden collapse and death	Extremely uncommon in cats, and not seen in native cats of Britain (the mosquito required for its transmission is not found in Britain)
Tapeworm	Diphyllobothrium latum	A very long tapeworm. Infection is acquired from fish	Usually mild, with loss of condition	Does not occur in Britain. Do not feed raw or undercooked fresh-water fish

After 1–5 days the oocysts become infectious, and other animals can become infected if they eat them. The oocysts mature and the parasite invades the tissues and forms cysts, mainly in muscles but sometimes in the brain. Cats may acquire infection by eating muscles of prey animals that contain cysts, or if the cat eats infected meat which is raw or undercooked.

Signs

Most toxoplasma infections in cats do not produce clinical signs, or they are so mild as to go unnoticed. Signs in the cat are extremely variable, depending on where the microscopic cysts form. More severe infection may be associated with a raised temperature, liver disease, pneumonia, vomiting, diarrhoea, abortion, heart disease and so on.

Action

None, since the infection can only be diagnosed by a veterinary surgeon.

Transmission to man

This infection can occur in man, and is particularly serious in pregnant women as it may affect the baby in the uterus. It is wise to take the precautions listed below to minimize the risk of human infection. This advice must be followed by pregnant women.

- Heat meat to 66°C (150°F) to kill toxoplasma cysts.
- Clean litter trays daily (oocysts are not infectious until 24 hours old).
- Use gloves to clean tray, and when gardening, and wash hands afterwards.
- Add boiling water to faeces, or burn them, as most disinfectants do not inactivate oocysts.

GIVING WORMING MEDICATION

Worming medication can come as liquid, powder or tablets. It is usually not necessary to starve the cat before worming. The instructions given by the veterinary surgeon should be followed to the letter.

Other Endoparasites

A number of other types of worm rarely infect cats in the UK, but are occasionally seen in cats entering Britain. Details of these are given in Table 9.1.

Ectoparasites

Ectoparasites are parasites that live on or in the skin. The major ectoparasites of cats are:

- Fleas
- Lice
- Ticks
- Harvest mites
- Ear mites
- Mange mites – *Notoedres cati*
  – *Demodex cati*
  – Cheyletiella species

Details relating to these parasites are given in Table 9.2.

Table 9.2. Ectoparasite infections of cats

Parasite	Life cycle	Signs shown by cat	Comment
Fleas Scientific name: *Ctenocephalides felis*, but also Spilopsyllus sp. (Rabbit flea) and *Archeopsyllus erinacei* (hedgehog flea)	The life cycle of the flea is completed off the cat. Eggs are laid on the cat, and in the environment on floors, furnishings and bedding. The eggs hatch in 2–16 days, into larvae which take 7–10 days to reach maturity and pupate. The adult fleas emerge from the pupae. Fleas may survive without food for 4 months. Fleas act as intermediate hosts for the tapeworm *Dipylidium caninum*	Thin, elongated, brown, wingless insects with 'long legs' which run rapidly over the skin and which jump when off the cat. They occur particularly along the back, around the neck, and on the belly. The clinical signs of flea infestation depend on the frequency of the flea's activities, and how the cat reacts to the flea saliva antigens. Many cats show minimal response to flea infestation. Cats that have an irritant or allergic response show small crusty lesions mainly over the back and neck. These lesions are called miliary dermatitis and can be felt by the owner	Flea droppings (dirts) are black, hard, comma-shaped and the size of sand grain. When placed on wet blotting paper, the blood they contain will leak out and stain the paper red. Treatment should be directed at ridding both the cat and its environment of the parasite. The house and upholstery should be vacuumed carefully, to remove any eggs, and treated with a suitable insecticide regularly throughout summer. The cat should be treated for fleas regularly. If feral cats visit your garden, sleep in your shed/summerhouse etc., then the places where they rest should be treated regularly as a source of fleas. Remember to treat dogs, rabbits and other pets at the same time as the cat
Lice Scientific name: *Felicola subrostratus*	A biting louse. Adult lice feed on the skin and lay white eggs (nits) which are glued on the cat's hairs. These hatch into young lice which resemble the adults. Lice cannot exist off their host for more than a few days, so infection is spread by close contact between cats	Small, light-brown, pear-shaped, wingless insects, with short legs, that move slowly on the skin surface. Clincial signs vary, and infection may be asymptomatic. Cats with lice may scratch at the areas infested and there may be crusty, papular lesions	Uncommon in cats. Treatment with most insecticides soon clears the condition. Since lice breed on the cat there is less need to pay attention to the environment than is the case with a flea infection

Table 9.2. (cont.)

Parasite	Life cycle	Signs shown by cat	Comment
Ticks Scientific name: Ixodes spp.	Cats occasionally become infected with ticks if they wander in fields where sheep or cattle (the natural hosts of the tick) have grazed. Eight-legged adult ticks lay eggs, which hatch into six-legged larval forms. Adults or larval forms may feed off the cat	Brownish-white or blue-grey round insects, usually found around the head and between the toes. They vary in size, from an unfed larval tick to a fully engorged adult female of 1 cm long. They lie attached to the skin by their heads, which are firmly embedded. Some discomfort may occur at the attachment site, but otherwise infection usually goes unnoticed by owners	Adult ticks can be removed by first applying a swab soaked in ether or surgical spirit to them. This causes the tick to loosen its hold on the skin, so that the tick can then be removed manually by grasping the head end as close as possible to the skin with tweezers or forceps, and pulling gently in a straight line. If the head is not removed completely, a local skin reaction may result. If in doubt, seek veterinary help
Harvest mites Scientific name: *Trombicula autumnalis* Colloquial names: chiggers, berry bugs, red bug, heel bug	This mite lives in decaying vegetation and is free-living as an adult. However, its larvae are parasitic. The larval mites occur most frequently in late summer and autumn, and their natural host is the field mouse	Larval harvest mites appear as orange or red specks, 0.2 mm in diameter, clumped in thin-skinned areas such as the webs between the toes and the small pocket that is present on the edge of the ear. They feed for 3 days, which results in severe irritation, self-excoriation, and the formation of sores with hard scabs or patches of raw skin. Harvest mites prefer chalk soil areas	The incidence of these mites is variable in different areas of the country, and is seasonal. Treatment with one application of suitable parasiticide is sufficient if reinfestation can be prevented as the adults are not parasitic and do not breed on the cat. Seek veterinary advice to obtain a suitable parasiticide. Humans can be infected with this mite
Ear mites Scientific name: *Otodectes cynotis*	The life cycle of the earmite occurs entirely on the host, feeding on the surface layers of skin. Inside the ear is the principal habitat, but it may be found on other areas of the body, particularly the head, paws and back. Adult mites live for 2 months, and lay single eggs that hatch in 4 days. The larval and nymph stages follow, which last 18 days until they develop into adults	The mite is white and just visible to the naked eye, and often causes no signs in the cat. In cases of severe infestation, and in some particularly sensitive cats, a thick, crumbly dark-brown waxy discharge is produced in the ear, which gives rise to the terms 'otitis externa' or 'canker'. This provokes the cat to scratch, and at least some of the inflammation and trauma which results is self-inflicted. Bacterial infection may follow	This mite can infest dogs, so it is wise to treat all dogs and cats living in the household, simultaneously. Ear treatments which will kill this mite are available through veterinary surgeons

Table 9.2. (cont.)

Parasite	Life cycle	Signs shown by cat	Comment
Mange mites Scientific name: 1. *Notoedres cati* (head mange, or feline scabies)	The life cycle takes place entirely on the cat. The female mite burrows into the skin, making tunnels in which she lays her eggs. Transmission of infection from cat-to-cat is by direct contact, as the mite cannot live for long away from the cat	Usually infects the head and neck area first, but can spread to legs. The infected skin becomes inflamed and itchy, then thickened, wrinkled and covered with crusts. Self-inflicted injury, hair loss and secondary skin infection with bacteria can occur. Some cats may be almost asymptomatic carriers of the mite	This disease is now rare in the British Isles. Diagnosis is confirmed by the demonstration of mites in deep skin scrapings. Parasiticidal treatment can be obtained from veterinary surgeons, and dogs, cats and rabbits in-contact should be treated. Treatment should be given at weekly intervals for 4–6 weeks
2. *Demodex cati*	The entire life cycle takes place deep in the cat's skin, and in hair-follicles	This mite is cigar-shaped with stumpy legs	A very rare condition in cats, more common in dogs
3. *Cheyletiella species* (walking dandruff mite)	The life cycle lasts 5 weeks, and takes place on the host, but adult mites may live off the body for up to 10 days. The eight-legged adult is surface-living, and draws fluid from the skin after piercing it with its mouth parts. Eggs are attached to the base of hairs, and a six-legged larva will emerge. This will moult through nymphal stages to reach the adult stage	Clinical signs of infection may be absent in the cat. With heavy infection, the usual sign is profuse skin scales (dandruff), particularly along the back and flanks. The cat may or may not be itchy	Diagnosis is confirmed by grooming the cat and examining the dandruff microscopically for evidence of mites. This mite can infect man, and lesions on owners are often the first indication that the cat is infected. The mite causes intensely irritant raised red spots, on hands, forearms and chest. The mite does not multiply on humans, and lesions tend to go as the cat is treated. The mites can infect dogs and rabbits, therefore these pets should be treated simultaneously, with a suitable parasiticide obtained from the veterinary surgeon. Treatment should be at weekly intervals, for 4 occasions

In general terms it can be said that ectoparasite infection is probably the major cause of skin disease in cats. A number of parasites can also cause problems in humans, so don't forget to tell the veterinary surgeon if you or any of your family also have a rash or skin problems.

Inherited diseases

When a deformed or abnormal kitten is born, a question then arises; has the defect been passed on from the queen or the tom, i.e. is the defect of genetic origin and can it be inherited? If an abnormality is present in the kitten at birth, it is described as congenital. Some abnormalities may be very obvious and can be spotted immediately, whilst others may be internal malformations, not necessarily apparent at the time, or conditions that develop as the kitten gets older; only as the kitten grows does it become increasingly more obvious that it is not normal or clinically healthy.

It is important to realize that not all congenital conditions are hereditary; a disturbance in the kitten's growth in the uterus can result in a congenital deformity. Examples of non-hereditary factors that can cause congenital deformities are viral infections during pregnancy, teratogenic drugs given during pregnancy (such as thalidomide administered to women), adverse environmental temperatures. Detecting the cause of a congenital deformity is often very difficult, and unfortunately with many of the conditions it is not known whether the problem is hereditary or non-genetic in origin. Congenital heart defects are also not necessarily hereditary, but it is not advisable to breed from affected individuals.

Table 9.3 deals with some conditions of cats that are thought to be inherited.

Zoonoses

Zoonoses, or zoonotic diseases, are those diseases and infections which can be naturally transmitted between vertebrate animals and man. The risk is minimal in respect of cats, if the following simple hygienic precautions are observed.

1. Keep your cat healthy, and have any signs of illness diagnosed and treated promptly by a veterinary surgeon.
2. Worm kittens vigorously against roundworm, and adult cats every 6–12 months against roundworms and tapeworms.
3. Groom your cat regularly.
4. Treat the cat and its environment regularly for fleas.
5. Wash cat bedding frequently.
6. Remove cat faeces from litter *daily*, wear gloves and wash your hands afterwards.
7. Insist that children wash their hands after handling cats, and especially so if the cat is ill.
8. Store cat food separately from human food and do not feed cats from household crockery.
9. Do not feed raw meat to the cat and, if possible, take the cat's prey away before it is eaten.
10. Wear gloves when gardening.
11. Try to avoid getting scratched or bitten. If this occurs, wash the wound thoroughly and apply antiseptic.

Table 9.3. Some inherited diseases of cats

Condition	Mode of inheritance	Clinical disease	Breed
Corneal dystrophy	Recessive	A bilateral corneal clouding that occurs from 4 months old	Manx
Deafness in white cats	Dominant white gene, W	Deafness resulting from a degeneration in the inner ear	Predominantly blue-eyed white cats, although odd-eyed and very occasionally orange-eyed white cats may also be deaf
Dermoid cyst	Multifactorial	An embryological defect of eye tissue which may involve the cornea, conjunctiva, third eyelid and eyelids, consisting of fibrous tissue and fat covered by skin, with hairs protruding from it	Birman especially
'Flat-chested' kittens	Possibly inherited	Extreme dorsoventral compression of the chest, which can cause difficulty in breathing and heart failure in affected kittens. First noticed at 2–6 weeks old, and affected kittens do not thrive well	Burmese particularly
Hydrocephalus	Recessive	Enlarged skull and forehead due to abnormally high fluid pressure within the brain. This may lead to blindness, ataxia, depression, convulsions or coma	All breeds
Lysosomal storage disease	Unknown	A nervous disorder, caused by absence of a particular enzyme. This leads to the accumulation of the material and enzyme would normally break down, which affects the central nervous system. The conditions may not be noticed until 4 weeks old	All breeds
Nasolacrimal duct deformity	Polygenic	Tear overflow (epiphora) may be seen in long-hair cats if a particularly flattened face has lead to deformity of the nasolacrimal ducts (which drain tears from the corner of the tye to the nose)	Long-hairs, particularly persian
Polydacty	Dominant, Pd	The possession of extra toes, usually the front paws	All breeds
Progressive retinal atrophy	Dominant	A bilateral, progressive blindness, due to degeneration of the retina. Affected kittens have dilated pupils with poor response to light	Abyssinian

Table 9.3. (cont.)

Condition	Mode of inheritance	Clinical disease	Breed
Spasticity	Possibly inherited	Noticed when 3 months old. Kittens are nervous, panicky, and have difficulty in getting up from recumbency. There is a marked bend in the neck near the middle, with the head kept tucked under onto the chest. The kitten may have a high-stepping gait, which usually affects the front legs, and the front legs may be weak, stiff or twitch. The kitten has difficulty in eating, may cough or retch for no reason, and tires easily	Devon Rex
Spina bifida	Dominant, M	Cats that inherit this gene have variable deformities of the tail and/or spine. The tail may be completely or partially absent. In its more severe form, spina bifida may result; cats have have abnormalities of the tail end of the spine, which can cause loss of bowel and bladder control, and hind-leg weakness, or a closed anus. Cats that are homozygous (i.e. MM) die in the uterus	Manx cat (Mm)
Split foot	Dominant, Sp	An abnormal cleft in one or both front paws	All breeds
Squints	Polygenic, but related to the Siamese (C^s) gene	An abnormality in the optic nerves, resulting in faulty connections between the eyes and the brain, causes some Siamese cats to try to compensate by developing a convergent squint	Siamese

These precautions should become a way of life in pet-owning households, and they should ensure that your cat will never be a health risk to you or your children. Most human disease is caught from other humans, so do not be too ready to blame your cat until there is positive laboratory-investigated evidence that the cat is the culprit.

Rabies is the most serious zoonosis. See details below. Rabies is kept out of Britain by a strong and continuing campaign by government, by the vigilance of customs officials, by the general public, and by our sensible quarantine laws.

Details relating to other zoonoses are given in Table 9.4.

Rabies

Rabies is a fatal infection caused by a virus transmitted in the saliva of many animals. Foxes are the most important carriers of infection in Europe, followed by dogs, cats and small rodents.

Incubation period Nine to 51 days.

Transmission The virus is present in the saliva of infected cats and is transmitted by biting, or through saliva entering a superficial wound already present. The virus travels via the nerves to the brain, where it causes inflammation (encephalitis), and subsequent nervous signs. It then spreads rapidly through the rest of the nervous system, to enter the salivary glands and other organs.

Major signs The course of rabies in cats progresses through three stages; a prodromal stage, an excitative period ('furious' rabies), and a paralytic period ('dumb' rabies). The prodromal stage lasts about one day, and the cat shows a change in behaviour. Quiet cats become alert, restless or friendly, whilst friendly cats may scratch or bite, become depressed and seek out dark places. Sometimes the furious form predominates, and the cat becomes irritable, vicious, with eyes flashing, mouth foaming, and an arched back, but more frequently the cat succumbs to the paralytic stage. At this stage the cat is not irritable, seldom bites and is constantly purring. Convulsions follow with gradual paralysis and finally death. The entire course is seldom more than 10 days.

Prevention We are fortunate in Britain that our island situation enables our government to take effective measures to keep rabies out of the country, by our quarantine regulations and by efficient detection by Customs and Excise at ports and airports. There are penalties of imprisonment and very heavy fines for those found attempting to smuggle cats, dogs and other pets into the country.

Table 9.4. The signs, treatment and prevention of some feline zoonoses which occur in the UK

Disease in cat	Transmission	Symptoms (humans)	Action to be taken (cat)	Action to be taken (human)	Prevention
Fleas	From the cat, and from the environment where the cat fleas are breeding	1. Typical irritating, red raised spot 2. Possibly a severe allergic reaction to the flea's saliva in some humans 3. The tapeworm *Dipylidium caninum* uses the flea as its intermediate host. Although a rare occurrence, ingestion of these fleas can lead to tapeworm in humans, and tapeworm segments may be seen in faeces	Anti-flea treatment of the cat and, most importantly, the environment	Possibly the application of anti-histamine creams. If any worms are noticed in human faeces, consult the doctor. However, threadworms in children, the most common human infestation, are *not* transmitted by animals	Regular flea treatment of all animals *and* environment
Cheyletiella infection	Transfer of 'walking dandruff' mite from coat of cat to human	Very irritating rash, often on forearms and chest, where cat has been held close to body. Mite can penetrate clothing	Identification of mite, and use of anti-parasite treatment provided by veterinary surgeon	Rash usually goes when mite has been eliminated from cat	Prompt attention to scurf-like deposits in cat's coat
Toxocariasis	Transmission more important from dogs. Mature roundworms inhabit the cat's intestine, and lay eggs which are passed in the faeces. The eggs, if eaten by man, hatch into larvae, which may travel around the body	Usually none, but migrating larvae may cause problems, for example if they settle in the eye	Regular worming of kittens and their mothers, with wormer provided by veterinary surgeon	None. Condition usually undiagnosed	Regular worming of cats. Prompt collection and disposal of cat faeces, wear gloves when cleaning litter tray and when gardening

Table 9.4. (cont.)

Disease in cat	Transmission	Symptoms (humans)	Action to be taken (cat)	Action to be taken (human)	Prevention
Toxoplasmosis	Infection is particularly serious in pregnant women. Transmission is by eating undercooked meat containing toxoplasma cysts, or from ingestion of infectious oocysts that have been passed in the faeces of infected cats	Usually none, but if transplacental infection does occur, the newborn child may have numerous disorders, which might include enlarged liver or spleen, hydrocephalus, blindness and convulsions	None, as most toxoplasma infections in cats do not give clinical signs. Signs depend on where the cysts form. If the condition is diagnosed by the veterinary surgeon, suitable treatment will be prescribed	None, as infection in man is usually undiagnosed	Heat meat to 66°C (150°F), before eating it – this kills toxoplasma cysts. Clean cat litter trays daily, use gloves to do this and when gardening. Add boiling water to faeces or burn them, to inactivate oocysts
Ringworm	Direct contact with an infected animal including cats	Non-irritating eroded patches on skin, probably the wrists, not necessarily circular	Positive identification as ringworm by laboratory tests, followed by specific treatment	Treatment by doctor	Avoid contact with animal which may be infected
Poxvirus	Transmission from cat to man is rare, but may be from direct contact with the scabbed and ulcerated skin lesions around the head and neck of the infected cat	Blister or ulcer with reddened edges which may resemble chicken pox, possibly fever	Positive identification as poxvirus infection by laboratory tests. No specific treatment	Treatment by doctor	Avoid contact with animals which may be infected
Salmonellosis, Campylobacteriosis	These bacteria are shed in the cat's faeces. Infection is transmitted to man by ingestion of the bacteria	Diarrhoea with campylobacteriosis; diarrhoea, vomiting and fever with salmonellosis	Laboratory tests on the cat's faeces to identify if the cat is the source	Treatment by doctor; probably laboratory tests to identify source	Strict hygienic precautions when handling animals and food

Table 9.4. (cont.)

Disease in cat	Transmission	Symptoms (humans)	Action to be taken (cat)	Action to be taken (human)	Prevention
Cryptosporidiosis	Oocysts of these coccidia are shed in the cat's faeces. Infection is by faecal-oral route	Watery diarrhoea, vomiting, abdominal pain	As above	As above	As above
Cat scratches or bites	The bacterium usually transmitted from the cat's mouth is *Pasteurella multocida*	Swollen, reddened, painful area around bite from cat; may suppurate	None; these bacteria are normally present in the cat's mouth	Treatment by doctor, if severe	All cat bites and scratches should be thoroughly washed and dressed immediately
Cat scratch disease	Usually by a cat scratch. Cause not known, but probably a bacterium	Lesion on arm or hand, usually from a cat scratch. The lymph node draining the region of the scratch is usually enlarged, tender and may suppurate	None; it has not been proven that the cat is carrying the causative organism	Treatment by doctor; possibly biopsy of the lymph node	As above

Given the serious nature of rabies, and our success at keeping it outside the British Isles, the Police should be informed immediately wherever there is any suspicion that foreign visitors have brought pets with them into the country, or people who have been abroad transporting pets with them, or acquiring pets while they were away.

No cat in this country will show signs of rabies unless it has been in a country where rabies is endemic, or it has been bitten or licked by an illegally imported cat.

Action If a cat is suspected of having rabies avoid touching it, barricade it by some means into a small room and tell the Police or a veterinary surgeon immediately – day or night.

There is no treatment for rabies, but if possible, affected animals are kept under very strict confinement on Ministry of Agriculture premises for observation as rabies can only be positively proven by laboratory tests on the brain of the cat after its death.

In-contact animals will also have to be kept in confinement for the full quarantine period of six months.

Precautions Rabies vaccines are only available in this country for cats which are being exported to countries where rabies is endemic and for use in imported cats when they are in quarantine kennels. MAFF will issue to your veterinary surgeon a specific dose for each cat due to be exported.

Comment Help keep rabies out of Britain by obeying the quarantine laws.

Further reading *Rabies – the facts you need to know* Henderson and White, (Barrie & Jenkins).

Vaccination and immunity

We are all under constant attack from the millions of micro-organisms which inhabit our world, so some means of protection is essential for survival. Healthy bodies are equipped with several defence mechanisms which are in operatioin all the time. The skin is a barrier to invasion by microbes; the mucous membranes in the nose trap foreign substances which are breathed in, and the cough reflex comes into play when throat and larynx are irritated and to prevent 'germs' getting into the lungs. The acidity of the stomach will kill invaders which get that far, and the quantities of mucus produced by the small bowel act as a barrier to infection. Other invaders will pass from the body in faeces and urine, while the liver will destroy toxins produced by bacteria. These defense mechanisms are similar in man and animals, and they work very well when health is good, but are not so effective when the body is in a run-down state, underfed or weakened, or when there is a state of mental or physical stress.

When an organism succeeds in passing these primary barriers, the body still has resources to use against the invader. The immune system comes into action to manufacture special and specific weapons – antibodies – to use against the organism making the attack.

Kittens

Kittens do have an immune system of their own at birth, but it is not fully developed. Thus nature has arranged for them to acquire some protective antibodies from their mothers. These are called passive antibodies since they have not been produced by the kitten itself. A modicum of passive 'maternal antibody' passes to the kitten while it is still in the uterus, but most comes via the colostrum, the first milk from the queen. Antibodies in the colostrum can only be absorbed by kittens for the first day or so after birth, so if a kitten does not suck this colostrum, it may be less resistant to diseases compared with its litter mates that have sucked or have consumed more.

The antibodies which the queen passes to her kittens will be to those diseases which she herself has encountered or been vaccinated against. If she has lived a very isolated existence away from other cats, made few excursions outdoors, and has never been vaccinated, she will have very little protection to pass on to her kittens, and they will be vulnerable to all the infectious feline diseases from their earliest days.

Maternally-acquired antibodies in the kittens will start to fade quite quickly, with blood levels of antibodies decreasing markedly every week. The kitten must then develop its own antibodies against specific diseases, either by encounter with the particular disease or by vaccination, if it is to be protected.

Adult cats

Most disease-causing organisms consist mainly of proteins. A healthy body is quick to detect proteins foreign to itself and to set about rejecting them by the production of specific antibodies to the invader. These active antibodies (i.e. created by the animal itself) are produced by specialized white blood cells found mainly in the lumph nodes and spleen.

The first time the body encounters a specific disease, or a vaccine, active antibodies may take as long as 10 days to be produced, but the next time that the disease is encountered (either as the infection or vaccination), memory cells come into action and antibodies are 'manufactured' very quickly, so that the disease does not have the chance to become established. This is why some diseases of man and animals occur only once in a lifetime.

Antibodies tend to be very specific and destroy only the microbe (the antigen) which stimulated their production. For some infectious diseases, a blood sample taken from the cat and processed at a specialist laboratory will show if a cat has antibodies to a particular disease, and sometimes sophisticated techniques can reveal whether the antibody has been made in response to a recent infection or has been present for some time. Antibody levels wane with time, but another encounter with the right antigen (i.e. a booster vaccination) will cause a quick resurgence of production.

Vaccines

Since we do not want cats to have to endure an episode of disease to develop their own protection, we turn to the creation of active immunity by vaccination. This is the deliberate triggering of the immune response by the administration of a low dose of the antigen, in order to stimulate the production of antibodies without causing the disease.

Essentially modern vaccines fall into five main classes:

1. Attenuated, or modified, living vaccines
Fortunately bacteria and viruses can be modified to reduce their ability to cause disease but at the same time maintain their ability to stimulate the formation of active antibodies. This is achieved by a process called attenuation and is usually brought about by growing the organism in an unnatural host, e.g. in hens' eggs, a different species of animal or in tissue culture. The amount of attenuation depends on how long the organism is maintained in the 'artificial' system. The aim is to get the right balance to achieve maximum antibody production in the animal given the vaccine and yet not cause the disease. The advantage of live vaccines is that usually only one dose is required in cats over 12 weeks of age to stimulate immunity.

2. Killed vaccines
These are made from organisms which have been killed, by heat or chemical agents such as formalin. Although the organisms are incapable of multiplying in the vaccinated animal, they are still able to stimulate the formation of antibodies. Two doses of the vaccine are normally required, and an adjuvant (additive) may be needed to enhance the effect. The immunity stimulated by killed vaccines is often not as long-lasting as that stimulated by live vaccines.

3. Toxoids
The lethal effect of some organisms is brought about by the production of poisonous substances called toxins. The body reacts to these by producing specific antibodies called anti-toxins, which are capable of neutralizing toxins. This can be done artificially by injecting a toxoid which is a detoxified toxin. Toxins are generally made by inactivating toxins either by heat or by chemical means and on injection they stimulate the formation of anti-toxin in the body. Two doses are normally required to stimulate immunity and booster doses may be needed over one, two or three years. Probably the most familiar example is tetanus toxoid.

4. Sub-unit vaccines
These vaccines, an example has just become available for use in cats, will probably be the vaccines of the future, where just the part of the organism that stimulates protection is selected, and genetically engineered so that it can be produced in large quantities. These vaccines are likely to be very efficacious and are of course much safer.

5. Mixed vaccines
Mixed vaccines may contain a mixture of live and dead antigens. Care is needed to ensure the compatibility of the antigens, and that protective antibody levels are produced to each component of the vaccine.

Methods of administration
Vaccines are generally given by subcutaneous or intramuscular injection, but in certain circumstances, where there is a need to stimulate local protection, they are given by other routes. For example, an intranasal vaccine is available to protect cats against respiratory virus infection. This stimulates the production of 'local antibodies' in the upper part of the respiratory tract within only a few days, just where they are needed. This is followed later by the production of antibodies in the blood stream.

When to vaccinate cats

There are currently only three viruses that cats and kittens can be vaccinated against; the respiratory viruses (calicivirus and herpesvirus) and feline enteritis (panleucopaenia) virus. Respiratory virus vaccine should be given from nine weeks old, with a second dose three to four weeks later. Enteritis vaccination usually involves giving a single dose from 12 weeks of age. It is wise to consult your veterinary surgeon as soon as you obtain your kitten or when you adopt an older cat so that he can discuss with you the most appropriate vaccination requirements for your circumstances.

Booster vaccination

Protection created by vaccines is generally not as long lasting as naturally-acquired immunity, so a booster dose is needed periodically, to cause a quick resurgence of antibody production. Different intervals are advised for the different diseases, and indeed by the different vaccine manufacturers.

In general, protective antibodies against the respiratory viruses tend to wane by one year, and booster vaccination should be given yearly. If the cat is to enter a boarding cattery, a booster vaccination two to three weeks prior to admission is recommended. Vaccination against feline enteritis (panleucopaenia) usually produces longer-lasting production, and in this case booster vaccination is usually recommended at one to two year intervals.

CHAPTER 10

FIRST AID AND NURSING

First aid principles

First aid for cats is based upon a number of priorities.

- Action to help the cat survive until it can be taken to a vet.
- Action to preserve life.
- Action to reduce immediate pain.
- Action to reduce the likelihood of further damage.
- Action to prevent helpers getting scratched or bitten.

In all but the most trivial injuries the cat will need to be taken to a veterinary surgery. There is little use in calling a veterinary surgeon to the site of the accident, especially a road accident, as the cat will, in all probability, need to be taken to the surgery for treatment.

It is however extremely important to make early contact with the veterinary practice, by telephone, so that the staff are ready to deal with the problem when the cat arrives. Furthermore you will get practical advice straightaway. If the cat is desperately ill or injured, ask someone else to make the call to warn the practice that you are on your way.

Carrying box

One of the best investments you can make when you first obtain your kitten is to buy a modern, plastic-coated wire carrying cage, of a size to fit an adult cat. You then have an easily cleaned and disinfected ‘house’ for your pet in any emergency and also a ready means of transporting your cat.

Cats being taken to a veterinary surgery, for whatever purpose, or going to a boarding cattery, or even visiting friends should always travel in a safe carrier. However sophisticated your cat is, you cannot depend on the behaviour of other animals or other people and many a tragedy has occurred through a cat leaping from its owner's arms when frightened by some incident which neither owner nor cat anticipated. And if you mean to show your cat, whether in pedigree or household pet classes, it must arrive in a carrier.

The plastic-coated wire carriers are much the best. Wicker baskets are impossible to clean and disinfect and are likely to snag clothing when being carried.

Most veterinary practices sell a purpose-made cardboard cat carrier which is useful in an emergency, but those do not clean well and they cannot be locked as can the wire ones.

Make a resolution that you will *never* lend your cat carrier to anyone. If you say this from the beginning you need never offend anyone. One reason is that however well cleaned, some small viruses can linger a long time and may pass on infection to the next cat that uses the box. Secondly, the whole purpose of owning a carrier is that it should be readily available at *your* home whenever *you* need it, however unforeseen that need may be.

All cat equipment should be kept exclusively for your own cats and, if at all possible, not contaminated by use by other cats.

First aid kit

A cat's first aid kit should contain the following items:

At least four 2.5–5 cm (1–2 in) bandages
A 5 cm (2 in) crêpe bandage
A roll of adhesive plaster 5–7.5 cm (2–3 in)
A supply of cotton gauze pads of varying sizes
A large roll of cotton wool
A pair of blunt-ended forceps (tweezers)
A pair of blunt-ended scissors, not used for anything else
A stubby-ended rectal thermometer
A suitable lubricant (e.g. 'Vaseline')
A steel comb and brush for removing matted hair
Sterile disposable syringes (bought from a veterinary practice) One 10 ml, one 5 ml and several 2 ml, all for oral dosing only
A bottle of safe antiseptic (e.g. 'Hibitane')
A bottle of simple kaolin mixture (*not* with morphine or similar)
A bottle of medicinal liquid paraffin
A styptic pencil or potassium permanganate crystals
A plastic eyedropper
Anti-parasite products safe for use on the cat and another that can be used on the environment (from veterinary surgeon)
A soothing but safe skin cream (check with veterinary surgeon)
Two small screw top jars for urine and faeces samples
Ear and eye drops as advised by veterinary surgeon
A notebook for details of treatment history and all telephone numbers of the local veterinary practice, including after hours services, as well as all the local taxi services.

The cat's first aid box should be kept separately from any human medicines and also separate from medication meant for dogs, as cats are so sensitive to many substances.

No human medicines should be used for cats, and everyone in the household should be aware that cats are unable to tolerate aspirin or any related compounds. Phenol (carbolic acid), often a component of disinfectants, is poisonous to cats.

Finding a vet in an emergency

Using the local veterinary practice is described elsewhere in this book, but in an emergency it may be necessary to find a vet in an unfamiliar area.

Consult the Yellow Pages directory, you will find a number of practices listed there. Always telephone first to confirm that a veterinary surgeon is available at the address you choose. Many veterinary practices have branch surgeries which are not always attended, but a telephone answering machine or answering service should direct you to where you can get help.

Police stations, post offices and village shops can often supply the information you need and you could ask other pet owners who should have local knowledge about veterinary practices.

Remember that, by law, only a qualified veterinary surgeon is allowed to diagnose and treat animals, and unqualified people may only render necessary first aid.

Dealing with a road traffic accident involving a cat

If an injured cat is found by the roadside take it out of the line of traffic or it may well be hit again. Also, take care of yourself, since whilst bending over the cat you may be almost invisible to motorists.

Take as much care as you can to avoid getting bitten or scratched, as the cat is likely to be in pain and frightened and it may take revenge on any human who comes near. If available put on gloves or cover hands and arms with towels or rugs, and avoid putting your face close to the cat.

Wrap the cat in a coat or rug or whatever fabric comes to hand, both to keep it warm and also to keep its limbs and claws close to its body. The head may be covered lightly to facilitate handling the cat but be careful not to prejudice the cat's breathing.

Lift the cat carefully, on a board or a shovel to avoid causing pain if the cat is badly injured. As cats are territorial animals it is quite likely that the cat's home is nearby. It is well worth spending a few minutes trying to locate the owner, who will no doubt be very concerned and will be able to take over the care of the cat.

A frightened cat may become aggressive and resent handling even by the owner. A lot of adrenalin is produced as the result of a stressful situation so the cat may be restless and try to run away. You can do most for the injured cat if you stay calm and cautious, and move slowly.

It is as well to be aware that if you take an accident case to a veterinary surgery, you may well be regarded as responsible for payment for the cost of the cat's treatment, although it will be usual for veterinary surgeons not to proceed with expensive repair work, such as pinning fractures, until the owner is found. In any case it is usual to let a cat rest overnight after an accident to get over the immediate shock, before undertaking fixation or fractures or other surgery.

If you volunteer to drive the cat to a veterinary surgery, try to obtain a large deep cardboard box for the cat to travel in, if a proper cat carrier is not available.

Put the box on the floor of the car rather than the seat or, if there is no help available to supervise the cat, put the box in the boot if the journey is a short one, so that the cat is contained while you are driving – but be careful when you open the boot in case the cat has escaped from the box.

Cats injured by traffic do not have to be reported to the Police in the United Kingdom.

Having moved the cat to safety, the first priority is:

● **Keep the airway clear**

The cat must be able to breathe even if it is unconscious. Clear the mouth, nose and throat of all blood, vomit and discharges, otherwise the cat may choke, but take care not to get bitten.

The cat's tongue should be pulled forward to allow it to breathe, perhaps by very gently using tweezers, pliers or food tongs, if you are in danger of getting bitten.

The act of pulling the tongue forward very often stimulates the cat to breathe and it may suddenly regain consciousness, so if you have your fingers in the cat's mouth at this time, you will have to withdraw them quickly. Keep the cat's head slightly lower than the body to allow fluid to drain away from the mouth and the blood to flow to the brain.

When a cat is unconscious it must not be allowed to lie on one side for more than 10–15 minutes or the lungs may become waterlogged. Turn the cat over gently at least four times every hour to avoid the complication of pneumonia.

● **Conserve body heat**

Any very sick or injured cat needs to be kept warm, but it should not be so muffled up that it cannot breathe freely. The best way is to wrap a small warm blanket firmly but not too tightly round the cat, turning in the end of the blanket over the legs and feet but leaving the head well clear. If nothing else is available, newspaper, plastic sheeting or even aluminium foil or a 'space blanket' will suffice.

Do not apply any direct heat, for instance a hot water bottle or a heating pad, as when the cat's body is short of blood all the supply available should go to the brain. If you heat up the skin, blood is diverted to that site.

If the cat is wearing a collar it should be cut off in case swelling makes it impossible to undo later. Cutting the collar also gives the opportunity to examine it for the owners name and address or the cat's name which may well be written on the inside of the collar.

● **Control any bleeding**

Unlike many dogs, cats do not usually bleed freely as they have fewer major blood vessels near the surface, so they are less vulnerable to life-threatening haemorrhage. When haemorrhage does occur it is usually internal and professional help is needed without delay. Suspect internal bleeding if the cat is collapsed and the mucous membranes of the mouth and eyes are very pale and cold.

External bleeding does however sometimes occur. If an ear or limb is bleeding, the application of a styptic pencil to small wounds can be a useful emergency measure. For more serious bleeding, make a big pressure pad of cotton wool to cover the whole limb and secure it with adhesive tape, a strip of material or even nylon tights as a temporary measure while the cat is being closely supervised. Pressure must be applied evenly so as not to constrict the limb. This procedure is only a stopgap while veterinary attention is being sought. Injuries which break the skin nearly always need to be seen by a veterinary surgeon, as wounds on cats very easily become septic.

Giving medication

Injections

Although an injection is the safest and surest way of administering medical treatment to cats, this is almost always done by a veterinary surgeon. The occasional exception being the long term treatment for diabetes. It is quite in order for an owner to give regular insulin. The technique is actually quite easy but must be taught by the veterinary surgeon attending the case.

Liquid medicine

Some owners find it easiest to give medicine in liquid form. It is best done with a small medicine bottle or a 2 ml plastic syringe which can be provided by your veterinary surgeon. The cat's head should be steadied and liquid squirted slowly but steadily just behind the large canine tooth on one side. The method is never accurate as there is inevitably a good deal of spillage. Care has to be taken to prevent the cat from tilting its head too far backwards as there is a danger of choking. A quiet cat can be given a simple kaolin mixture or fed liquefied food in this way quite easily.

Giving tablets

A fairly quiet cat can be dosed without too much difficulty if it is done quickly but gently. The longer the cat is wrapped in a blanket or towel the more likely it is to struggle and a fierce struggle does not do the cat or owner any good at all. The cat's mouth can be opened by placing the first finger and thumb alongside the whiskers (taking care not to stroke the whiskers forward). The third and fourth fingers are then placed behind the ears so that the whole head is boxed in by four fingers. The head can then easily be tilted back and the mouth will open automatically. The other hand or a pair of blunt forceps is used to place a tablet at the very back of the mouth. A cat will swallow if the throat is gently stroked or the owner blows gently in the cat's face. Alternatively a small dosing 'gun' can be made by cutting the top off a 2 or 5 ml plastic syringe. These can be obtained from veterinary practices. The tablet is placed in the barrel and 'fired' into the mouth which is opened with the other hand.

Medicated food

It is possible to give a semi-solid food by squeezing a tube of say fish paste or cheese onto the cat's tongue. Medicinal liquid paraffin can be added to the food for cats which are constipated. Unlike almost every other medicine the majority of cats seem not to dislike its presence in their diet.

Skin dressings

These need to be applied directly to the skin and not just to the fur. This usually means cutting some hair away to get down to the skin.

Eye and ear drops

Similarly eye and ear drops must get to the site of the problem. It is useless to apply them just to the eyelid or earflaps.

- By far the best strategy is to seek the veterinary surgeon to demonstrate exactly what is required for the administration of any medicine.
- It is important to continue with medication even though the cat may seem to be better.
- It the cat shows some ill-effects from medication or gets very much worse, it must be seen again by the veterinary surgeon without delay.
- If you have any doubt about whether your cat is receiving the proper dose of medicine tell your veterinary surgeon. He may be able to give you a different preparation which is more easily administered.

Accidental poisoning

All our houses, gardens and garages contain substances which can be poisonous. Luckily cats are careful and fastidious about what they choose to eat and are therefore, in general, unlikely to knowingly consume poisonous substances – particularly those with an unusual or offensive smell or taste. However, under certain circumstances, cats may be at a greater risk of ingesting toxic materials, for example:

- A cat's natural instinct to hunt small prey means that poisoned rodents may be consumed on occasion, resulting in secondary poisoning of the cat.
- Coat contamination with toxic materials can result in poisoning due to the frequency and thoroughness of self-grooming in the cat.

In addition, cats are only poorly able to metabolize and thus detoxify many drugs and chemicals in comparison with other animals such as dogs. This means that cats can on occasion succumb to much smaller amounts of potentially poisonous substances, and therefore should *never* be dosed with any medicines designed for human use unless the owner has been specifically instructed to do so by a veterinary surgeon. Cats are especially sensitive to aspirin, which must never be given to them. Disinfectants based on phenol (carbolic) should not be used in cat-owning households.

Signs of poisoning

Among the signs of poisoning will be sudden, violent vomiting and/or diarrhoea, fits, excessive salivation, staggering gait, collapse, and coma, but all these signs may relate to other conditions and may not be caused by poisoning. All will require immediate veterinary help.

HISTORY TIP

If the cat's illness is thought to be associated with access to a dangerous substance, or if the cat is found with a container or packet, take all the associated material, packaging, and any vomit with you to the veterinary surgeon, to help in identifying the specific cause and in finding a possible antidote.

Table 10.1 overleaf lists some common poison risks.

Coping with the suspected poisoning case

Get advice from the local veterinary practice as soon as possible. Do not attempt treatment yourself or do anything aimed at trying to make the cat

Table 10.1. Common poison risks

Situation	Poison
Garage	Engine oil Petrol Antifreeze (ethylene glycol) Lead paint Paint remover Wood preserver Glue Tar and creosote (phenol) Putty
Kitchen	Detergents Disinfectants Carbon monoxide (from leaking coal/gas appliances or those burning Calor gas, oil or solid fuel without proper ventilation) Bleach
Bathroom	Medicines Bleach Disinfectant
Garden sheds	Herbicides (sodium chlorate, arsenicals, paraquat and diquat) Insecticides and fungicides (particularly those containing organochlorines, organophosphates and carbamates) Molluscides – slug killers (metaldehyde) Rodenticides – rat and mouse poison (antu, calciferol, alphachloralose, warfarin, arsenic, thallium, strychnine)
Other rooms in the house; conservatories	House plants, e.g. Diffenbachia (Dumb Cane) Detergents Dyes Lead Naphthalene (found in moth balls)
Garden	Fungi/toadstools Laburnum Herbicides Slug pellets Rodents which have ingested rodenticides Cyanide (products used to destroy wasps' nests)

vomit. Put the cat in a quiet dark room, especially if it is having a fit, whilst you are waiting for the vet to call or whilst you are getting a suitable container to take it to the surgery.

Common plants – poisonous, and possibly fatal, to cats

Anemone
Buttercup
Clematis
Christmas Rose
Crocus
Daphne
Delphinium
Dumb Cane
Foxglove
Holly
Hyacinth
Hydrangea
Impatiens (Busy Lizzie)
Larkspur
Lily-of-the-Valley
Mistletoe
Morning Glory
Philodendron
Poinsettia
Rhododendron
Snowdrop
Sweet Pea
Wisteria
Yew

Home nursing

Since most owner nursing is carried out in relation to surgical operations, the information in this chapter is given with that in mind. Some information on nursing is given in the 'What if' section of Chapter 8 and reference should also be made to the relevant section there. *If in doubt consult your veterinary practice* – a short telephone call to the surgery will ensure that mistakes are not made and will help set your mind at rest.

Care of the cat before and after a surgical operation

Most cats will need surgery under full anaesthetic at some time in their lives. The care that you will give your cat before and after the operation will contribute greatly to the successful outcome.

Cats make much better surgical patients than humans, possibly because, unlike us, they do not anticipate the event. Some individuals have a high pain threshold and will behave entirely normally two or three days after surgery.

Small animal veterinary surgery has now reached a high degree of sophistication, but there is always some risk involved in a full anaesthetic.

Before surgery

If the operation is non-urgent ('elective' or 'cold' are words used in this context), plan to have a few days free when you have plenty of time to devote to your cat after the operation.

If you are unable to keep close observation on the cat in the post-operative days, it may be wise to ask the veterinary surgeon to keep it as an in-patient. Cats usually leave wounds alone but it is not unknown for cats to burst their sutures, or to remove them, if they are left alone to their own devices.

Pre-operative starvation

Your veterinary surgeon or the veterinary nurse will give precise instructions on withholding food and drink, usually for 12 hours, possibly longer, before the operation.

It is very important that these instructions are carried out, as otherwise the cat may choke on vomit during the anaesthetic.

Tell the veterinary surgeon if a mistake has been made as it may be better to postpone the operation.

Tell the veterinary surgeon if your cat has ever had special problems in recovering from an anaesthetic.

If the cat is on medication, ask the veterinary surgeon whether it should be withdrawn.

On the operation day

1. Arrive at the surgery at the time requested.
2. Provide a telephone number where you can be contacted all day.
3. Be aware that the hair will have to be shaved from around the operation site. If you hope to show the cat again soon, ask if as little hair as possible can be removed, but the needs of surgery must come first.
4. The cat will probably be given a 'pre-med' tranquillizing injection and you may be asked to wait while this takes effect.
5. You will probably be given a time at which you may telephone to enquire about your cat.

After surgery

Collection of the cat after surgery

Cats vary in the time they take to recover from an anaesthetic. They should remain under skilled supervision until they are fully conscious.

Before your cat is handed over to you, make sure you have all the information you will need. Never be afraid to ask!

1. Ask about food and fluid – what should be given and when.
2. Ask about medication – when should you start giving what is prescribed.
3. Ask about contacting a veterinary surgeon should the cat develop problems after it reaches home.
4. Ask about exercise.
5. Ask when you are to report progress and when the sutures (stiches) are to be removed. The cost of suture removal and post-operative checking are often included in the operation fee. You may wish to ask if this is so.

The journey home

1. Keep the car warm but well-ventilated.
2. Transport the cat in a suitable container; ask your vet for advice and read the section on carrying boxes, Chapter 10.
3. Prevent post-operative shock with hot-water bottle and blanket.
4. Be aware that the cat may relapse into a deeper sleep when in familiar surroundings.

Post-operative care

1. The cat's first need will be to pass urine. Support may be needed to enable it to use a litter tray.
2. Make up a comfortable bed in a warm, quiet, dry area. Use plastic protection as the cat may pass urine while in a deep post-operative sleep.
3. Unless instructed otherwise by the veterinary surgeon, after major operations offer small quantities of water/glucose solution (one tablespoonful of glucose to one pint of boiled water) or an electrolyte solution provided by the veterinary surgeon, every hour.
4. Give small amounts of easily digested food every three to four hours, unless instructed to the contrary. Make a mousse out of kitten food, warm to blood heat and feed, little and often.
5. Be prepared to support the cat to pass urine and faeces for 24–48 hours after surgery. If balance has not been regained by that time, tell the veterinary practice.
6. Be aware that the cat may have a slight cough, caused by intubation from the anaesthetic, for two to three days after surgery, and the throat may be sore making eating difficult.

Post-operative nursing

Veterinary surgeons often say, 'Give me a ring if you are worried!' The following conditions will give reason for post-operative concern and should be reported to the veterinary surgeon.

1. Sinking deeper into unconsciousness.
2. Cold, clammy feel to the paws, pale gums and lips.
3. Still not fully conscious and only cautiously active by 48 hours post-operation.
4. Persistent retching and vomiting, the cat not retaining even small quantities of water.
5. Failure to regain limb control in 48 hours.
6. Passing faeces with blood content – estimate how much.
7. Acute swelling and redness around wound site or unpleasant smell from wound.
8. Convulsions or seizure.

9. Allergic reactions, such as bumps or wheals appearing on skin, or acute swelling of face, mouth or throat.
10. Removal of the sutures by the cat.

Medication
Before you leave the surgery, make sure that the name of each drug is written on the container, together with its use, e.g. to stop vomiting, antibiotic etc. Enter the names of the medication in your cat's records, it may be invaluable to you later on.

If the tablets are supplied to you in an envelope, transfer them to a clean, dry bottle, sticking the vet's envelope securely on the outside.

Make a chart for the dosage, marking off each time you give a dose.

If you have more than one pet, make sure the medicine gets to the right animal.

Control of water intake
Cats which have become dehydrated during surgery will be very thirsty, but water in large quantities may make them vomit.

Remove all water bowls, flower pots and vases, and prevent access to puddles, ponds and water butts.

Give fluid in appropriate quantity, one teaspoonful every hour by the clock. After two hours, if the cat is not vomiting, the quantity may be doubled, and thereafter increased cautiously until the cat is able to drink freely.

Fluid may be given in a hypodermic syringe (without a needle in place) if the cat finds it difficult to raise its head.

Dressings
If the cat has a dressing on a leg or foot, it may be kept clean when the cat goes outside by putting the foot into a plastic bag, secured loosely by sticky tape. Remove the bag and tape immediately on return to the house and put them in a safe place. Elastic bands are bad news for animals so do not use them to secure the bag! If the dressings are becoming soiled but are still in place, another layer of conforming bandage may be put on top. It is important not to allow dressings to become wet.

Sutures
If the sutures are well-positioned and not too tight, most cats tolerate them well. The leg of a pair of tights make a useful body stocking to keep dressings in place.

If the cat is inclined to worry about the sutures, try putting a bandage on a front paw to offer a distraction. An Elizabethan collar is another solution but this must only be fitted by a veterinary surgeon. When this device is in place the cat will not be able to reach any part of the body, but these collars are tolerated surprisingly well.

Kittening

Signs of pregnancy

Cats are induced ovulators, which means that eggs are released by the female on the stimulation of mating. Fertilization takes place 24 to 36 hours later. With calling continuing for at least five days, a cat that is free to roam can be mated several times and may have kittens by a number of different tom cats in the same litter.

Most, but not all, cats will kitten about 63 days after mating, but there can be variations of several days on either side.

The first signs of pregnancy are that the nipples become a deeper shade of pink and more prominent. This occurs about three weeks after mating. By feeling across the abdomen with the thumb and finger of one hand, it is often possible at about 3–3½ weeks to identify the young in the womb (the pregnant uterus feels like a short necklace of quite widely spaced beads). Extreme caution is advised when attempting pregnancy diagnosis like this as heavy manipulation can cause damage or even abortion. Later the pregnant queen starts to fill out and the body angles get progressively more round.

Giving birth

The first indications of the impending arrival come when the queen starts to search around for a convenient place to have her kittens and begins to shred material such as newspaper into pieces. This is called first stage labour. Expensive kitten boxes are often purchased and totally ignored; the queen usually preferring an inaccessible corner with newspaper or a cardboard box. She will have her kittens where she wants to and no amount of persuading or cajoling will alter her determination. The best advice is to wait until she settles and put clean newspaper down around her. The second stage of labour is indicated by obvious abdominal straining and it is helpful to keep a note of when this started. Normally a fluid-filled sac will appear at the vulva ahead of the first kitten, which will be wrapped in another fluid-filled membrane, the amniotic sac. The queen should break open the sac with her teeth to release the kitten, and she will then lick the kitten clean and dry. The kitten may squeal while this is being done but this is a healthy sign as a certain amount of what appears to be rough treatment helps to get the kitten's lungs working. The queen should then bite off the umbilical cord about 2 in from the kitten, so separating it from the afterbirth. If the queen cannot do these things herself the owner must take over, cleaning the kitten's eyes, nose and mouth with tissues to remove all mucus, and severing the cord carefully and slowly with sterilized scissors. It is best to try to crush the cord as it is severed rather than making a clean cut, extra sharp new scissors are best avoided. Then the kitten must be rubbed dry with towels and left to warm in a blanket whilst later arrivals are dealt with. A pair of sterilized scissors, cotton wool, and dry towels should be to hand if needed just in case. The placenta would, in the wild or feral cat, provide a useful form of nourishment while the queen is unable to hunt, and there is no harm in allowing a domesticated queen to eat the placenta and foetal membranes if she wants to do this.

Kittens have been arriving by their own devices for a long time, and it is best to leave the queen to get on with it, while at the same time keeping a discrete eye on the proceedings. Not all cats like human company at this time, but some demand it apparently for no other reason than to show how clever they are. Generally, the queen needs little help, only encouragement, and it is a good idea to avoid touching or interfering in any way. Whether or not to call the vet is so often a vexed question, and particularly so in the middle of the night. The best indicator is the queen herself. She should purr happily throughout the delivery with only occasional interruptions in the pitch as another kitten arrives. If the queen is in distress, it is usually obvious by her manner and actions. If constant unsuccessful straining occurs for more than thirty minutes and is accompanied by much moving around and being unable to settle, the time has come to talk to the veterinary surgeon on the telephone. Be prepared to take the cat to the surgery where everything is to hand to help your queen. Wrap up warmly any kittens that have already been produced and take advice from the receptionist or nurse on whether or not you should take them to the surgery as well. As long as they are kept warm, kittens can survive quite well for some hours before first feeding. Above all don't panic.

Check List – Kittening

When to seek veterinary advice:

1. When straining has gone on longer than 30 minutes without production of a kitten. Telephone the vet.
2. If you see a foul-smelling, dark-coloured discharge from the queen on the second or later day after kittening. Take the queen to the vet.
3. If the kittens cry continually, and feel cold and damp to touch. Ask about the possibility of a home visit by the vet.
4. If, at any time during lactation, the queen has a raised temperature, and one or more teats are hard and inflamed. Take the queen to the vet.

What if I find a kitten partially born but the queen seems unable to deliver it completely?

This is a comparatively rare happening but if it does occur the owner must be prepared to assist, as it will be impossible to get veterinary help in time to save the kitten.

Using a clean handtowel or face flannel, get a firm but not too forceful grip on the kitten, and give a gentle pull in the line of the kitten's girth, downwards and away from the spine. No force must be used as this will damage the kitten and the queen as well, but a gentle pull may be exerted as the queen strains.

What if a kitten appears to be stillborn?

Kittens may sometimes appear to be dead, this can be because the environment is too cold, or the queen is too disturbed to deal with her kittens properly.

Another reason for apparent stillbirth is that the kitten's airway is blocked by foetal membranes or fluids.

Keep the room where the birth is taking place warm and dry, without draughts at floor level. Clean the kittens' airways if the queen is neglecting this task, and put the kittens in a warm box lined with plenty of bedding. Individual kittens which seem moribund may be held up by the back legs for a few seconds to stimulate breathing, followed by rubbing with a warm towel.

They must be encouraged to feed from their mother as soon as possible.

What if my cat has kittens unexpectedly? How do I find homes for them?

You should not expect a rescue organisation to take over the litter, and you may well find more satisfaction, and even more success in finding homes for the kittens yourself.

Many local newspapers have free advertising columns for pet livestock, and this is probably the best way to make the litter known to prospective buyers, but it is also useful to let your veterinary surgery know you have kittens.

It is said that it is better not to make a charge for non-pedigree kittens, because if you are prepared to give them away, you can select from suitable applicants, while if you seek to sell then you may find it difficult to refuse those who offer to buy. Expect to give new owners advice on the care and upbringing of the kitten and be prepared to take the kitten back if for any reason the new owners find it unsuitable for their way of life.

Do not forget to point out that while the kitten is free, its upkeep is not. Vaccination, neutering and spaying, and holiday boarding must be allowed for, as well as feeding and provision of litter.

What if my female cat appears pregnant again but I have not been able to find homes for the first litter yet?

This is one of the facts of life of owning a female cat. It is essential to prevent the queen from roaming freely while she is rearing kittens. Ask your veterinary surgeon's advice about getting her spayed either now, or when the next litter has been reared, otherwise finding homes for kittens is going to become a way of life for you.

CHAPTER 11
FURTHER USEFUL INFORMATION

Veterinary services

Veterinary surgeons

Animals may only be treated by a qualified veterinary surgeon, except that an owner may diagnose and treat illness in his own animals, and anyone may give first aid to an animal in distress. Boarding kennel owners, trainers and people working in grooming businesses are acting illegally if they diagnose a condition and prescribe or apply medication to a cat that is not owned by them.

On graduation from veterinary college, the new graduate becomes a Member of the Royal College of Veterinary Surgeons (MRCVS). These initials will follow those which denote the university attended, e.g. London University Veterinary School, also known as the Royal Veterinary College, grants the degree of Bachelor of Veterinary Medicine (BVetMed). Fellowship of the Royal College of Veterinary Surgeons (FRCVS) is granted for services to the profession or by thesis. Recently new postgraduate studies have been recognized by the granting of certificate or diploma grades in certain veterinary specialities. You may see these distinguished as, for example, Cert SAD (Certificate in Small Animal Dermatology), or DV Ophthal (Diploma in Veterinary Ophthalmology.) Other postgraduate qualifications are in cardiology, orthopaedics, anaesthesia, radiology, as well as others applicable to large animal veterinary care.

The Royal College of Veterinary Surgeons is the governing body of the veterinary profession and one of its important roles is acting as mediator and investigator in response to complaints from the public. The vast majority of these complaints stem from poor communication between the client and the veterinary surgeon, and it is hoped that some aspects of this situation may be eased after a study of this book.

Every veterinary practice, whether it is run single-handed by one person, or whether it is owned by several partners employing a number of assistants and lay staff, is a small business which must pay its overheads, allow a reasonable profit for its principals and a return on the capital invested in equipment. Veterinary fees are worked out upon this basis; there is no nationally agreed scale of fees.

Where wide differences in charges are found, this may reflect the amount and standard of the equipment provided and the additional services offered, as well as the amount of skilled lay help available for the care of animals. Of course the area of the country will affect the fees charged. It is usually much more expensive to have cats treated in the London area.

Veterinary nurses

The Royal College of Veterinary Surgeons supervises the training and examinations for veterinary nurses who become, after qualification, members of the British Veterinary Nursing Association. Full details of the course of tuition can be obtained from RCVS, 32 Belgrave Square, London SW1.

However, many veterinary surgeons train lay assistants to their own needs and do not require them to be formally qualified. The number of people looking for this type of work always greatly exceeds the number of posts available.

Fees

If you feel that you have been charged too much for veterinary services remember:

- You can always ask about the cost of treatment in advance. To be cautious about what you may be required to pay will not be taken as lack of concern for your cat.
- You can ask for an itemized bill to see how the total accumulated.
- Veterinary medication is often expensive to manufacture because in comparison with human needs, demand is low.
- Unlike private medical consultations and drug prescriptions, VAT is charged on all veterinary services.
- If the treatment advised is really more than you can afford, your veterinary surgeon may be able to refer you to one of the animal charities which are able to help.

Insurance

In order not to have the risk of embarrassment you may wish to take out an annual insurance policy which covers veterinary fees for illness and accident, as well as other benefits. Your veterinary surgeon will have proposal forms from several companies offering different levels of cover. All the companies exclude preventative vaccinations and elective spaying and neutering.

Most companies have an upper age limit beyond which they no longer accept for enrolment, but it is important to choose a company which will insure your cat for life if it is enrolled when young. It is often the early years, and again old age, which prove to be the most expensive in terms of veterinary fees.

One company will also insure your queen for veterinary fees which may occur during pregnancy and kittening, so it is worthwile reviewing all the policies on offer, and also asking your veterinary surgeon which company he finds the most satisfactory to deal with.

Consulting the veterinary surgeon

Find out from the surgery whether an appointment is necessary, or whether open surgeries are run between certain hours. With the latter system, it may be necessary to wait a short while for attention.

If you have any way of getting to the veterinary surgery, it is preferable to do so, rather than request a house call which may prove to cost more than you expect, as house calls are an extravagant use of the veterinary surgeon's time. Furthermore the veterinary surgeon can do relatively less for a sick or injured cat at your home. All the diagnostic and treatment equipment, as well as trained assistance, is available at the surgery. If you have no transport, the receptionist may well be able to tell you of a taxi service.

If at all possible the person who knows the cat best should take it to the surgery. Other people may not be able to supply in detail the information the veterinary surgeon needs. Have no hesitation in writing down the history of the illness and other information about the cat, so that you do not forget what you mean to say.

Expect to pay in cash or by cheque at the conclusion of the consultation. Small animal veterinary surgeons do not expect to send out accounts for payment, and may make an extra charge if they have to do so. Some veterinary surgeons accept credit cards, but find out in advance whether your vet does.

If you have an particular phobia about injections or the sight of blood, the veterinary surgeon would much rather you explained and then waited outside while your cat is attended to. You are not the only one, by any means!

British veterinary surgeons usually dispense medication and treatments, rather than writing prescriptions for the chemist to fulfil. Ask for the name of the medication to be written on the envelope it is packaged in, and make sure you know what the dosage regimen is to be, and when you are to start giving the medication.

Skin dressings and medicated shampoos sometimes have a complicated method of application. Ask for the instructions to be written down if you fear you have not understood or may forget. No one will think the worse of you.

Second opinions

There is, as yet, no veterinary 'Harley Street' where you may take your cat for a consultation with a 'specialist', although this may come about in time.

When it is felt that a case would benefit from the opinion of a veterinary surgeon who has taken a great interest in one aspect of feline disease, it is usual for the veterinary surgeon in general practice to refer his client to one of the university veterinary schools, or possibly the Animal Health Trust or to a colleague in private practice. At a veterinary school the case will be seen by a lecturer in veterinary medicine and surgery, often accompanied by students, or a veterinary surgeon researching a particular disease.

You may request that your cat is referred for a second opinion but you cannot make the approach on your own. Arrangements have to be made through your veterinary surgeon and the findings of the person giving the second opinion will be communicated to your own home practice. The account will also be sent to your own vet, who will pass it on to you.

Changing practices

It is a very important part of ethical veterinary behaviour that clients shall not be 'poached' from one practice by another. It is also not in the best interests of a sick cat to be subjected to a variety of treatments given in ignorance of what has been done before. Therefore trying to change practices, unless for a valid and obvious reason such as moving house, may be obstructed, for the very best of motives, by the practice you are trying to change to.

If you feel unable to tell your current veterinary surgeon that you want to go somewhere else, the most tactful time to make the change is when your cat is not suffering from an illness.

The Royal College of Veterinary Surgeons decrees that every practice must offer a service to sick animals 24 hours a day, 365 days a year. In order to comply, the one or two person practice may employ part time veterinary help, or may enter into arrangements with neighbouring practices to cover 'out of hours' work on a reciprocal basis. This is the reason that emergency calls are often re-routed to a telephone number and a veterinary surgeon with whom you are unfamiliar.

For non-urgent consultations, it is always possible to telephone the surgery to ask when the veterinary surgeon who has examined your cat before will be on duty.

Veterinary hospitals

Some veterinary practices are entitled to term themselves 'Veterinary Hospitals'. This special status is granted by the Royal College of Veterinary Surgeons to premises where the building and the facilities reach a standard of excellence laid down by the College. Among the requirements are provision for the proper care of animals as in-patients, and there must be at least one trained veterinary nurse employed.

The veterinary hospital is not comparable with an NHS district hospital for humans. It is not the specific place to take cats which have had an accident or are seriously ill, and it would be a mistake to think that the personnel who own or work in the hospital are necessarily of greater competence or have higher qualifications than veterinary surgeons in other practices.

Veterinary hospitals function in every way as other general practices do, having their own clientele, except that they are able to offer nursing facilities to those clients who are not able to look after their sick cats at home, or for those cats which require expert nursing care.

Finally, being a veterinary surgeon involves more than just curing disease in animals; it means helping owners at times of worry and stress. Communicate with your veterinary surgeon. Establish a relationship based on your common interest – your pet. Such mutual understanding and respect will pay dividends for everyone.

Cat Fancy

In Britain the main organization catering for the cat is the Governing Council of the Cat Fancy (GCCF), which was formed at the beginning of the century. It is a body which deals with all the administration of the cat world, from registering cats' pedigrees, to licensing shows.

Made up of delegates from the many cat clubs, the Council sits four times a year to consider a variety of matters including: policy decisions on rules governing showing, registration, disciplinary matters; the appointment of judges; and the approval of the standard of points on which cats are judged. The day-to-day running of the council is carried out by an annually elected executive committee. Owners' individual prefixes are registered as well as the names of pedigree cats and kittens, and the transfers of ownership when cats are sold.

The GCCF grants licenses to affiliated clubs, so that they may run shows for which they engage judges who are also licensed by the GCCF to judge specific breeds of cats.

There are three levels of cat shows, only one being allowed to award certificates which count towards championship status of the individual cat. The GCCF holds an annual show only for qualified cats and kittens from which the top winning cat of Great Britain is elected.

Members of the Cat Fancy are bound by the rules and regulations of the GCCF, and for any breaks in the code of behaviour, there exists within the constitutions a series of disciplinary procedures.

Cat shows

Showing cats is a fascinating hobby which can become to some extent somewhat addictive. Shows are held each weekend throughout the country, some open to all breeds of cat and others for specific breeds or for non-pedigree cats, known as household pets.

Structure of a cat show

The GCCF licences three types of cat show: exemption, sanction and championship. At all of these shows, judges assess the cat or kitten in order of merit according to a set standard of points for the particular breed. Depending on the status of the show, GCCF certificates may be awarded by the judge in open classes to a cat that has attained the level of excellence required. These classes are for one breed only and certificates count towards the status of the cat: three challenge certificates for a champion, three grand challenge certificates for a grand champion. There is a parallel system for neutered and spayed cats with their certificates called 'premiers'. Many shows have a section for the non-pedigree cats though no actual certificates can be awarded, as assessment is on a personal basis and cannot conform to a standard of points.

At shows all cats must remain in individual wire cages, supplied by the show management for the duration of the show, usually from 9 a.m. to 5 p.m. The shows are very often held on Saturdays.

One side benefit of cat showing as a hobby is the opportunity to get to know unfamiliar towns, as exhibitors are not allowed to remain with their cats while judging is in progress. Many exhibitors fill in the time by shopping or exploring in the neighbourhood.

First time showing

Before being able to enter a show, pedigree cats must be registered with the GCCF in the name of the owner and be of a breed that is recognized by the GCCF. Though not essential, joining a breed or area club has distinct advantages. Apart from meeting other breeders and cat lovers, the clubs usually have reduced entry fees to their shows for members. Non-pedigree cats do not have to be registered with the governing body and can be entered into any show that puts on the appropriate classes for non-pedigree cats.

How to enter your first show after obtaining a list of shows from the GCCF:

- Send for a schedule enclosing an SAE to the show manager at least two months before showdate.
- Complete an entry form with the requested details of the cat which are found on the pedigree form.
- Select the classes you wish to enter, remembering that the main class is the open which is for the specific breed. There will be a minimum number of classes the cat must enter, a section of definitions for other classes is printed in the schedule.
- Return the entry with the correct fee and a stamped addressed postcard for confirmation of the entry being accepted.

The closing dates for shows is usually approximately six to eight weeks before the show day. This gives plenty of time for preparation of the cat.

Types of show

Exemption

The name implies the status of the show. It is exempt from the rules of competition which govern the other shows. Judges may judge cats in breeds which they are not formally licensed to judge and the club may offer extra prizes. There are no certificates and wins do not count towards champion status. Clubs and societies use this form of show to build up to championship status, as it shows the governing body the club is capable of running a show. Often shows of this kind are very friendly affairs with the organizing committee putting a lot of effort into every detail.

Sanction

This is similar to championship show but still without the certificates. Clubs have to adhere strictly to the rules concerning running a show by producing a schedule of the correct classes with judges on the particular breed lists.

Championship

Certificates are awarded to the winners of the open classes, and these count towards championship or premier status of the cat.

All the shows mentioned can have a best of breed or best in show and offer either prize money or rosettes for classes other than the open class.

Preparation

The judges will be looking for excellence in the breed and assessing the cats in order of merit against a set standard of points. Temperament is not included in the standards, though judges cannot fail to be impressed by the good example of the breed which has a gentle demeanour and purrs throughout. Show preparation is vital as well as time consuming; it is never wasted. Longhaired cats are usually prepared at least two weeks before with a bath which is followed by powdering and grooming. Preparation of shorthaired cats takes rather less time but is just as meticulous.

Veterinary inspection

The main hurdle many exhibitors dread is the veterinary inspection before entering the show hall. This is one element in a two-part process that aims to prevent disease and infection being spread at cat shows. The first part of this on-going campaign is a rule that forbids cats being showed more than once in a fourteen day period, so that any disease which may be being incubated should begin to show positive signs before the next cat show. The second part is a screening process on arrival at the show by a team of veterinary surgeons who look for obvious signs of illness or parasitic infestation. Because of time factors, the examination cannot be made in great detail so only those cats showing obvious signs of illness are prevented from entering the show although incidents of disease spreading within a cat show are rare and provide sound endorsement of this policy. The exhibitor should be aware of the general health of the cat and examinations of the ears, eyes and the coat for evidence of fleas or other external parasites should be attended to before the cat is presented to the vet on the morning of the show. A cat with serious illness or infestation that requires a long period of treatment should never be taken to a show. The owner who takes a chance on doing this risks answering to the disciplinary procedures of the GCCF in a serious breach of the rules.

Having passed the veterinary inspection, the cats are put in numbered cages known as pens. Judging is carried out round the pens and on the basis of anonymity, with the pens bearing no distinguishing marks or labels. All the accessories in the pen, blanket, litter tray and water bowl, must be white, and may not bear any individual or distinguishing marks. Judges and stewards wearing white coats for hygiene and distinguishing reasons, are given the pen numbers of the cats they have to judge, and take with them a wheeled trolley on which to stand the individual cat while they judge its merits.

Cat owners must leave the hall when judging starts and are not re-admitted until midday when the general public may come in too. Many of the awards, in the form of cards, rosettes and ribbons will already be in place on the pens by this time, although the judging of minor classes will still be going on. This procedure ensures, as far as is humanly possible, that judging is not influenced by recognizing the cat or knowing to whom it belongs. The stewards who accompany the judges to help with handling are often learner-judges who must steward at a number of shows before they can apply to be considered as judges for specific breeds. The steward will disinfect the judges' trolley between cats, open the cage and extract the cat and endeavour to display the cat so that the judge can assess its quality. This process can take a long time if the cat is shy and reluctant to be handled. Unlike dog shows, the judge cannot always compare likely winners side-by-side. If a judge wants a second look at a cat, the trolley must be trundled back to its cage. When the important classes have been judged the cat may be fed and can have its toys in the pen for the rest of the day. Cats cannot be taken home until the show closes, usually about 5 p.m., so going to a cat show is a full and sometimes exhausting day.

The above applies to all sections of cats, pedigree and non-pedigree, though not all shows include a non-pedigree section.

The GCCF's own show is held usually in May. Entry is restricted to cats and kittens which have qualified by winning an open class at one of the championship club shows held during the year. The show, the Supreme, is a knock-out competition and the winning cat takes the title 'Supreme Adult'.

Charities and feline organizations

Charities and organizations abound for the cat with virtually every aspect now catered for, though this has not always been the case, with feline medicine in particular having been the poor relation for many years.

There is now much more knowledge available about the health problems of cats and much of the recent interest is due to the work of the Feline Advisory Bureau. This is a charity maintained by cat owners who raise enough money to support one, or sometimes two, post-graduate scholars at Bristol University Veterinary School specifically to study feline medicine.

Names and addresses

Cat Fancy

Governing Council of the Cat Fancy,
4–6 Penel Orlieu, Bridgwater, Somerset TA6 3PG
Tel: (0278) 427575

Cat Association of Britain,
CA Central Office, Hunting Grove, Lowfield Heath, Crawley, Sussex
Tel: (0293) 23470
(*This is an alternative association to the parent body. The Cat Association registers cats and holds its own shows, but cats and kittens registered with GCCF may not be shown at Cat Association shows unless special dispensation is given by the parent body.*)

Cat press

Cats,
5 James Leigh Street, Manchester M1 6EX
Tel: 061–236 0577
(*Weekly with reports of cat shows. Editor: Brian Doyle*)

Cat World,
Scan House, Southwick Street, Southwick, Brighton BN4 4TE
Tel: (0273) 595944
(*Monthly with some results of shows. Editor: Joan Moore*)

Feline Advisory Bureau Bulletin,
76 Oliver Road, Shenfield, Brentwood, Essex CM15 8QD
Tel: (0277) 225426
(*Quarterly with scientific reports of feline investigations and general cat news. Available only to subscribers to FAB. Editor: Barry Kirk*)

Veterinary bodies and associations

British Small Animal Veterinary Association,
5 St George Terrace, Cheltenham, Glos. GL5 3PT
Tel: (0242) 584354

British Veterinary Association,
7 Mansfield Street, London W1M 0AT
Tel: 01–636 6541

Feline Advisory Bureau,
350 Upper Richmond Road, Putney, London SW15 6TL
Tel: 01–789 9553

Welfare associations

Blue Cross,
1 Hugh Street, Victoria, London SW1V 1QQ
Tel: 01–834 5556

Cats' Protection League,
17 Kings Road, Horsham, West Sussex RH13 5PP
Tel: (0403) 65566

People's Dispensary for Sick Animals,
PDSA House, South Street, Dorking, Surrey RH4 2LB
Tel: (0306) 888291

Royal Society for the Prevention of Cruelty to Animals,
RSPCA Headquarters, The Causeway, Horsham, West Sussex RH12 1HG
Tel: (0403) 64181

Further reading

Genetics for Cat Breeders, Roy Robinson. Pergamon Press, Oxford (1977)
Excellent, understandable book on genetics.

Standard Guide to Cat Breeds, Ivor Raleigh and Grace Pond. Macmillan, London (1979)
Recent guide to pedigree cats with standard of points for each breed.

Book of the Cat, Michael Wright and Sally Walters. Pan (1980)
Comprehensive book covering many aspects of cat ownership.

For cat care information, including free leaflets and details of free loan video service (suitable for group viewing only), please write to the following address. Your request should be coded after the PO Box number with either a (CP) if you are a cat owner, or (SS) if you are a teacher:

Pedigree Petfoods Education Centre,
Freepost,
PO Box 77,
Burton-on-Trent DE11 7BR

APPENDIX I
GLOSSARY

What did the veterinary surgeon mean?

Inevitably veterinary surgeons will use long or difficult words to describe various conditions and procedures. The glossary below is provided to help cat owners understand what is meant and should be used *in conjunction with* the Index of Diseases and Conditions Affecting Cats.

aberrant	varying from the norm.
acquired immunity	immunity resulting from either vaccination or a previous attack of the disease which makes the body resistant to further infection.
acute	severe and short course – applied to disease or condition.
adhesions	the joining together of tissues, usually applied to organs in the abdominal cavity, and which may occur after an abdominal operation.
adipose tissue	fat.
aetiology	the cause (of a disease or condition). Sometimes spelt 'etiology'.
afterbirth	the membranes (placenta) expelled with the kittens during birth.
albino	an animal lacking in the pigment melanin, so it is white (no colour in skin, hair, nails or eyes).
anabolic steroid	a hormone which promotes growth. Anabolics are used only in very specific situations by veterinary surgeons.
anaerobes	bacteria which like to grow in the absence of air. They are often associated with inflammation of the gums.
analgesic	a medicine which relieves pain.
aneurysm	a dilated blood vessel.
anomaly	marked deviation from the normal.
anorexia	loss of appetite.
anoxia	lack of oxygen.
anthelmintic	a worm remedy.
antibiotic	a substance produced by micro-organisms which inhibits the growth of, or destroys,

	bacteria, e.g. penicillin. Antibiotics may be given by injection, by mouth, or applied locally.
antihistamine	a medicine which counteracts the effect of histamine, a substance released locally in cases of insect bites or stings, and which causes inflammation in the tissues.
antipyretic	substances which lower body temperature in fever.
antiseptic	a substance that kills or inhibits the growth of micro-organisms.
antiserum	blood serum containing high levels of antibody – used sometimes as a treatment for virus infections.
antitussives	substances which suppress coughing.
ataxia	loss of the power of movement resulting in staggering and inco-ordination.
aural resection	an operation to open up the external ear canal to allow it to be exposed to the air – used to cure chronic ear disease.
autogenous vaccine	a vaccine prepared from a micro-organism isolated from animals affected by an outbreak of disease.
bacteria	unicellular micro-organisms.
benign	not malignant, recurring, or spreading. Usually applied to tumours.
biopsy	a minor operation to take part of an affected tissue to diagnose the cause of the lesion and reach a prognosis.
cachexia	debility and wasting.
callus	the swelling which develops around a fractured bone as part of the healing process.
canker	a term used sometimes to describe inflammation of the external ear canal (otitis externa).
carcinogenic	cancer producing.
carcinoma	a type of malignant tumour.
cardiac	pertaining to the heart, e.g. cardiac failure.
cautery	the destruction of tissue, usually to prevent bleeding, by applying a caustic substance or a hot instrument.
chronic	persisting over a long period of time, applied to a disease.
C.N.S.	central nervous system.
coitus	sexual intercourse.
congenital	present at birth.
contagious	capable of being transmitted from one animal to another. Applied to a disease, e.g. feline influenza.
corticosteroids	medicines which mimic the action of the steroid hormones produced by the adrenal

	cortex. They are used most frequently for their anti-inflammatory action.
cryosurgery	the application of intense cold to destroy diseased tissue.
cutaneous	appertaining to the skin; subcutaneous – under the skin.
cyanosis	used to describe tissues which have turned purple or black due to an inadequate blood supply.
cyst	a closed cavity filled with fluid.
dew claw	an extra claw near the carpus or below the hock.
diathermy	the destruction of tissue, usually to stop bleeding, by using a high frequency electric current to generate heat.
dilation	an increase in the size of a structure.
diuretic	a medicine which increases the production of urine.
dys-	a prefix meaning painful or difficult, e.g. dystocia – difficult birth.
ecbolic	a medicine which makes the uterus contract.
E.coli	a bacterium, present in the intestines, which may become pathogenic.
electrocardiogram (E.C.G.)	a record, made by an electrocardiograph, of the heart's performance.
electroencephalogram (E.E.G.)	a record, made by an electroencephalograph, of brain function.
electrolytes	substances that split up into ions when dissolved in water. Electrolyte solutions are often used as transfusions in dehydrated animals.
Elizabethan collar	a collar made from cardboard or plastic fitted over the head which prevents the cat interfering with wounds, dressings, etc., but still allows normal feeding.
embolism	a plug, usually a blood clot, blocking a blood vessel.
emaciation	excessive thinness or wasting.
endemic	usually applied to a disease which is present in an area at all times. Endemic is truly a medical term – the veterinary equivalent is in fact *enzootic*.
endocrine glands	glands which secrete hormones into the blood to act as chemical messengers.
endoscope	an instrument for looking inside the body, usually through a natural opening, e.g. the vagina, but possibly through an artificial opening, e.g. a surgical wound.
enterotomy	an operation involving cutting into the intestines.
etiology	see 'aetiology'.

euthanasia humane killing.
expectorant a substance used to clear phlegm.

first intention applied to a wound that heals promptly.
fistula an abnormal opening or duct leading into a natural canal, hollow organ or other part of the body.
fomites inanimate objects which may act as carriers for infectious agents.

gangrene death and putrefaction of tissue.
gastric pertaining to the stomach.
gestation period of development of the young in the womb.
granulation tissue tissue containing large numbers of blood vessels which occurs when wounds fail to heal promptly. It is seen particularly in large open wounds which need to heal from the bottom.

haematology examination of the blood.
haematuria blood in the urine.
hormone a chemical messager transported by the blood and produced by an endocrine gland.
hydrocephalus a condition involving the accumulation of large amounts of fluid within the brain cavity.
hyper- used as a prefix to mean excessive, e.g. hyperthyroid, hyperactive.
hyperplasia excessive growth of tissue.
hypertrophy increase in size of an organ or tissue.
hypervitaminosis an excess of a particular vitamin.
hypo- used as a prefix to mean deficient or low, e.g. hypothyroid.
hypotension lowered blood pressure.
hypothermia lowered body temperature.

iatrogenic caused by medication.
idiopathic of unknown cause.
immunization to make an animal resistant (immune) to disease.
infectious caused by disease producing micro-organisms. Infectious diseases are not necessarily contagious.
intra-articular given into a joint cavity. This route is not commonly used.
intramuscular given into the muscle. Intramuscular injections are usually given into the hind leg. This route is used generally where a quick action is required.
intranasal through the nose. This route of adminstration is used for vaccines designed to give local protection of the respiratory tract.
intraperitoneal into the abdominal cavity. This route of injec-

tion is used very infrequently.

intubation placing a tube in the trachea to facilitate breathing whilst under an anaesthetic.

lance applied to a surgical incision made into an abscess to allow the accumulated pus to drain away.

laparotomy the surgical opening and closing of the abdomen.

larva an immature stage in the development of an insect or worm.

lesion a pathological change to a tissue, e.g. a wound.

malignant severe, life-threatening, capable of spreading. Applied to tumours.

metastases tumours arising as a result of malignant cells spreading to other parts of the body.

micturition the act of passing urine.

mucus fluid produced by a mucous membrane, e.g. the lining of the vagina.

necropsy a post-mortem.

necrosis death of a tissue.

neonatal newborn

neoplasia formation of a neoplasm or growth (tumour).

nystagmus a condition in which the eyeballs show fine, jerky, involuntary movements.

ophthalmoscope an instrument used for looking into the eyes.

oral pertaining to the mouth, given by mouth.

orthopaedics treatment of bones and joints.

paraplegia paralysis of the rear end of the body.

parenteral the administration of a substance by a route other than the digestive tract, e.g. by injection.

paresis partial paralysis.

parturition giving birth.

pathogen a micro-organism capable of causing disease.

pericardium the membrane that encloses the heart.

perinatal in the period around birth.

perineum the region between the genitals and the anus.

pheromone a chemical substance secreted externally by an individual, the odour of which causes a response in another member of the same species.

photophobia fear of intolerance of light.

placenta see 'afterbirth'.

pneumothorax air in the chest. Usually occurs after a puncture wound to the chest.

polydipsia excessive thirst.

polyuria excessive urination.

prognosis the expected outcome of a disease, condition or operation.

prolapse protrusion, to the outside, of an abdominal organ, e.g. uterus or urinary bladder.
prophylaxis prevention of a disease.
prosthesis an artificial part, e.g. an artificial hip joint.
purulent containing pus.
pus a secretion from inflamed tissue, usually sticky and creamy, which contains white blood cells, serum and bacteria.
put down to painlessly destroy. (Also: 'put to sleep'.)
pyrexia raised body temperature, fever.

renal pertaining to the kidney, e.g. renal failure.
resection the removal of part of an organ.
rhinitis inflammation of the lining of the inside of the nose.

sepsis bacterial infection usually causing pus to be formed.
septicaemia blood poisoning by bacteria and their toxins.
serology the examination of blood for the presence of antibodies to disease.
side effects effects of a drug other than those desired.
spaying the removal of the uterus and ovaries of the queen.
sporadic occurring occasionally.
squamous cell carcinoma a type of skin cancer. Commonly seen on the tips of the ears or on the nose or lips of white cats living in sunny climates.
staphylococci bacteria which commonly occur, particularly in association with skin disease.
staring coat a dry, dull coat.
stenosis narrowing of a canal, e.g. the intestines.
streptococci commonly occurring bacteria which can cause disease in cats.
subacute between acute and chronic.
subclinical applied to a disease in which the signs are not obvious by clinical examination.
subcutaneous under the skin. Subcutaneous injections are used very commonly where a rapid effect is not required, since this route of adminstration tends to be less painful.
sulphonamides chemical compounds which are used to kill or suppress the growth of bacteria in the body.
superficial on the surface. Often applied to a wound.
suppurative producing pus. Applied to a wound.
syncope fainting.
syndrome a set of signs which occur together indicating a particular condition or disease.
synergistic acting together to increase the effect, e.g. penicillin plus streptomycin.

tachycardia increased heart rate. The opposite is called 'bradycardia'.

tachypnoea increased rate of breathing.

taurine an amino acid which the cat requires in the diet as it cannot produce it itself. Lack of taurine produces visual disturbances.

teratogenic capable of producing abnormalities in kittens in the womb, applied to a medicine, e.g. thalidomide.

thrombus a blood clot occurring in a blood vessel or the heart.

tissue an aggregation of similar cells in the body, e.g. a muscle.

topical a drug applied to the outside of the body.

toxaemia a spread of bacterial products (toxins) in the blood from a source of infection.

trauma injury, wounding, shock.

tumour a growth, neoplasm.

ulcer break in the surface of an organ, e.g. corneal ulcer.

umbilicus the point of the abdominal wall where the umbilical cord emerges.

uraemia a build up of waste products in the blood due to kidney disease.

villus small, finger-like process projecting from the wall of the intestine (pural: 'villi').

virus a sub-microscopic agent which infects animals, plants and even bacteria.

viscus any large internal organ (plural: 'viscera').

Wood's lamp a lamp that emits ultraviolet light. Used to diagnose some forms of ringworm.

zoonosis a disease that can be transmitted from animals to man.

APPENDIX II

INDEX OF DISEASES AND CONDITIONS AFFECTING CATS

Disease/condition	Definition	Further Information
ABORTION	Loss of kittens (foetuses) whilst still in the womb possibly as a result of trauma, or an infection.	See 'What if' No. 45
ABRASION	A superficial wound.	See 'What if' No. 35
ABSCESS	A septic region caused by a bacterial infection, which consists of a pool of pus surrounded by a wall of fibrous tissue. An accumulation of pus which is walled off by fibrous tissue and is not inflamed is called a 'cold abscess'.	See 'What if' No. 34
ACNE	An accumulation of 'spots' and pustules in the skin.	
AELUROSTRONGLUS ABSTRUSUS INFESTATION	Infestation with the cat lungworm.	See 'What if' No. 15 and Chapter 9
AGALACTIA	Failure to produce milk possibly caused by stress, mastitis or generalized disease.	
ALLERGY	Hypersensitivity to various 'allergens' which may be contained in food, environmental objects, or in the air; may be manifest as skin disease or gastroenteritis.	
ALOPECIA	Hair loss, which can result from a great number of different causes.	See 'What if' Nos 16 and 17
ANAEMIA	Reduced number of red cells in the blood. There are many causes and diagnosis can be difficult.	See also Feline Infectious Anaemia, Chapter 9
ANAPHYLAXIS	Hypersensitivity to injected foreign material (usually shown as shock).	
ANOREXIA	Inappetence – failure to eat.	See 'What if' No. 3
APNOEA	Cessation of breathing.	See 'What if' No. 42
ARTHRITIS	Inflammation of a joint.	See 'What if' No. 29
ASCARID INFESTATION	Roundworm infection.	See Chapter 9
ASCITES	Accumulation of fluid in the abdominal cavity which can be associated with heart disease, liver disease, or feline infectious peritonitis.	See 'What if' No. 28

Disease/condition	Definition	Further Information
ASPIRIN POISONING	Ingestion of aspirin or aspirin derivatives. Cats are particularly sensitive to aspirin poisoning because of their poor ability to metabolize and excrete the compound.	
ASTHMA	Hypersensitivity to various allergens manifested by breathing difficulties.	See 'What if' No. 15
ATAXIA	Unco-ordinated gait.	See 'What if' No. 43
AUJESZKY'S DISEASE	A disease which in the cat is characterized by intense itching with self-mutilation, fever, dullness, salivation, facial oedema, convulsions and death. It is caused by a virus infection, usually from contact with infected pigs.	
AUTO-IMMUNE DISEASE	A condition where the body rejects its own tissues. The basic cause is a failure of the cat's immune system.	
AVITAMINOSIS	Vitamin deficiency.	See Chapter 6
BLEPHARITIS	Inflammation of the eyelids usually secondary to conjunctivitis.	See 'What if' Nos 9 and 10
BRAIN LESION	Brain damage – see also C.V.A.	See 'What if' Nos 13 and 33
BRONCHITIS	Inflammation of the bronchi.	See 'What if' No. 15
BRUISING	A 'contusion' caused by a blow from a blunt object inflicting damage to the tissues under the skin.	
BURN	An injury caused by dry heat.	See 'What if' No. 35
BURSTITIS	Inflammation of a 'bursa', a fluid-filled sac which is present to protect a vulnerable part usually a bony structure, e.g. the elbow, from trauma.	
CALCULUS (plural: CALCULI)	A stone which is formed in the urinary bladder or gall bladder.	See 'What if' No. 25
CANKER	A lay term which used to be used for inflammation of the ear (otitis externa).	See 'What if' No. 12
CARBON MONOXIDE POISONING	A form of poisoning caused by breathing carbon monoxide gas.	See Chapter 10
CARDIAC ARRYTHMIA	Irregular heart beats.	
CATARACT	An opacity of the lens in the eye.	See 'What if' No. 10
CAT 'FLU	See Feline Influenza.	See 'What if' Nos 7 and 9
CAT LEPROSY	A bacterial skin disease of cats causing lumps or swellings to appear usually around the head or limbs.	
CERVICAL SPONDYLITIS	Fusion of the vertebrae in the neck region as a result of new bone being formed at the joints. This is a feature of an excessive amount of vitamin A being consumed over a long period.	See 'What if' Nos 43 and 49
CHEYLETIELLA INFESTATION	An infestation of the skin with cheyletiella mites.	See Chapter 9
COCCIDIOSIS	An infection with coccidial parasites. In severe cases diarrhoea may be seen.	
COLITIS	Inflammation of the colon.	
COMA	Unconsciousness.	See 'What if' No. 38

Disease/condition	Definition	Further Information
CONGENITAL CEREBELLAR HYPOPLASIA	Failure of the cerebellum (an area of the brain associated with co-ordination of movement) to develop properly. Can be due to infection of the foetus or very young kitten with feline infectious enteritis virus.	See 'What if' No. 43 and Chapter 9
CONJUNCTIVITIS	Inflammation of the conjunctival sac in the eye which may be caused by virus or bacterial infections, foreign bodies or malformed eyelids.	See 'What if' No. 9
CONSTIPATION	Failure to pass faeces. There are many causes of this sign.	See 'What if' No. 22
CONTUSION	A bruise by a blow with a blunt object which leads to rupture of the small blood vessels under the skin.	See 'What if' No. 35
CORNEAL ULCERATION	Ulceration of the front of the eye – the cornea.	See 'What if' No. 10
CRAMP	An uncontrolled contraction of a muscle.	See 'What if' No. 39
CUSHING'S SYNDROME	Excessive production of the hormones produced by the adrenal cortex causing increased thirst, more frequent urination, enlarged abdomen, symmetrical hair loss and skin changes. This condition is not common in cats.	
C.V.A.	Cerebro vascular accident – a blood clot in the brain as a result of rupture of a blood vessel.	
CYSTITIS	Inflammation of the urinary bladder possibly as a result of bacterial infection.	See 'What if' No. 25
CYSTS	Swellings, usually under the skin, which contain fluid.	
DEHYDRATION	Water and salt depletion in the body.	See 'What if' No. 2
DEMODECTIC MANGE	A rare skin disease caused by the mange mite, *Demodex cati.*	See Chapter 9
DENTAL CALCULUS	An accumulation of a hard deposit (tartar) on the teeth.	See 'What if' No. 30
DERMATITIS	Inflammation of the skin possibly caused by bacterial or fungal infections, skin parasites, contact irritants, hypersensitivity and self-inflicted trauma.	
DERMATOPHYTOSIS	Ringworm infection.	See Chapter 9
DIABETES INSIPIDUS	Lack of the hormone which prevents excessive loss of water through the kidneys resulting in excessive thirst and urination.	
DIABETES MELLITUS	Lack of insulin production by the pancreas or failure of tissues to respond to the effects of the hormone leading to, particularly, raised sugar levels in the blood, excessive thirst and increased frequency of urination.	See also 'What if' No. 6
DIARRHOEA	The frequent passage of abnormally soft faeces. This sign can be associated with a number of infectious diseases and other conditions of cats.	See 'What if' No. 20
DISLOCATED EYE-BALL	Eye displaced from its socket.	See 'What if' No. 10
DISLOCATION	Separation of the bones forming a joint.	See 'What if' No. 29
DYSPNOEA	Respiratory distress.	See 'What if' No. 14
DYSTOCIA	'Difficult birth' which may be associated with inertia of the womb, or due to kitten oversize or incorrect presentation.	

Disease/condition	Definition	Further Information
EAR MITE INFESTATION	Infestation of the ear canal by the mite *Otodectes cynotis*.	See Chapter 9
ECLAMPSIA	A nervous disease in lactating queens caused by an imbalance of calcium in the blood sometimes called 'lactation tetany'.	
ECZEMA	Inflammation, usually acute and wet, of the skin.	
EMACIATION	Over-thinness – underweight.	See 'What if' No. 40
EMESIS	Vomiting.	See 'What if' No. 2
ENCEPHALITIS	Inflammation of the brain.	
ENDOCARDITIS	Inflammation of the lining of the heart.	
ENDOMETRITIS	Inflammation of the womb usually after kittening. But see also pyometra.	See 'What if' No. 51
ENTERITIS	Inflammation of the intestines usually associated with diarrhoea.	See 'What if' No. 20
ENTROPION	Inturned eyelids.	See 'What if' No. 9
EPILEPSY	Fits caused by abnormal electrical discharges in the brain.	See 'What if' No. 33
EPIPHORA	Tears coming from the eyes – may be associated with over-production of tears or because the ducts, which carry them away to the nose, are not functioning efficiently.	See 'What if' No. 9
EPISTAXIS	Nose bleed.	
FAINT	A temporary loss of consciousness.	
FALSE PREGNANCY	Signs of pregnancy in queens, usually which have been mated and failed to conceive. Also sometimes called phantom pregnancy or pseudo-pregnancy.	
FELINE DYSAUTONOMIA	See Key-Gaskell Syndrome.	See 'What if' Nos 2, 10, 22 and 24
FELINE INFECTIOUS ANAEMIA	An infection with *Rickettsia* (a micro-organism midway between a bacterium and a virus) causing an increased destruction of red blood cells. This disease is transmitted between cats by fleas and sometimes other blood sucking insects.	See 'What if' Nos 2 and 37, and Chapter 9
FELINE INFECTIOUS ENTERITIS	A severe viral enteritis in cats which can be fatal. Effective vaccines are available against this disease.	See 'What if' Nos 2, 20 and 39, and Chapter 9
FELINE INFECTIOUS PERITONITIS	A viral infection often resulting in the accumulation of large amounts of fluid in the abdomen and possibly also the chest.	See 'What if' Nos 28 and 43, and Chapter 9
FELINE INFLUENZA	An upper respiratory tract infection caused most frequently by a virus or viruses.	See 'What if' Nos 7, 9 and 15, and Chapter 9
FELINE LEPROSY	See Cat Leprosy.	
FELINE LEUKAEMIA	A malignancy of the white blood cells caused by infection with a virus (feline leukaemia virus).	See 'What if' Nos 2, 20, 37 and 45, and Chapter 9
FELINE MILIARY DERMATITIS	Numerous scabs mainly along the skin of the back caused by an allergy to flea bites or flea excreta.	See 'What if' Nos 18 and 36

Disease/condition	Definition	Further Information
FELINE PNEUMONITIS	The name sometimes given to a respiratory disease caused by a *Chlamydia psittaci.*	See Chapter 9 and 'What if' No. 45
FELINE SCABIES	See Notoedric Mange.	
FELINE UROLOGICAL SYNDROME	An irritation or blockage of the bladder caused by the build-up of a sandy crystalline material in the urine.	See 'What if' Nos 23, 25, 36 and 39
FELINE VIRAL RHINOTRACHEITIS	A viral upper respiratory tract infection involved in the feline influenza disease complex.	See 'What if' Nos 7, 9 and 15, and Chapter 9
FITS	Convulsions – see also Epilepsy	See 'What if' No. 33
FLATULENCE	Passage of wind associated with indigestion.	
FLEA INFESTATION	Presence of cat fleas on the skin. Occasionally hedgehog or rabbit fleas may be involved.	See Chapter 9
FRACTURE	A broken bone.	See 'What if' No. 29
FUR BALLS	Accumulation of hair in the stomach and intestine caused by the cat grooming itself during periods of excessive shedding of hair.	See 'What if' Nos 1, 2, 16 and 22
GASTRITIS	Inflammation of the stomach.	
GINGIVITIS	Inflammation of the gums, mostly associated with the accumulation of dental calculus (tartar).	See 'What if' Nos 30, 31 and 32
GLAUCOMA	Increased pressure in the eye leading to a blueing of the cornea.	See 'What if' No. 10
GLOSSITIS	Inflammation of the tongue.	
HAEMATEMESIS	Vomiting blood – may be associated with gastric ulcers, acute poisoning or severe infections. *This is a serious sign.*	See 'What if' No. 2
HAEMATOMA	A blood clot under the skin – most commonly seen under the skin of the ear flap as a result of a head shaking/ear scratching.	See 'What if' Nos 13 and 34
HAEMATURIA	Passage of blood in the urine.	See 'What if' No. 25
HAEMOPHILIA	An inherited defect of blood coagulation.	
HAEMORRHAGIC GASTROENTERITIS	A severe condition of cats whereby there is vomiting and bloody diarrhoea of sudden onset accompanied by dehydration – *an emergency situation.*	
HAIR BALLS	See Fur Balls.	See 'What if' Nos 1, 2, 16 and 22
HARDERIAN GLAND ENLARGEMENT	Swelling (hypertrophy) of Harder's gland which is situated on the back of the third eyelid.	See 'What if' No. 10
HARVEST MITE INFESTATION	Infestation particularly between the toes and on the ear flap with the harvest mite *Trombicula autumnalis.*	See Chapter 9
HEART DISEASE	Usually a disorder of the heart muscle in cats.	

Disease/condition	Definition	Further Information
HEAT STROKE	Collapse as a result of exposure to too high an environmental temperature. Cats with heat stroke often have a body temperature of greater than 106°F and need to be cooled rapidly. *Seek veterinary advice instantly.*	See 'What if' No. 38
HORNER'S SYNDROME	Drooping of the lower eyelid and protrusion of the third eyelid caused by damage to the nerve supply to the eye.	
HYPERAESTHESIA	Increased sensitivity to external stimulae (sound, touch, light).	
HYPERPNOEA	Rapid breathing.	See 'What if' No. 14
HYPER-SEXUALITY	Excessive sex drive (libido).	
HYPERTHYROIDISM	Excessive production of thyroid hormone resulting in increased drinking, weight loss, restlessness and increased heart rate.	
HYPOGLYCAEMIA	Lack of glucose in the blood.	
HYPOSEXUALITY	Lack of sex drive (libido).	
HYPOTHERMIA	Lowered body temperature.	
ICTERUS	Jaundice – a yellowing of the tissues as a result of an excess amount of bile in the blood. Possibly associated with liver disease, haemorrhage, or possibly feline infectious anaemia.	
INCONTINENCE	Involuntary passage of urine.	See 'What if' No. 24
INCO-ORDINATION	A staggery gait – ataxia.	See 'What if' No. 43
INFERTILITY	Inability to reproduce.	
INTUSSUSCEPTION (intestinal)	Telescoping of one section of the intestine into another often as a result of severe enteritis.	
JAUNDICE	See Icterus.	
KERATITIS	Inflammation of the cornea.	See 'What if' No. 10
KEY-GASKELL SYNDROME	A degenerative condition of certain nerves controlling unconscious activities like intestinal muscle contraction, etc. The cause is unknown, but could possibly be due to either a toxin (poison) or infection. The condition is usually fatal.	See 'What if' Nos 2, 10, 22 and 24
LACERATION	An irregular shaped wound with jagged edges. Often with loss of skin. Often caused as a result of road traffic accidents.	
LACTATION TETANY	See Eclampsia.	
LAMENESS	Inability to put a leg to the ground or to bear full weight on it.	See 'What if' No. 29
LENS LUXATION	Dislocated lens in the eye.	
LEPROSY	See Cat Leprosy.	

Disease/condition	Definition	Further Information
LICE INFESTATION	Infestation with lice (pediculosis).	See Chapter 9
LICK GRANULOMA	A chronic wound producted by continued licking.	
LUNGWORM	See Aelurostrongylus abstrusus Infestation.	See 'What if' No. 15 and Chapter 9
LYMPHOSARCOMA	A malignancy of the lymphoid tissue associated with infection with feline leukaemia virus. See Feline Leukaemia.	See 'What if' Nos 2, 20, 37 and 45 and Chapter 9
MAMMARY NEOPLASIA	Tumour in the mammary glands. Such tumours often spread secondarily to the lungs.	See 'What if' No. 48
MANGE	A parasitic skin disease of cats caused by various mange mites.	See Chapter 9
MASTITIS	Inflammation of the mammary gland.	See 'What if' No. 48
MEGAOESOPHAGUS	Enlargement of the oesophagus with food due to blockage or failure of the normal muscular constractions which move the food along. Can be associated with the Key-Gaskell syndrome.	See 'What if' No. 2
MENINGITIS	Inflammation of the outer covering of the brain.	
METRITIS	Inflammation of the uterus – see also Pyometra.	See 'What if' No. 51
MILIARY ECZEMA	See Feline Miliary Dermatitis.	See 'What if' Nos 18 and 36
MISALLIANCE	Mismating.	See Chapter 7
MYASIS	Fly strike – flies lay eggs on soiled or damaged areas on the skin; these hatch into maggots which live on the cat's tissue. *Very prompt veterinary consultation is needed.*	
MYOCARDITIS	Inflammation of the heart muscle.	
MYOSITIS	Inflammation of skeletal muscle causing acute pain.	See 'What if' No. 39
NEOPLASIA	Tumour (growth) formation.	
NEPHRITIS	Inflammation of the kidneys.	
NOTOEDRIC MANGE	Infestation, usually around the head and ears with the cat head mange mite, *Notoedres cati.*	See Chapter 9
OBESITY	Overweight.	See Chapter 6
OEDEMA	Accumulation of fluid under the skin mostly associated with kidney disease or local obstruction to blood supply possibly as a result of an insect bite or local infection.	
OSTEOMYELITIS	Inflammation of the bone marrow, usually associated with a bacterial infection.	
OSTEOSARCOMA	A bone tumour.	
OTITIS EXTERNA	Inflammation of the external ear canal.	See 'What if' No. 12

Disease/condition	Definition	Further Information
OTITIS INTERNA	Inflammation of the inner ear usually as an extension from otitis externa.	See 'What if' No. 13
OTITIS MEDIA	Inflammation of the middle ear usually as an extension of infection through the ear drum from an otitis externa but possibly from infection via the eustachian tube.	
OTOCARIASIS	Infestation of the ear canal with the ear mite *Otodectes cynotis*.	See Chapter 9
OTODECTIC MANGE	Inflammation of the ear canal caused by the ear mite *Otodectes cynotis*.	See Chapter 9
PANCREATITIS	Inflammation of the pancreas accompanied by severe abdominal pain, vomiting and possibly sudden death.	
PANLEUCOPAENIA	See Feline Infectious Enteritis	See 'What if' Nos 2, 20, and 39 and Chapter 9
PANSTEATITIS	An inflammation of subcutaneous fat related to vitamin E deficiency.	
PAPILLOMAS	Warts.	
PARALYSIS	Inability to move.	See 'What if' No. 43
PARONYCHIA	Inflammation of the nail or claw beds.	
PERIODONTAL DISEASE	Inflammation of the gums around the teeth.	See 'What if' No. 31
PERITONITIS	Inflammation of the peritoneum, the lining inside the abdomen which also covers the outside of the abdominal organs.	
PHARYNGITIS	Inflammation of the pharynx usually associated with generalized disease.	See 'What if' No. 15
PICA	Depraved appetite.	
PNEUMONIA	Inflammation of the lungs.	
POLYDIPSIA	Drinking excessively. There are many causes but this may be a serious sign.	See 'What if' No. 6
POLYPHAGIA	Increased appetite.	See 'What if' No. 5
POLYPS	Benign growths often seen in the ear canal.	
POLYURIA	Increased frequency of urination.	See 'What if' No. 24
P.R.A.	Progressive retinal atrophy. An hereditary eye condition.	See 'What if' No. 11
PRURITUS	Itchy skin. There are many causes of pruritus.	See 'What if' No. 18
PSEUDO-PREGNANCY	See False Pregnancy.	
PTOSIS	Inability to raise upper eyelid.	
PYLORIC STENOSIS	Contraction of pyloric valve in the stomach.	See 'What if' No. 2
PYOMETRA	Accumulation of pus in the uterus. This is a serious condition. *Seek veterinary advice without delay*.	See 'What if' No. 51
RABIES	A fatal virus disease of cats and all warm-blooded animals.	See Chapter 9 and 'What if' No. 33
RHINITIS	Inflammation of the nasal cavities.	See 'What if' No. 7
RINGWORM	A fungal infection of the skin.	See Chapter 9

Disease/condition	Definition	Further Information
RODENT ULCER	An enlarging ulcerated area, usually seen on the lip. Cause unknown, but possibly allergic in nature.	See 'What if' No. 30
SALIVARY CYST	A cyst in the salivary gland caused by an obstruction of the salivary duct.	
SALMONELLOSIS	An infection with salmonella bacteria causing, principally, an enteritis.	See Chapter 9
SEBORRHOEA	A dry or greasy scaling condition of the skin.	
SHOCK	Collapse of the circulation resulting from haemorrhage, trauma, burns, anaphylaxis, accumulation of toxins in the blood, cardiac failure, etc.	See 'What if' No. 38
SINUSITIS	Inflammation of the nasal sinuses, usually occurring following a bacterial rhinitis.	
SLIPPED DISC	Dislocation of the disc between the spinal vertebrae.	
SPONDYLITIS	Inflammation of the vertebrae and spinal joints leading to rigidity of the back.	
SPRAIN	An over-stretched or torn ligament.	See 'What if' No. 29
STEATITIS	See Pansteatitis.	
STOMATITIS	Inflammation of the mouth usually as an extension from gingivitis or periodontal disease.	See 'What if' No. 31
STRAIN	An over-stretched or torn muscle.	
TAPEWORM INFESTATION	Tapeworm in the small intestine.	See 'What if' Nos 19 and 46, and Chapter 9
TENESMUS	Straining to pass faeces.	See 'What if' No. 22
TETANUS	Infection with the bacteria *Clostridum tetani*, resulting in the accumulation of toxins in the blood causing muscle stiffness, rigidity and spasm. Rare in cats.	
TICK INFESTATION	The presence of one or more ticks on the skin.	See 'What if' No. 34 and Chapter 9
TONSILLITIS	Inflammation of the tonsils, may be associated with a local bacterial infection but is more often a sign of a generalized infectious disease.	See 'What if' No. 15
TOOTH DECAY	Dental caries.	
TOXOCARIASIS	Infection with the roundworms, *Toxocara cati* and *Toxascaris leonina*.	See Chapter 9
TOXOPLASMOSIS	Infection with the parasite *Toxoplasma gondii* causing general illness, loss of weight, raised temperature, pneumonia and a range of other signs.	See Chapter 9
TROMBICULOSIS	Infestation with harvest mites, sometimes also called berry bugs or chiggers.	See Chapter 9
URTICARIA	Sudden appearance of itchy, raised wheals on the skin caused by contact allergy, stings, bites or hypersensitivity to ingested allergens or drugs. Prompt administration of an antihistamine under veterinary guidance may be required.	
UTERINE INERTIA	Lack of uterine contractions during kittening; may be due to physical exhaustion or psychological stress. See also Dystocia.	

Disease/condition	Definition	Further Information
VAGINITIS	Inflammation of the vagina generally caused by a bacterial infection.	
VOMITING	Regurgitation of the stomach contents. This sign is common to a great number of diseases and conditions.	See 'What if' No. 2
WARTS	Papillomas (benign skin growths) which may be caused by a virus infection.	
WOUNDS	See Contusion, Laceration and Abrasion.	See 'What if' No. 35
YELLOW FAT DISEASE	See Pansteatitis.	

INDEX

For specific diseases and conditions see also separate index, pages 197–206.
(*KEY: IDC – Index of Diseases and Conditions*)
For definitions and further entries, *see also* Glossary, pages 190–196.

Contributors (continued) . . .

DAVID SUTTON qualified as a veterinary surgeon from the Royal Veterinary College London in 1982. He initially spent some time in private practice in East Anglia where he was directly involved in treating a wide range of domestic species, but fostered a particular interest in feline medicine. Currently he works in industry being employed as Technical Services Manager for Mycofarm Ltd, a veterinary pharmaceutical company which manufactures a range of antibiotic and hormonal preparations for the practising veterinary surgeon. Apart from his professional commitment he has a deep personal affinity for felines and has owned a large number of both pedigree and non-pedigree cats over the years.

GEOFF SKERRITT Mr Skerritt graduated in veterinary sciences from Liverpool in 1971. After a short period in small animal practice he returned to the University of Liverpool as a member of the academic staff in the Department of Veterinary Anatomy. He has a special interest and responsibilities in clinical neurology and gained his Fellowship of the Royal College of Veterinary Surgeons in 1985 for his thesis on neurological disease.